FLIPPING HOUSES
QuickStart Guide®

FLIPPING HOUSES

QuickStart Guide®

The Simplified Beginner's Guide to
Finding and Financing the Right Properties,
Strategically Adding Value, and Flipping for a Profit

Elisa Zheng Covington, MBA

Editors: Bryan Basamanowicz, Jesse Hassenger, Marilyn Burkley, Danielle Anderson
Cover Illustration and Design: Katie Donnachie, Nicole Daberkow, Copyright © 2022 by ClydeBank Media LLC
Interior Design & Illustrations: Katie Donnachie, Brittney Duquette, Copyright © 2022 by ClydeBank Media LLC

First Edition - Last Updated: August 17, 2023

ISBN: 9781636100302 (paperback) | 9781636100326 (hardcover) | 9781636100340 (audiobook) | 9781636100319 (ebook) | 9781636100333 (spiral bound)

Publisher's Cataloging-In-Publication Data
(Prepared by The Donohue Group, Inc.)

Names: Covington, Elisa Zheng, author.
Title: Flipping houses QuickStart Guide: the simplified beginner's guide to finding and financing the right properties, strategically adding value, and flipping for a profit / Elisa Zheng Covington.
Other titles: Flipping houses Quick Start Guide
Description: [Albany, New York] : ClydeBank Finance, [2022] | Series: QuickStart Guide | Includes bibliographical references and index.
Identifiers: ISBN: 978-1-63610-030-2 (paperback) | 978-1-63610-032-6 (hardcover) | 978-1-63610-033-3 (spiral-bound) | 978-1-63610-031-9 (eBook/ePub)
Subjects: LCSH: Flipping (Real estate investment)--Handbooks, manuals, etc. | Real estate investment--United States--Handbooks, manuals, etc. | House buying--United States--Handbooks, manuals, etc. | House selling--United States--Handbooks, manuals, etc. | Dwellings--Remodeling--United States--Handbooks, manuals, etc. | LCGFT: Handbooks and manuals. | BISAC: BUSINESS & ECONOMICS / Real Estate / Buying & Selling Homes. | BUSINESS & ECONOMICS / Real Estate / Commercial. | BUSINESS & ECONOMICS / Investments & Securities / Real Estate.
Classification: LCC: HD1382.5 .C68 2022 | DDC: 332.6324--dc23

Library of Congress Control Number: 2022940869

Author ISNI: 0000 0005 0373 5106

For bulk sales inquiries, please visit www.go.quickstartguides.com/wholesale, email us at orders@clydebankmedia.com, or call 800-340-3069. Special discounts are available on quantity purchases by corporations, associations, and others.

Copyright © 2022
www.quickstartguides.com
All Rights Reserved

ISBN-13: 978-1-636100-32-6

OVER
850,000

READERS **LOVE** *QuickStart Guides.*

Really well written with lots of practical information. These books have a very concise way of presenting each topic and everything inside is very actionable!

– ALAN F.

The book was a great resource, every page is packed with information, but [the book] never felt overly-wordy or repetitive. Every chapter was filled with very useful information.

– CURTIS W.

I appreciated how accessible and how insightful the material was and look forward to sharing the knowledge that I've learned [from this book].

– SCOTT B.

After reading this book, I must say that it has been one of the best decisions of my life!

– ROHIT R.

This book is one-thousand percent worth every single dollar!

– HUGO C.

The read itself was worth the cost of the book, but the additional tools and materials make this purchase a better value than most books.

– JAMES D.

I finally understand this topic ... this book has really opened doors for me!

– MISTY A.

Contents

PART II – TRANSFORMING A HOUSE

PART III – FINDING A BUYER AND TURNING A PROFIT

PART IV – LEGAL AND BUSINESS CONSIDERATIONS

BEFORE YOU START READING, DOWNLOAD YOUR FREE DIGITAL ASSETS!

 Case Study Library

 Prepare for Closing Checklist

 House Flip Deal Analyzer

 Staging Examples

TWO WAYS TO ACCESS YOUR FREE DIGITAL ASSETS

Use the camera app on your mobile phone to scan the QR code or visit the link below and instantly access your digital assets.

SCAN ME or go.quickstartguides.com/flipping **VISIT URL**

Introduction

Five years isn't very long in the grand scheme of things, but the last five years completely changed my life. A half decade ago, I was trapped in a dead-end job with a tech company, working nine to five along with everyone else, and wondering how I could change the course of my life. My job in Silicon Valley was okay, but I wasn't passionate about it. It was just something I did to earn an income and support my lifestyle. More senior positions at my company didn't look appealing because the higher pay didn't seem like proper compensation for how stressful and demanding the jobs appeared to be.

There was also a lingering uncertainty, sadly common in plenty of twenty-first-century jobs, about where the company was headed and how its direction would affect employees. Silicon Valley businesses are notorious for laying off employees, to the point where people joke that if you've never been laid off, your career is not complete. Looking back, it seems like everyone around me—including myself—was simply living up to the societal expectation of earning a degree, finding a job, going to work, and getting a salary. It matched Robert Kiyosaki's description of the "rat race" in his highly successful personal finance book *Rich Dad Poor Dad*. I was certain that I didn't want to remain in the rat race for the next 20 or 30 years, but I was unsure how to escape it.

I had gotten interested in real estate investing by this time and dreamed of leaving my job to pursue it full time. I was drawn to the idea of being my own boss and being responsible for my own success instead of showing up to work every day for a company that could fire me tomorrow. But I lacked the confidence or knowledge to follow my dream. So I became a landlord and eventually started flipping houses on the side while hanging on to a job that I didn't find at all inspiring but that came with a salary and benefits. As I completed my first two flips, I thought constantly about quitting my full-time job but just couldn't seem to pull the trigger. And then, just before Thanksgiving in 2017, I got laid off.

In hindsight, the layoff was the best thing that could have happened to me, as it freed me up to pursue what I knew I really wanted to do. But at the time it was tough, and I felt that I was at a low point in my life as I realized that for seven years I had spent most of my time and energy at a company that found me disposable. I felt as if I had no control over my own career. I wish I had avoided the humiliation by leaving on my own before I was laid off, but I guess I wasn't quite ready. Five years later, I am flipping houses full time and can now embrace the fact that my career is firmly in my own hands instead of under someone else's control. I wake up every morning eager to begin work, and I enjoy nearly every aspect of what I do. Being my own boss also enables me to control my schedule and take time to enjoy my family, friends, and favorite activities.

If you are in a situation that sounds similar to where I was—dissatisfied with your career, feeling like you're doing things just to keep up with expectations—I want you to know that you have the power to change it. Leaving a job to pursue something on your own is a leap of faith, to be sure. I remember how scary the idea felt and how anxious it made me. Some people with good intentions may try to discourage you from taking the leap, out of concern for your financial security. They'll say you are going into a risky venture and gambling with all your savings or that you won't be able to find enough deals to earn a sustainable income—the same things that people told me. We'll discuss those and other myths of house flipping a little later, but I'm here to tell you that with the right guidance and a lot of hard work, you can overcome the challenges associated with flipping houses and be a success. I spent a lot of money trying to learn the business from the gurus who offered seminars and other trainings, but in hindsight I don't think I got my money's worth. This book and other inexpensive sources will provide valuable information to get you started and help you build the confidence you need. Flipping houses isn't rocket science. It seems complicated and intimidating when you're just starting out, but you should have faith in yourself and believe that you can do it, because many people have managed to succeed, including myself, who was a total newbie not long ago. My only regret is not starting sooner! Let me tell you a little more about my journey from working a nine-to-five job to becoming a seven-figure house flipper in just a few years.

House Hacking and Landlording

By 2012, I had finally saved enough to purchase my first property, a two-bedroom, two-bathroom loft in a nice part of San Francisco. It was not a smooth or easy purchase, to say the least. The loft was listed as a short sale, and the complex's homeowner association (HOA) was suing the developer for water damage in the building. There were few banks willing to lend me money to buy this property, but I fell in love with the place, and it was a bargain I couldn't pass up, because the real estate market was at rock bottom at that time and the property was listed at 20 percent below market value. To make a long story short, I made an offer and was turned down, only to find out a month later that the other offer had fallen through and my offer was accepted. It took six months to close on the property due to the lengthy short sale process, but finally it was mine.

I decided to **house hack**, which means renting out part of the house while living in the other part. Not wanting to take the chance of renting to someone I didn't know, I offered one bedroom and bathroom to a friend who was looking for a place to live. That turned out to be a mistake, as she was not nearly as neat as I am, didn't clean up after herself, and on multiple occasions left the door standing open when neither of us was home. I had to ask her to find another place, meaning I ended up losing both a renter and a friend. It made me realize that being a landlord is not easy, but the rent money helped me pay down the mortgage every month, which allowed me to continue saving a big chunk of my income.

Property values started going up shortly after my purchase, and in 2014, the appreciation on my loft made it possible for me to get a **home equity line of credit (HELOC)**, a type of loan that uses some of the equity in your home to give you a revolving line of credit. I used the HELOC to purchase a rental property, a one-bedroom condo that my then-boyfriend-now-husband and I spent two months remodeling (see the before and after photos of our kitchen in figure 1). I realized later that doing it on our own was another mistake. We both had full-time jobs and could only work on the project on weekends, which made it very stressful, and it took a lot longer than it should have. Hiring contractors to do the work would have saved us time and, ultimately, money.

OUR KITCHEN REMODEL

fig. 1

I furnished the apartment and offered it as a high-end rental, which ended up being a good experience. The monthly income gave me good cash flow, and I enjoyed the tax benefits of a rental. With property values still rising, however, I decided in 2015 to sell both the loft and the rental. The value of the rental had appreciated by 40 percent and the value of loft by 80 percent. I decided at that point that I definitely liked real estate, and the capital from the sales made it possible for me to continue investing.

HGTV and High-Ticket Courses

It was about this time when my husband turned me on to the house flipping shows on HGTV. I know that sounds cliché, but once I started watching them, I became hooked on the idea of getting into real estate in a bigger way. I was glued to the TV, getting inspired by *Flip or Flop*, *Fixer Upper*, *Property Brothers*, and other shows. I was intrigued by the process of flipping houses and impressed with the success of the flippers on the shows. And then, in 2016, I experienced one of those light bulb moments when suddenly everything becomes clear. I realized I was good at making real estate deals and managing properties and that those skills could be applied to a new career. For the first time, I considered the idea of becoming my own boss and flipping houses as a business.

Other than what I saw on HGTV, I had no idea what flipping houses entailed or how I might get started in the business. I was desperately trying to learn about these things when I saw an ad for a free seminar hosted by my favorite HGTV personalities that promised to teach me. The seminar was eye-opening, as the presenters shared case studies demonstrating how lucrative the business can be. They would not, of course, give out all their secrets for free, and I was prompted to learn more by signing up for a three-day course that cost $1,000. Those classes got me really pumped up, as a lot more success stories were shared. I was convinced that an additional advanced course would be a good idea and signed up for one that cost $25,000. I learned a lot from those courses, and they gave me all the fundamentals I needed to get started, but as I mentioned earlier, in hindsight I don't believe it was necessary to spend that kind of money.

MY TAKE

Only after I had spent $25,000 on the advanced course did I realize that most of the information I got from it can be found elsewhere for a much lower cost, or even for free. Most of the house flipping information you'll need can be found in this book, and if you need more knowledge on real estate basics or home remodeling, you can find pretty much everything in books, websites, YouTube videos, and other sources. There's a lot of free information available, and you get to pick and choose what's interesting and pertinent to you. We'll suggest some helpful resources in chapter 15.

Side Hustle Turned into a Seven-Figure Career

It took a while, but I finally decided I had spent enough time sitting on the sidelines. Despite dire warnings of a downturn, the real estate market had continued its upward trajectory in 2016. I had completed courses, read book after book, listened to dozens of podcasts, and attended countless real estate meetings. I had explored real estate strategies other than flipping houses, including mobile home parks, apartment buildings, and commercial real estate, and decided that house flipping was the form of investing that made the most sense for me. I was ready to find my first deal!

I knew flipping houses would be an intense undertaking while working a full-time job, but I was so excited and passionate about it that I couldn't wait to get started. I knew that I'd need some help, so I started looking for a mentor (something I strongly suggest that you do as well). I had the good fortune to meet my mentor at a real estate meeting where he was the guest speaker. I connected with him after the meeting, followed up with a phone call, and asked him if he'd be willing to mentor me. He agreed, and just a few phone calls with him provided me with knowledge and insights I hadn't gleaned during that $25k course! I credit my mentor for providing the foundation I needed for a successful career and remain grateful for his guidance and encouragement.

At my mentor's suggestion, I started looking for agents who could bring me deals. You'll read a lot about finding deals and working with agents throughout this book, but for now I'll tell you that it's not an easy task when you're working full time. For months I spent every lunch hour and break locked in a conference room cold calling agents. I called literally thousands of agents and was turned down multiple times a day, but my determination paid off. I eventually found hundreds of agents who were willing to look for deals for me. The time and effort I put into finding them—a process I call "massive action"—was worth every minute.

I found my first deal after just a month of cold calling. I'll save the story of my first flip for later in the book, but it was truly a nightmare, and everything that could go wrong did go wrong. Despite all the difficulties and setbacks, though, I truly enjoyed the process of turning a neglected house into a dream home, and I looked forward to putting the experience I gained into good use on my next flip. See the before and after photos of the kitchen from my first flip (figure 2).

OUR FIRST KITCHEN REMODEL

fig. 2

The kitchen of my first flip, before and after renovations.

One deal led to another, and my job started to get in the way of the side hustle I had going. I don't know how long it would have taken me to finally get the courage to quit and start flipping full time, but as I mentioned, getting laid off put me in a position to make that decision sooner than I might have otherwise. It still seemed scary at that point, but after careful consideration, I decided I was done with the corporate life and would trust myself to establish and operate a successful business.

I'm not going to tell you that what I've done was always easy, or that every flip has gone smoothly. There have been bumps in the road and I've had to work very hard, but working for myself keeps me motivated and excited about what I do. I've found immense satisfaction in building my business, and the rewards have been great. Since 2019—just my third year in business—I've made a seven-figure profit every year.

I live in the San Francisco Bay Area, which has some of the highest real estate prices in the country. That means that my potential for making a profit or taking a loss is higher than it would be for someone flipping houses in pretty much anywhere else in the country where prices are lower. My experience is that I'll have to spend a million dollars to buy a house that I'll renovate and resell at a profit. All the information in this book, however, is transferable to lower-priced markets found in many areas of the country. I'm very aware that the median home price in the United States is $269,000, according to Zillow. While it's likely you'll be working with lower numbers than I do, the formulas for figuring out whether or not a deal will work and the process of transforming a home and turning a profit are the same. You may just have to do a larger volume of deals to achieve profits similar to what I generate, but on the other hand, the risk you incur on each deal will be lower.

Myths about House Flipping

When I started flipping houses, I heard the same things over and over again. House flipping is too risky. You'll lose everything. You need too much money to get started. You'll have to work every minute. There are no deals. It's too late to get into the business because the market is going to turn soon. Well, none of those things turned out to be true. Yes, my first couple of flips were difficult, but looking back, I attribute that to a lack of experience and not having the strong team that I do today. If any of these limiting beliefs is preventing you from getting started in house flipping, take a minute to read why they are simply not true.

You Need a Fortune to Start

Sure, you need money to buy a property and get it fixed up and ready to sell, but there are various ways to find money to fund your deals without using much—or any—of your own. You'll read in detail about how to do this later in the book.

A lot of flippers get **hard money loans**, which are short-term loans (usually one year or less) issued by a company, investor group, or licensed mortgage broker—not a bank. I normally fund up to 85 percent of the cost of my deals with hard money loans. Other funding sources that I'll explain in further detail include private investors, loans from family members, a personal line of credit, a HELOC, savings, a conventional mortgage, and even crowdfunding. If you can get a hard money loan for 85 percent of your deal and 100 percent of the rehab cost and then find another source, such as a loan from a family member or a home equity loan, for the other 15 percent of the purchase price, you can fund a deal with no money of your own. You'll read more about it later, but I've flipped a few houses without using my own money, even when I was just starting out and didn't have a lot of experience.

It's Too Much Work

This is a fear for many new house flippers who imagine they'll have to spend every waking minute of the rest of their lives working because there are a lot of moving parts and they are ultimately responsible for the deals.

I'll be honest with you: the first few flips I did were difficult and time consuming, and my first year as a house flipper was busy and stressful, but that's because I was still trying to figure out the best practices and build my team. Once I became more experienced and got a good team in place, the time I needed to spend decreased dramatically. When you get a trustworthy team established, team members take a lot of the work off your hands and free up your time significantly.

At this point in my house flipping career, I only work about ten hours a week on average, relying on my team members to carry the rest of the weight. Agents in my network find deals and bring them to me, and they also assist me with getting top dollar for the completed flips. I rely on my contractors to do the renovation work and keep the projects on time and on budget—although I do like to get involved with some of the design aspects because I enjoy picking out floors, tiles, lighting, paint colors, and so forth. I hire professional stagers to furnish and decorate the houses and make my properties look their best so I can get the highest prices possible. I rely on a business planning and consulting firm to handle my entity formation and asset protection, and I rely on my CPA for bookkeeping and taxes. My team members are professionals who excel in their lines of business. I know them and trust them to do their best work, enabling me to work less and enjoy life more.

It's Too Risky

A lot of beginners are afraid to take the first step because they believe flipping houses is too risky. It may come as a surprise to you, but I'm actually a risk-averse person. If I had thought that house flipping was overly risky, I wouldn't have tried it in the first place. As with any investment, there are risks associated with real estate investing and house flipping. But I'm convinced that if you know what you're doing and are smart when analyzing deals, there's less risk in flipping houses than with many other types of investment. Real estate is a tangible asset, and though its value goes up and down, it's normally less susceptible to the wild swings that we sometimes see with the stock market or cryptocurrency.

People who think flipping houses is a risky business are usually those who don't know much about it. If you know the ins and outs of flipping, you'll know what crucial things you must do to mitigate certain risks. While that doesn't guarantee that you'll never lose a penny in the house flipping business, reducing and controlling your risk can minimize any loss you might incur.

Risk mitigation gets plenty of coverage throughout the book—we even include a chapter on the risks of house flipping and how to alleviate them. You'll read about how fluctuating markets, problems with contractors, legal issues, and other factors can trip up a deal you're working on. But you'll also read about how it's possible to minimize those risks and increase the chances of making money on every deal.

There Are No Deals

When I was exploring different avenues of real estate investing, many investors and agents told me that housing inventory was too low, competition was too fierce, and it was impossible to find deals. That really messed with my head and caused me to look elsewhere for investing opportunities, delaying my start into house flipping. Fortunately, I found a mentor, who convinced me I would be able to succeed. I found my first deal after just one month of looking.

It's definitely true that good deals are hard to come by, but if you use the right methods and employ some perseverance, you'll see that good deals are everywhere.

Since I've started flipping houses, I've had consistent deal flow nearly all the time. But I still often hear people repeating the notion that there are no deals to be had! I've come to believe that the people who say that are just not looking hard enough or aren't using the right techniques to find deals. Some new investors I've mentored started locating deals after just a couple of months of work, proving that there are plenty of opportunities available.

In the book, we talk about various ways to find deals. You've already learned that I rely on agents to bring me deals, but some investors are very successful without an agent, finding houses on the market on their own or scouting out off-market deals from homeowners who, for various reasons, are looking to unload their houses.

It's a Bad Time to Start Flipping

The limiting belief that my timing was off delayed my career by almost a year. Aspiring house flippers often question at what point they should jump into the business. When the market is good, as it has been for years now, they worry that it might be too late in the market cycle to start flipping and the market could turn on them. If the market is declining, they reason, they could be stuck with a house they'll end up selling at a loss. If that's you, I understand; I thought the same thing in 2016 when

I was contemplating getting started but was worried that after four solid years of market growth, a downturn had to be just around the corner. I ended up waiting until 2017 to take the plunge, losing my chance to get in on continued market appreciation, during which time many house flippers made a killing.

The real estate market has been robust since recovering from the Great Recession of 2008. Lower inventory and higher demand mean that house flippers have had to pay more for their deals, but the completed flips have sold quickly and for top prices, resulting in profits. Eventually, though, the market will take a turn for the worse. You'll read more about this in chapter 14, but the short answer is that when the market cools off, rehabbed houses may take longer to sell and sell for less than today's prices, but deals will be easier to find and less expensive to get. If your analysis and numbers are right, which they will be if you follow the instructions in this book, there's still a very good chance that you can profit in a down market.

After all I've learned, I've concluded that trying to time the real estate market just isn't a good idea. Many factors, including interest rates, demographics, the state of the general economy, and catastrophes like the pandemic can affect the real estate market, and it's impossible to predict what might happen that could drive it up or down. The beauty of house flipping is that it's on both the buying and selling sides of business, so the risk of changing market conditions is canceled out. You need to be aware of what's going on and employ different strategies depending on the state of the market, but I believe there is no bad time to flip houses. If the market has been booming for years, like our current market has, chances are that home prices are at their peak and it's possible the market could shift downward at any time. That means you'll want to be proactive and incorporate a worst-case scenario into your deal analysis. If we were coming out of a recession and prices were likely to be increasing, you could relax a little bit with your analysis and not be overly concerned if you ran into a few unanticipated expenses. I'm convinced that a good house flipper can not only survive but also prosper in almost any real estate market.

How This Book Is Organized

The intent of this book is to help you understand the business of house flipping and to provide a step-by-step guide you can use to navigate the process. I hope that sharing my experiences and providing recommendations based on what I've personally found to be successful will give you some confidence when you flip a house, whether or not you've ever done so before.

The book is divided into four parts. The first part, "How to Find, Analyze, and Fund a Deal," starts by letting readers know about the two main categories of house flipping: rehabbing, also known as fix-and-flip, and wholesaling. Most people associate flipping with rehabbing, but there are many flippers who work in wholesaling, either exclusively or in addition to rehabbing. Most of the material in this book applies to the rehab model of flipping houses, but I wanted to give you some information about wholesaling as well. Moving on, you'll learn about various means of locating deals, whether you elect to use an agent (which I highly recommend) or choose another strategy such as buying properties at auction or sending out mailers to homeowners. You'll learn the advantages and disadvantages of buying houses both on-market and off-market, and why location is so important. Part I also deals with the essential topic of how to analyze a deal and make sure your numbers add up so they result in a profit, which, of course, is the goal of flipping houses. Earlier in this introduction you read about funding your flips, which is another topic covered in part I. Finally, I'll walk you through the process of making an offer and buying a house.

Part II, "Transforming a House," is meant to guide you through the process of planning the necessary renovations, finding contractors to work with you, and getting the house ready to put on the market. This stage of flipping houses is critical because it's important that you stay on track with your time and budget. Encountering common pitfalls like getting scammed by a dishonest contractor or dealing with a serious problem with the house that you hadn't anticipated can result in your being over time and over budget, turning your flip into an extremely stressful experience (ask me how I know) or even a loss. Having this part of the flipping process proceed smoothly can ensure that you stay on track and avoid having to pay expenses such as financing costs, taxes, utilities, and insurance for any longer than necessary.

In part III, "Finding a Buyer and Turning a Profit," we'll look at the advantages of using a real estate agent to help you sell a house, while also considering other methods of listing and selling. You'll learn what's involved in the process of selling a home and getting top dollar—everything from getting it listed to negotiating and closing on the sale. Part III also provides guidance to help you assess a house flipping experience, regardless of whether you have already done so.

Part IV, "Legal and Business Considerations of House Flipping," is included to help you understand the importance of protecting yourself and your business. Though flipping houses is not as risky as many people think (and I'll explain more about why!), getting some sort of business structure in place can help protect you in the event of legal or financial issues because it separates your personal assets from your business assets. I hope you'll earn a lot of money through flipping houses, which is a good thing but also means you'll need to deal with the taxes you'll have to pay. Fortunately, there are ways you can minimize those tax bills. Some of the information in the last two chapters of part IV might sound familiar because they recap some material included earlier in the book with additional insight and detail. It's information I thought was important and wanted to expand on.

Chapter by Chapter

» **PART I: How to Find, Analyze, and Fund a Deal**

» Chapter 1, "The House Flipping Business Model," discusses the two main ways that real estate investors flip houses. While most TV shows feature the rehabbing model, also known as fix-and-flip, some flippers prefer wholesaling, in which they locate deals on discounted properties, agree to buy them, then sell the deal to another investor, usually without making any improvements to it and often without ever taking possession of the title. There are advantages and disadvantages of wholesaling, but it can be a good way to break into the business of flipping.

» Chapter 2, "Scouting Out Potential Deals," delves into the issue of finding agents to work with, something I feel is a critical step when you're starting to flip houses. Locating good deals is one of the most difficult aspects of house flipping, and good agents can help you tremendously in doing that. Some house flippers, however, choose to seek deals on their own, often looking for homes that are in foreclosure, being sold at auction, real estate owned, or have owners who for one reason or another need to sell the house—often as-is and below market value.

» In chapter 3, "Analyzing a Deal," I explain how to successfully analyze a potential deal, which is crucial to success in house flipping. If your numbers aren't right, you won't be able to establish an accurate maximum offer price for a deal you want. That could result in your offering too little for the house and losing the deal, or paying too much for the house, which can minimize your profit or even result in a loss.

» You'll learn about different methods of financing a deal in chapter 4, "Funding the Flip," along with why you don't need to have as much of your own money to get started as many people believe. There are a variety of ways to secure financing, and we'll explore some of the advantages and disadvantages of a number of them.

» Chapter 5, "Making an Offer and Buying the House," explores the process of building trust with a potential seller and working together to make the selling process successful. It also looks at the importance of fairness, both to the homeowner and to yourself, when making an offer. I always want my offers to be fair to the homeowner, but you still need to stick to your maximum asking price for the deal to make sense. And we'll have a look at how a house closing works.

» **Part II: Transforming a House**

» Renovating a house is a lot of work, especially when you're new to house flipping. In chapter 6, "Planning the Renovation Project," I make the case for hiring professionals instead of trying to do the work yourself. I speak from personal experience, and I hope you'll heed my advice. You'll learn how to determine the scope of work that is necessary for fixing up the house and how to create a budget that enables you to get all the necessary repairs done while keeping your deal on track financially.

» Chapter 7, "Finding a Contractor," is an important, practical chapter that looks at what type of contractor you might need and how to meet and screen contractors. It explains how to review contactors' bids to ensure you're comparing apples to apples, and the importance of getting a good contracting agreement in place so the project moves along smoothly and stays on schedule.

» In chapter 8, "Getting the House Ready to List," you'll read about the importance of getting your house to look its absolute best. I take special pains to do this because I've found that many buyers react emotionally to a house that's in tip-top shape, and it increases the price they are willing to pay for it.

» **Part III: Finding a Buyer and Turning a Profit**

» Some house flippers think it's a good idea to forgo the services of a real estate agent when selling a house, and others wouldn't consider trying to go it alone. In chapter 9, "Use an Agent or Sell it Yourself?" we'll explore the pros and cons of selling a house on your own and some techniques you can use to help you do that if you decide not to have a real estate agent. You'll also read about what an agent can offer and what to consider when hiring one.

» Chapter 10, "Selling the Flip," deals with questions such as the best time to list a home, what disclosures you may need and how to fill them out, and how to get your property listed on the open market. You'll learn about a few different ways of marketing your property and the ins and outs of reviewing and negotiating offers.

» Chapter 11, "Looking Toward Your Next Flip," challenges readers to assess their experience once they've completed their first flip and provides suggestions for doing so. This chapter also delves further into the importance of having the right team members in place and examines the topic of real estate market cycles. Understanding where we are in those cycles can help you know what to watch for to mitigate risk and increase profitability.

» **Part IV: Legal and Business Considerations of House Flipping**

» In chapter 12, "Establishing a Business Entity," you'll learn how having a business structure can protect your personal assets in the event you are sued or run into financial trouble. There are different types of entities, so we'll consider the advantages and disadvantages of each. We'll also discuss the importance of keeping your personal finances separate from your business finances and how to accomplish that.

» Chapter 13, "Tax Implications of Flipping Houses," looks at how taxes can take a bite out of your profits and presents some methods of reducing the amount of taxes you'll need to pay. You'll also learn about the importance of finding the people you need to help you with tax issues.

» While chapter 14, "Risks of House Flipping and How to Mitigate Them," acknowledges and discusses some risks associated with flipping houses, it also makes the argument that flipping houses carries less risk than many people assume. I believe that when done correctly, real estate investing, including house flipping, is less risky than many other types of investments.

» Chapter 15, "Preparing for a Career in House Flipping," provides some practical ideas for how you can continue moving toward a house flipping career, even if you aren't quite ready to get started. With a focus on education, networking, and identifying people who can help you, the information in this chapter is intended to keep you interested and motivated until you're prepared to take the plunge.

» I hope that reading this book gets you excited about the prospect of flipping houses and motivates you to get started. There's a lot to learn, but with some good, basic knowledge, you'll be able to get started and you'll continue learning as you go. With careful planning and some hard work up front, house flipping can be an interesting, lucrative, and rewarding venture. Let's get started!

PART I

HOW TO FIND, ANALYZE, AND FUND A DEAL

I 1 I
The House Flipping Business Model

Chapter Overview
  » The Two Models of House Flipping
  » Wholesaling: Contract Assignments and Double Closings
  » Pros and Cons of Wholesaling and Flipping

Real estate investors have long been attracted to flipping houses, and there is no indication that interest is declining. In 2020, nearly six percent of all housing sales in the United States were flips. If that doesn't sound like a lot, consider that six and a half million homes were sold that year, meaning that flips accounted for 390,000 of them. So if you're interested in flipping houses, you're in good company.

This first section of the book deals with the process of locating deals and how to analyze and fund them—crucial steps for house flippers to understand. Before you start learning about those steps, however, I'd like to tell you a little bit about the two different models for flipping houses. If you've watched HGTV shows like *Flip or Flop* or *Property Brothers*, you've seen the hard work that goes into planning and executing the rehab of a house—often a house that needs a whole lot of renovating before it will be ready to sell. That model of house flipping is known as **rehabbing**, or fix-and-flip, and it's what we'll spend most of our time discussing in this book. When people mention house flipping, they're usually referring to this model. But it doesn't hurt to understand the other model, which is called wholesaling, because it's simpler and more beginner friendly.

Not every house flip involves renovating a property before it's sold. **Wholesaling** is the process of locating a discounted property, signing a purchase agreement with the owner, and selling the deal—usually as-is—to another investor. There are a couple of ways to do this, which I'll discuss in this chapter, but in some cases the wholesaler never takes possession of the property, instead simply agreeing with the seller to come up with a particular asking price provided by the end buyer. As you can imagine, wholesaling is not nearly as labor-intensive as rehabbing, but it still requires knowledge, skills, and a good understanding of the various ways it can be done.

Wholesaling and rehabbing do share some common ground. Both involve acquiring a property and selling it for a profit in the shortest possible amount of time. In both cases, faster is better because you incur costs such as insurance, financing charges, property taxes, and utilities while holding a property. But there are also distinct differences in how these two processes work, and both come with advantages and disadvantages, which we'll examine. And because the rest of the book mostly deals with the rehabbing model of house flipping, we'll focus more on the wholesaling model in this chapter. I'll start by explaining a little more about what wholesaling entails and why it's a great way for certain investors to flip.

The Wholesaling Model

Wholesaling is really the act of finding deals for other investors. As a wholesaler, you locate a property that can be acquired at a good price. After signing an agreement of sale with the owner, you locate an interested investor and offer to sell the property at a price that's higher than the owner's asking price (but still an attractive price for the investor). If the investor agrees to pay you the higher price, the deal can proceed in one of two ways. One way is for you, the wholesaler, to *assign the contract* you've agreed upon with the seller, which means passing the contract along to the investor, who agrees to pay you a fee to get it without you yourself ever closing on the deal. The other major way to proceed is to *double close*, which is the process of the wholesaler buying a property from its owner and immediately selling the same property to an investor for a higher price. The process involves two closings, that of the wholesaler and that of the investor—hence the term "double close." We'll take a closer look at these two methods of wholesaling a little later in this chapter.

Before locking in a deal, a smart wholesaler will have already targeted investors who might be interested in buying the property, because, depending on the terms of the contract, once the wholesaler's purchase agreement is signed, they may have only a few days to find a new buyer. If no buyer is found, the wholesaler may need to exercise a contingency clause to back out of the contract, or come up with some sort of financing so they are able to close on the house themselves. Many wholesalers enter into purchase agreements without having funds to use in the event that they can't find someone to take the property. They count on the fact that having a contingency built into the agreement with the homeowner will enable them to simply walk away from the deal if a buyer is not located in time. Smart wholesalers usually maintain a list of potential buyers, negotiate a long enough contingency period to find a buyer, and make sure to cancel a contract before any deposits they make become nonrefundable.

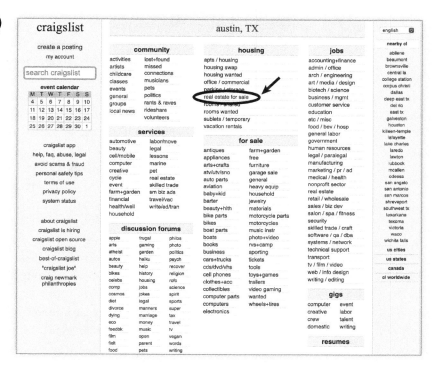

fig. 3

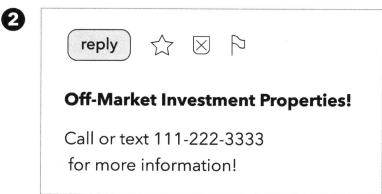

To submit a free Craigslist post, go to the home page, select your location, click on "real estate for sale," and create your post.

I'm a fan of real estate investment clubs, which tend to attract like-minded people who want to get to know each other. These club meetings can be opportunities for wholesalers to meet investors who are interested in purchasing fixer-uppers, either to sell or to hold and rent. It's a great way to work on building your network, even before you get your first deal. Once you have a property locked down, you can use the open mic portion of a meeting to share your deal and encourage interested parties to contact you. Other ways to locate investors include the classified ads on Craigslist, asking real estate agents to share the names of investors in their network, or finding them on online forums or social media sites. To run a classified ad on Craigslist, go to the "real estate for sale" section and post something like "Off-Market Investment Properties! Call or text me at 111-222-3333!" (see figure 3).

When you talk to or correspond with potential investors, you'll want to identify promising prospects and weed out those who might waste your time. Do this by asking some pointed questions, such as these:

» Do you have cash, or will you need to arrange financing? (This could affect how quickly you'd be able to complete the deal.)

» How quickly would you be able to close on a deal?

» Are you only interested in certain locations? (This helps you know who to contact depending on where your deals are located.)

» What types of properties are you interested in (single-family homes to flip and sell, rental properties, multiunit properties, etc.)?

» How extensive of a renovation are you able to handle? (Again, this will help you know who to contact depending on the condition of the property.)

» How many houses do you typically buy in a year?

» What percentage below market value must the deal be for you to consider pursuing it?

Retain all the information you collect on prospective end buyers, as this will help you build a network you can consult whenever you have a deal to offer. The information you'll get from these questions will help you understand which potential buyers would most likely be interested in a particular type of property and at what price.

Wholesalers shouldn't limit themselves to one type of deal, such as buying distressed properties to sell to rehabbers. There are all types of properties for sale and plenty of investors who are looking for them. Don't rule out rental properties or even commercial properties. Oftentimes you'll see that rehabbers have more strict criteria than buy-and-hold investors, and it's much easier to find properties with favorable rental prospects than ones with rehab potential.

As for where to find properties to buy in the first place, wholesalers typically find deals the same way any house flipper does, and that's a process you'll learn about in the next chapter. Analyzing a deal, the topic of chapter 3, is also largely the same for wholesalers and rehabbers. A wholesaler should analyze a deal just as if they were going to fix and flip the property. Once they've determined what the maximum offer price will be for a rehabber, they'll deduct a portion of it for their wholesaling fee. Wholesalers can face a fine line between earning their targeted fee and driving away potential buyers, who may be flippers mindful of how a high wholesaling fee will cut into their profits. Finding deals that are as much under market price as possible is vital for wholesalers because that allows them to charge a higher fee without deterring flippers. It's important to make sure what you offer to sell the house for is enough to cover the wholesaling fee you'll charge.

Wholesaling can be a great way to break into the real estate investment field, but it requires skill, knowledge, and a big network. Let's examine the two sale methods typically used in wholesaling: assigning the contract and double closing.

Assignment of Contract

Assignment of contract is the process of selling a contract to buy a home to another investor. A wholesaler who assigns the contract to someone else isn't actually selling the home because they don't own it yet; they're just selling the contract. The end buyer closes directly with the owner. In essence, the wholesaler is the middleman who simply matches a home seller with a home buyer, taking a fee for their services. That fee can vary depending on circumstances but often ranges from $5,000 to $10,000.

Many wholesalers like the assignment of contract model because they don't have to fund or own the property throughout the process, which keeps the risk at a minimum. The end buyer pays the sales price for the house, along with a fee to the wholesaler for the contract. The wholesaler never buys or takes title to the property, and the assignment of contract doesn't show up in the property's title chain, meaning the wholesaler is not really part of the paperwork. It is the responsibility of the wholesaler, however, to conduct title research and make sure the contract is complete and legal. The wholesaler needs to make it clear to the seller that the contract may be assigned to another buyer before the closing date, and to use "and/or assignee" after their name as the buyer when signing the contract. They also need to make sure to use a contract that's assignment-friendly, as some standard contracts do not allow assignment. Other contracts may allow assignment, but only if the seller agrees to it.

An agent I work with once brought me a deal for a 900-square-foot fixer-upper in a desirable part of town. The seller had inherited it and had rented the house for many years, and it had not been well maintained. I agreed to pay $1.125 million for the property with the intention of flipping it, because I knew the location of the house would attract many potential buyers. Things changed, however, after I posted information about it on Facebook and another house flipper reached out with interest. He offered to take the house off my hands and give me a $75,000 assignment fee. Even though I knew I could have made more by renovating and flipping the house, I decided to take him up on his offer because I didn't have to do any work or take any risk. We signed an agreement, I passed along the contract, and he was able to close on the deal and pay me the $75,000 within a week. Because an agent brought me the deal, I made sure my agreement with the flipper included my agent being the one to list the house once the rehab project was done. This way, my agent still earned a double commission even though I didn't rehab the house myself. (If you plan to rely on agents to bring you deals, you'll need to work it out with your buyer to make sure the agent gets the flipped listing so you don't burn your bridges.) I was well satisfied with the quick profit I made and will continue to use this wholesaling strategy from time to time if the circumstances are right.

Assignment of contract isn't always trouble-free. Contract assignments can be hard to sell; some investors shy away from them. And in some real estate markets, like the San Francisco Bay Area, discounted properties, on which wholesalers depend, can be hard to come by. Buyers sometimes back out at the last minute, leaving wholesalers scrambling to find another buyer and at risk of losing any deposits they've made on the house. Using the assignment of contract wholesaling method is beginner-friendly, but it's not something you should attempt without full awareness of how it works and what you need to do to ensure it proceeds smoothly.

Double Close

In a double-close deal, sometimes called a back-to-back closing, a wholesaler buys a property—often one that is distressed—and quickly sells it to another investor. This model differs from the assignment of contract in that the wholesaler actually takes possession of the house, although for only a short time. That does not occur in a situation in which a contract is assigned to an end buyer. Let's break down the process that results in a double-close transaction.

» The first step of a double close is for a wholesaler to find a homeowner who is anxious to get rid of a property and willing to sell at well under market value.

» Next, the wholesaler must find an end buyer who agrees to purchase the property. Because the wholesaler is going to close on the purchase of the house, they can wait until after closing to start looking for buyers. If holding costs will be higher than the wholesaler can pay, however, it would be better to start looking for a buyer before closing on the home.

» The wholesaler needs to finance the purchase. There are various ways to do that, including borrowing through a traditional lender, such as a bank, and borrowing from a hard money lender or private lender (which we will talk more about in chapter 4). Once funds have been obtained, the wholesaler buys the property from the seller.

» Finally, the wholesaler sells the property to the end buyer. In some cases, the selling process is reversed, with the end buyer buying the property first, after which the wholesaler immediately turns the money over to the seller. This is known as a *single-source funding plan*, sometimes employed when the wholesaler doesn't have funds available to purchase the property. The title officer must agree to the process, something that doesn't always happen since not all closing agents are investor-friendly or familiar with how single-source funding works.

The concept of double closings can seem a little confusing, but when you think about it, the process of a wholesaler buying and selling a house using the double-close method is similar to the process employed by a house flip that involves rehabbing; the wholesaler just skips the rehab step as part of an accelerated timeline. Like a house flipper, a wholesaler needs to have financing lined up to purchase the house, which is then sold—usually to another investor. It's the same process, although the time frame for wholesalers buying and selling properties is usually much shorter than that of a house flipper because there is no rehab work involved. See figure 4 for a graphical representation of these two wholesaling processes.

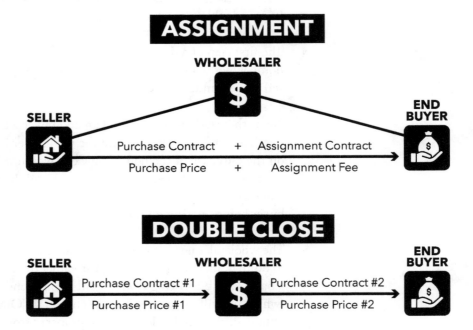

fig. 4

Some wholesalers have a strong preference for either contract assignment or double close, though many are open to both options, depending on the circumstances of the deal. Generally, the double-close method is popular when there is more money at stake for the wholesaler, usually $10,000 or more, as it's considered less risky than contract assignment. If less money is involved, assigning the contract is the more widely used method.

Wholesaling vs. Rehabbing: Pros and Cons

Wholesaling can be a great way to break into real estate investing because it doesn't require as many skills as are necessary for flipping houses. You don't need an eye for design or project management skills to wholesale properties. You don't need to be able to maximize the potential of a house to sell it for top dollar. The only skill you need for wholesaling is to be really good at finding deals—a skill that is also essential for house flippers. However, while wholesaling can be easier than fix-and-flip, there are some downsides. I'd like to take a little time to review the pros and cons of the two methods of wholesaling you've learned about and show how they compare to the practice of fixing and flipping houses. As you read the rest of the book, which deals almost entirely with rehabbing, you'll get a better sense of all that process entails and how it is different from wholesaling.

Pros and Cons of Contract Assignment Wholesaling

Contract assignment is a popular method of wholesaling for several reasons. It carries low financial risk because there is little or no money needed to get a deal. There is no market risk, as you're never owning the property, and no project management risk because there is no rehab involved. And because the process of finding a deal and assigning the contract usually moves quickly, you realize profits in a short amount of time.

Another advantage of contract assignment is that it's easy to get out of a deal that doesn't work out. As you read earlier, getting a few days' contingency in place when negotiating the contract gives a wholesaler the ability to walk away from the deal if they're unable to find an end buyer for the house.

On the downside of contract assignment is a high risk of losing the deal, either because an end buyer cannot be located before the contract contingency expires or because an unscrupulous buyer approaches the seller directly and offers them a little bit more than what you agreed to. If the seller withdraws from the contract they have with the wholesaler and takes the higher price offered by the end buyer, the wholesaler is cut out of the deal. You might be surprised to hear that this occurs, but real estate investing, like nearly every industry, has its share of shady characters. The practice of a buyer swooping in to offer the seller a slightly better price can be enabled by the process of contract assignment; to allow a potential buyer to do their analysis and due diligence before committing to taking over the contract, you must disclose the address of the property for sale, and the buyer will also be aware of what you paid for the contract and how much profit you stand to make. This presents the opportunity for the buyer to go behind your back and try to make a deal directly with the seller. That's why good wholesalers curate a short list of buyers they know and trust, and why they don't like to broadcast their deals.

Here's another potential complication: if you rely on agents to find deals for you, the agents may not want you to wholesale a property because, as mentioned in the example, their commission on the resale of the house can be jeopardized. I personally know a few house flippers who have a reputation for cutting agents out of the deal when they wholesale properties. And guess what? Fewer and fewer agents still bring deals to them. So it's important to include the agent's relist commission in your negotiation if your buyer plans to flip the house. If your buyer plans to keep the house as a rental, you should compensate the agent properly in another way, such as providing them with another listing or offering a cash payout.

Finally, profits on contract assignment deals tend to be low, because you always have to leave enough meat on the bone for the end buyer. Charging too much for the contract will discourage other buyers from considering it, leaving you with no choice but to walk away from the deal.

Pros and Cons of Double-Close Wholesaling

While contract assignment involves the significant risk of having a deal fall through, double closings come with low risk. The risk is much lower because the wholesaler purchases the house and holds it until a buyer is located, eliminating the possibility of someone trying to deal directly with the original seller. Double closings also tend to be more discreet than contract assignments because the end buyer typically doesn't know how much the wholesaler paid for the property until the original sales price is made public, a process that varies from state to state. This gives the wholesaler more control over the deal and increases the chances for a bigger profit than what might be realized with a contract assignment.

So, with time between closings on the shorter side, there's little to no market risk and quickly realized profit. There's also no project management risk, as wholesalers typically don't renovate before reselling the house. Nonetheless, double-close deals do not come risk-free. There can be significant capital required to get a deal, and a wholesaler who pays too much for a house may find it hard to find a buyer and end up having to lower their asking price. If the wholesaler has borrowed money that needs to be paid back quickly, these transactions can be stressful, to say the least. And as with contract assignment, you usually end up leaving some potential profit on the table because you need to balance what you make with what the next buyer expects.

There's also the matter of outside costs, like closing costs and real estate agents. Closing costs are not an issue with a contract assignment as the wholesaler neither buys nor sells the property—only the contract. With a double closing, on the other hand, the wholesaler normally has to pay closing costs twice, once when buying the property and again when selling it.

The situation is reversed for the use of a licensed real estate agent: an agent is needed for a contract assignment, but not for a double closing. For a contract assignment, a licensed agent normally must be present to actually assign the contract, handle the payment, and broker the deal. With a double closing, the wholesaler is buying the property and then selling it (a practice for which an agent is not required). Naturally, not requiring an agent appeals to some wholesalers. However, if you've told an agent who brings you a deal that you'll pay them commission on both the purchase and resale sides, you should honor that agreement. It's never a good business practice to back out of an agreement, and if you do, you shouldn't expect the agent to work with you again. Even if you're not legally obligated to pay commission on the resale side because you're selling to a wholesaler, you should.

Another con of double closings is that they tend to come with a single exit strategy. If you rehab a property and have trouble finding a buyer, you can always rent it or move into it yourself. With a property that is not rehabbed, you have to either sell it to another investor or rehab it yourself, which can be difficult if you are not prepared for it.

If you plan to wholesale using the double-close process, consider the possibility of having a rehab strategy in place, in case you can't find a buyer for a house that hasn't been renovated. This gives you an option and increases your opportunity to maximize your profit.

Pros and Cons of Rehabbing

Of course, as I mentioned, wholesaling is not necessarily what people have in mind when they talk about flipping houses. More often, they're referring to the rehabbing/fix-and-flip method, which is when a house flipper finds a deal and purchases a house, rehabs it, and resells it to a buyer in a relatively short period of time. And as with wholesaling, there are pros and cons to this method of house flipping that will inform your decision about whether to pursue it. Perhaps the biggest advantage of the fix-and-flip method is the potential for the highest profit possible.

In a good market, a house flipper can get top dollar for a house that has been carefully renovated and properly marketed. That means you're in a better position to maximize profit than wholesalers are. As with nearly any financial venture, incurring greater risk raises the chances of greater reward, and house flipping is no exception. Flipping houses requires significant capital, which introduces risk, but the potential for reward is great.

Fix-and-flip also relieves certain pressures. Owning the property gives you greater flexibility than wholesaling. This includes multiple exit strategies, as mentioned above. If the market goes down during your rehab period, you can scale back the scope of work to save money and reduce risk, as I've done many times. If it becomes difficult to find a buyer after the rehab, you should be able to rent it, as rental demand typically increases in times when people are hesitant to buy. When the market comes back up, you can decide whether to continue renting or to sell the house.

Finally, a word about a less practical, more emotional advantage of flipping houses. I make a lot of money doing what I do, but I also enjoy participating in a process that brings a tired, neglected house back to life in order to provide a home for an individual, couple, or family.

A major downside of fix-and-flip, as mentioned, is the financial risk involved. Because you need both the purchase price of the house and the funds to renovate it, rehabbing a house requires significant capital. You'll learn some ways of obtaining financing in chapter 4, and I'll share with you a method for financing a fix-and-flip with no money of your own.

In addition to financial risk, rehabbing houses for flipping includes project management risk. You don't have to talk to many house flippers to hear stories of unreliable and untrustworthy contractors, thefts from properties being renovated, workplace accidents, and other problems that occur during the fix-and-flip process. Fortunately, most of these risks become more manageable as you gain knowledge and experience.

Another disadvantage of the rehab model is that it takes longer to realize your profits than when wholesaling a house. Although you can't anticipate every issue you might encounter, you can realize your profit as quickly as possible by sticking as closely as you can to the timetable you set for getting the house ready to sell.

Whether you decide to wholesale or rehab houses will depend on factors such as your risk tolerance, what financial resources you have available, your ability to borrow money, how much time you want to commit to each deal, the level of savviness with which you can manage a rehab project, and others. For some people, wholesaling is a good way to start out because you can gain knowledge, skills, and experience without having to commit a lot of capital. Once you're comfortable with wholesaling, it can be easier to move up to the next level of real estate investing. That next level is fix-and-flip, and that's what we'll explore in greater detail in the chapters to come.

Chapter Recap

» The two primary methods of flipping houses are rehabbing (or "fix-and-flip") and wholesaling.

» The purpose of a wholesaler is to match a seller with an end buyer.

» Assignment of contract and double closing are the most common methods by which a wholesaler transfers property to an end buyer.

» When assigning a contract, a wholesaler never purchases the property.

» There are advantages and disadvantages associated with both wholesaling and rehabbing houses.

» Rehabbing is more hands-on and labor intensive than wholesaling, but it includes significant rewards.

| 2 |
Scouting Out Potential Deals

Chapter Overview
- » Where to Buy
- » What to Buy
- » Houses for Sale
- » The Not-Yet-for-Sale Market

Flipping houses can seem like a daunting proposition when you're just starting out; believe me, I've been there. My first flip was more than a hundred years old, and I didn't have the right contractors to help; it was, to say the least, nerve-racking. Once you get a feel for the market and gain some confidence, however, flipping can be an exciting and rewarding process, and one that's more collaborative and less solitary than it might initially appear. You'll quickly learn that house flipping requires a network of reliable individuals whom you trust and are comfortable working with. That network will include agents who can help you find deals, lenders who can help fund those deals, reliable contractors who will provide quality work within budget and on schedule, a mentor who can advise and guide you, and others. I have been fortunate enough to find people who have helped me tremendously and who remain instrumental in my success with flipping houses. Some of the most important have been the agents who brought me great deals that often allowed me to realize hundreds of thousands of dollars in profits.

Finding good deals is one of the most challenging aspects of flipping houses, but it's certainly possible once you have a game plan in place. You'll need to have avenues where you'll learn about properties for sale or connect with homeowners directly. You'll need to know how to tell if a deal is good, and how to make fair and appealing offers to get sellers to agree to sell you their houses. Beginners often stress about getting financing, but the truth is, once you have a good deal in place, other aspects of house flipping tend to fall in line fairly easily. As long as your deal is solid, there will be investors who are more than willing to work with you.

A word of caution about finding great deals: it can be a frustrating and exhausting process that requires a good amount of patience and stamina until you've acquired some experience and have a system in place. When I was starting out, I decided that I would rely on real estate agents to bring me deals because it doesn't require any marketing and it's free. I realized on my very first flip that I would need to contact a great many agents to get enough leads to eventually be able to land a project. Depending on where you are, the availability of deals, and the competition in your market, your deal funnel may look different, but my starting formula was that I initially needed to contact about one hundred agents to get 20 leads. Those 20 leads would then result in my making 10 offers, nine of which would not lead to a purchase agreement. The funnel shown in figure 5 illustrates the process of working with agents to find a deal, but it could apply to other methods of securing deals as well. Every method of locating a good deal takes a lot of effort, but it will be worth it when one lines up and you're on your way.

fig. 5

In this chapter, we'll look at the art and methodology of locating a deal. Not all these methods will involve working with agents—although that is my preferred method and it's completely free. The housing market has been on an upward trajectory for almost a decade and good deals have not always been easy to find, but understanding where and how to look will give you a big advantage. Let's get started.

Location, Location, Location

Maybe you've heard of what's referred to as the three golden rules of real estate: location, location, location. Location is a big deal in most aspects of real estate, and your search for a deal is no exception. Location includes not only the city or town in which you're looking for a deal, but also the neighborhood and the location *within* the neighborhood. Understanding and being familiar with the important characteristics of your territory is crucial to your success as a house flipper. Is the house you're looking at on a quiet street or one with double yellow lines down the middle and two or three lanes on each side? If you're in an urban setting, what's the proximity of the house to public transportation, restaurants, and other amenities outside the home? These types of location-based details can significantly increase (or decrease) the value of the house you're considering.

One important issue is the safety of the neighborhood. If local crime statistics are available, be sure to examine them. There are websites available that enable you to research the safety of a particular neighborhood. Some, such as SpotCrime, collect police and crime report information and allow you to enter an address and get a report on recent nearby crime activity. I've looked at houses in neighborhoods where I wouldn't even feel comfortable having contractors working there. I would have worried about materials being stolen and the house vandalized while it was on the market. And, of course, many buyers stay away from areas that aren't considered safe, reducing your chances of a quick sale.

Also be aware that what's considered safe can change from block to block. Many areas contain micro-neighborhoods with varying degrees of safety. If you're not familiar with an area, be sure to make yourself aware of crime statistics that apply to it. Visit the area, preferably at night, to get a sense of how safe it seems.

In addition to safety, the overall condition of a neighborhood should be considered when you're looking at a potential deal. In general, living conditions vary significantly between urban, suburban, and rural areas, and everyone has their own preference for the type of area in which they want to live. In the suburban areas where I do most of my house flipping, for example, a neighborhood in which homes and yards are well cared for is more appealing to buyers than one where properties are neglected, and the number of vehicles parked on the street would be expected to be low, especially compared to a more urban area with a greater population density. And in just about any area, windows can be a telltale sign: windows that are partially open or uncovered indicate a peaceful environment, and a lot of boarded-up or security-barred windows might raise concerns for some buyers.

This is not to say that you should never flip a house in a neighborhood that's considered less safe or desirable than others. But, to avoid overpaying for deals, be well aware of these signs and know that the appeal of the location and the neighborhood ultimately determines the price point of the homes. So you don't overpay for deals.

When doing your research about a particular location, it's important to understand what the supply and demand for housing is like in that area in order to determine if a house flipping business is feasible. If you find many other houses in the area for sale and they've been sitting on the market for a while, it's a sign that there's an oversupply, and you may have a lot of competition when you're ready to sell. The oversupply may also be an indication that the homes in that area are not in demand. Low demand and oversupply cause home prices to drop. You can (and should) assess the availability of homes and the demand for them by looking at inventory levels and ***days on market (DOM)***—the number of days between the time a house is listed for sale and when it goes under contract. If there are tons of properties for sale and it's taking months to sell them, then you probably want to look elsewhere.

You'll also want to consider market and demographic trends, which are often entwined. Is the population of the area growing, or are people moving out? Try to construct an overall profile of homeowners in the area where you're looking. Are most of the homes occupied by families, or is there a large population of singles or elderly people? Families will be concerned with the quality of schools, while that may not be a concern for singles. Also, singles and young couples might prefer an open-concept living space for entertaining purposes, while, in my experience, families with kids usually like separate living rooms and family rooms. If most neighborhood residents have two cars, it's likely that potential buyers will be interested in a garage. But if it's an urban neighborhood and cars are a luxury, nearby public transportation will be what people are looking for. All these factors play into the type of buyer who will be interested in the property and will determine the type of renovations you'll need to do and the price you should be willing to pay for a house.

Also consider what companies are located near the area in which you're considering buying. Large employers attract workers who will want to live close to where they'll be working, which increases demand for housing.

When Google first announced plans for its San Jose, California, headquarters in 2017, home prices in the adjacent neighborhoods went up by 20 percent.

All these tactics contribute to the same goal, which is learning as much as you can about potential buyers and what they'll be looking for in a house. That information will help you gauge the desirability and value of your flip and make it appealing to as many potential buyers as possible.

Deciding on Distance

Most house flippers prefer to get deals that are close to where they live, as this enables them to be close to the property and oversee contractors while renovations are underway. That's a great situation, and the one I absolutely recommend for beginning investors. However, I understand that it's not always feasible. If you live in an area where real estate is so expensive that you're unable to find deals you can afford, you could consider looking in another part of your state or in a different state.

In the San Francisco Bay Area, where I live and flip houses, the median price of a single-family home in June 2021 was $1.2 million. But prices vary depending on the location within the Bay Area. In the City of San Francisco, for instance, the median home price was $1.83 million, while in Contra Costa County, about an hour east of San Francisco, the median home price was a far more manageable $805,000. Flipping a house in San Francisco might require $400,000 or more in down payment and rehab costs, while a flip in Contra Costa County would take only half the capital. If you go even further out to Stockton, a city located about an hour and a half from San Francisco (as seen in figure 6), where the median sales price is $420,000, you can cut your investment in half again.

fig. 6

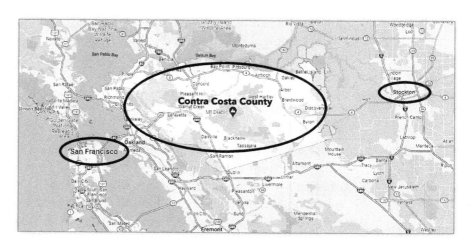

Some investors choose to buy in other areas because there's not enough demand for properties in their immediate locale. They'll go out an hour or two to an area that's more populated and there's greater demand. While that's not an ideal situation, it's probably doable if you plan accordingly and are able to manage your time and projects efficiently.

You can also flip in another state that has affordable real estate prices, but you've got to know what you're doing if you choose to go that route. You'll need someone you can absolutely depend on to be your local representative. This person would need to take photos and video of the property, check up on contractors, make sure the project timetable is on schedule, and keep you informed of any issues or problems. Some investors find a real estate agent or a contractor to do this, but there are other options. You could ask a family member or friend to be your project manager. You could use your network to try to find someone who is interested in getting into the business of flipping houses and could learn from you while overseeing your projects. There are house flipping investment groups in many areas, which could be a good starting point for finding someone to be your local connection to a project. Try a Google search to find one, or check a networking platform like Meetup. You could also advertise on Craigslist and interview those who respond. Choose carefully, and always hold the person accountable for keeping the project on time and within budget.

Obviously, if there is an abundance of good deals, you'll choose one that's in a great location—close to jobs, good schools, transportation, and so on. But more often than not, you'll realize that good deals are hard to come by and you'll need to be flexible in your search to make it work, especially in the beginning. I recommend that beginners keep an open mind and start by looking for deals within a broad geographic area. Once you start to get leads, you can afford to be a little pickier.

What to Buy

Once you've decided on an area in which to look for a deal, you'll want to narrow down the type of property you want. It's important to understand what an average house in the area is like, as that will be what a typical buyer is looking for. In the Bay Area, for example, an average home is a single-story ranch-style house with three bedrooms and two bathrooms and is between 1,200 and 1,500 square feet (see figure 7). If you flip a home that's similar to what's average, you'll have a big buyer pool and the house will typically sell quickly. If the house is much bigger—say 2,500 square feet with five bedrooms and three baths, and the neighboring houses are 1,500-square-foot three-bedroom homes—it's probably overpriced for the neighborhood and will be difficult to sell because of a limited buyer pool.

GRAPHIC

fig. 7

AN AVERAGE HOME IN THE BAY AREA

- Single Story
- Ranch Style
- 3 Bedroom, 2 Bath
- 1,200 – 1,500 sq ft

You'll also want to know the local median sales price, because that's the price most buyers in that area will qualify for. If the median home price in your area is $300,000 but you over-improve a home in the hope of a resale value of $400,000, your buyer pool will be much smaller, if not nonexistent, and your flip may sit on the market for a while until you finally have to lower the price. You can easily find local housing market reports that include the median sales price on sites such as Redfin, Zillow, and Trulia.

NOTE

PRO TIP: When you're starting out, I recommend flipping an entry-level home that's of average size and has a resale value that's around the median sales price for the area. Avoid houses that are too big, too old, or have specific architectural features that may not appeal to many buyers.

Also consider the extent of renovations that will be necessary. If you're new to flipping, it's probably best to look for a house that doesn't need extensive rehab work. There's enough to learn during your first couple of deals without having the added stress of dealing with heavy repairs, especially if you weren't anticipating them.

EXAMPLE

CASE STUDY – My First Flip: Just one month after I'd started looking for deals, an agent I had connected with told me about a property he was listing. It was a large Victorian-style house that had been a home to three generations. The seller was the grandmother who wanted to cash out, retire, and move to Mexico. My first deal! I was excited to get started, but before long I felt overwhelmed and frustrated (see figure 8).

THE NUMBERS

Purchase Price	$1 million
Estimated Rehab Cost	$100,000
Final Rehab Cost	$120,000
All Other Costs*	$136,000
Estimated After-Repair Value (ARV)	$1.35 million
Sales Price	$1.35 million
Profit	$94,000

*Other costs include commissions, closing costs, financing costs, insurance, utilities, staging, and miscellaneous costs

Challenges: The house was more than one hundred years old, with a tiny kitchen, an outdated electrical system, and an awkward upstairs layout that forced me to move many walls and update the infrastructure. It was a lot more work than I'd anticipated.

Unfortunately, I didn't have good contractors for this flip. They scammed me, which led to the project being delayed and the rehab budget being exceeded. I was still working full time at this point, so practically every minute that I wasn't at my job, I was checking on and worrying about the project. It was extremely stressful. Luckily, I had brought my mentor in as a partner to guide me through the deal in exchange for a percentage of the profit. If it wasn't for my mentor's guidance on this deal, I probably would have lost a lot of money and never wanted to flip another house!

On top of all that, I was too green to realize that the deal was a niche home that would only appeal to a narrow subset of potential buyers. This slowed down the sale of the house once it finally got on the market. It was an exhausting project, but well worth the effort in terms of learning and experience. Plus, when the house went on the market and the previous owner came to an open house for a look, she cried because she loved what we had done and couldn't believe it was the same house—a response I found very gratifying after all the work and hassle involved with that flip.

Takeaways:
» Start with standard-sized, entry-level homes.
» Get references for contractors, and screen them; this is crucial.

> » Partner with an experienced mentor on your first deal to learn on the job and help you through rough spots.
> » Always budget for unexpected costs.
> » Don't expect to make money from your first few deals. If you do, consider it a bonus.

To view before-and-after photos of my first flip, go to the Case Study Library included with your Digital Assets at go.quickstartguides.com/flipping. To watch the video I made about this experience, look for "My Nightmare 1st House Flip" on my YouTube channel: www.youtube.com/transformrealestate.

All that being said, buying a house that requires more extensive work, like gutting the kitchen or replacing the electrical system, may be unavoidable if you don't have access to many deals. If you find yourself in that situation, you should at least understand the potential risks you are taking on, including unexpected costs and longer-than-anticipated construction time, which could lead to higher holding costs and increased exposure to market risk. If you enter a deal in which extensive renovations are necessary, I highly recommend having a good, trustworthy contractor lined up before closing on the house.

The most complicated flips are those with structural issues. Normally, you can acquire these houses at reduced prices, but repairing structural issues usually requires working with a structural engineer and can be expensive and time consuming, especially when permits are required. These types of major repairs can add value when you sell the house, but you need to be sure you have someone who can perform the work the right way while staying on time and on budget. Be sure you understand the risks associated with the condition of the house.

When deciding on the type of homes to flip, consider that single-family homes are generally more desirable to buyers and hold their prices better in a market downturn than townhomes and condos, but townhomes and condos are more affordable and cost less to remodel because you are not responsible for all the infrastructure. Some house flippers avoid condos and townhomes due to HOA rules and fees, but, depending on your budget and risk appetite, they may be worth your consideration. For a quick look at the pros and cons of these various properties, take a look at figure 9.

The following are some features to watch for when you're checking out a house. Some features are likely to encourage potential buyers, and others may be warning signs that the house could be difficult to renovate and sell.

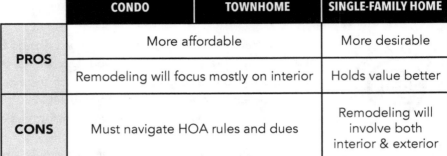

	CONDO	TOWNHOME	SINGLE-FAMILY HOME
PROS	More affordable		More desirable
	Remodeling will focus mostly on interior		Holds value better
CONS	Must navigate HOA rules and dues		Remodeling will involve both interior & exterior

A walk-in closet in the master bedroom

Ceiling fans that can help lower energy costs

Exterior lighting

Hardwood floors in the main living area

A covered front porch

Energy-efficient **appliances and windows**

A **patio** large enough for picnics and cookouts

A **kitchen** that's large enough to eat in

Energy-efficient **lighting**

A **dining room**

A full **bath** on the main level of the house

A walk-in **kitchen pantry** that's large enough to accommodate nonperishables and kitchen items such as containers and small appliances

A double, side-by-side **kitchen sink**

A **laundry room** where dirty laundry can be stored until it's washed, dried, and ready to be put away

A **garage** large enough to include storage space in addition to housing cars

What Buyers Want

It can be helpful to keep up with trends and preferences when you're in the market for deals, as you can keep an eye out for specific desirable features and whether there's potential to add them to a house that you're checking out. Figure 10 lists the top 15 features that home buyers look for, according to the National Association of Home Builders (NAHB), a trade association based in Washington, D.C.

This is a good reference list, but I think you should take it with a grain of salt. Not all those features carry the same importance, and priorities and preferences vary from location to location and from buyer to buyer. For instance, I rarely put ceiling fans in my flips because of the mild weather in the Bay Area, but in other parts of the country, ceiling fans are a common and desirable feature. Also, pantries are rare in my area due to limited indoor space, and walk-in pantries are even less common. But in places where homes are much larger, they are a highly desirable feature. Hardwood floors are a big deal in California, and I often install them or refinish existing ones when I'm flipping a house. In states like Louisiana and Texas that get a lot of rain, tile floors are far more desirable than hardwood. What buyers are looking for varies significantly depending on location and other factors.

Watch Out for These Red Flags

Chances are you'll look at houses that contain some of the features that buyers want, or at least have the potential for adding some desirable elements. On the flip side are features that could discourage buyers or cause you more problems than you are willing to deal with. We've already mentioned red flags like structural issues. What follows are some other features or characteristics that could be troublesome as you proceed through renovations and attempt to sell the house. I'm not suggesting that you give up on a deal if you run into one or more of these—just warning that they're issues that deserve serious thought.

1. Widespread mold, especially the black mold *Stachybotrys*, which is considered a health threat. Small patches of mold under a sink may not be a problem, but if the mold is widespread it should concern you because you may have to resort to professional mold remediation specialists.

2. A tiny kitchen that cannot be expanded. A big part of my rehab involves enlarging and redesigning kitchens to improve functionality. Usually I can borrow from a nearby space to do this, but in some cases, despite my best efforts, I just can't make a kitchen big enough for the size of the home. Because a good-sized kitchen is usually on the top of buyers' lists, this can make the house much harder to sell.

3. Too few bathrooms for the size of the house. A three-bedroom house with just one bathroom means there's not a bedroom with its own bath, which normally would serve as the master bedroom. That situation typically doesn't function well for a family with kids, and the house is likely to be passed over if buyers can afford better options. Sometimes, though, you can come up with a creative way to add a bathroom and significantly increase the value of the home. Be sure to read the "Spanish Flip" case study later in this chapter to find out more about this.

4. A low-pitched or flat roof. These roofs are usually cheaply constructed using less material and are more liable to cause drainage problems; they also provide less indoor space and less insulation than steeply pitched roofs. They are usually not attractive to buyers and thus lower the resale value of the house. See more information about this in the case study titled "Low-Pitched Roof Flip" in chapter 3.

5. No garage. This is less of a problem in some urban settings where many people don't have cars and garages aren't necessary—but in an area where most properties come with garages, not having one is a disadvantage. An investor I know lost a couple hundred thousand dollars on a flip because he didn't realize his target buyers weren't interested in a house without a garage.

6. A funky floor plan that can't be easily fixed. This could include irregularly shaped rooms, awkward additions, the lack of a bedroom with its own bathroom, etc. Fixing a poor floor plan sometimes requires load-bearing walls to be removed, which necessitates the involvement of a structural engineer and plan reviews for permitting, which can get expensive and time consuming.

7. Excessive noise, especially in an area where other streets are quiet. Excessive noise can come from a highway or busy road, a nearby

ambulance service or fire station, an entertainment venue, a school, or other factors. Read about how this affected a deal I did in the case study "Twice Flipped," later in this chapter.

8. A nearby property that is run-down and disreputable-looking. This can be a big turn-off for potential buyers, as they usually want to avoid neighbors who don't take care of their property. This problem is also addressed in "Twice Flipped."

9. An oddly shaped lot or one that is much smaller than average for the area. Most home buyers want a yard that is big enough for some outdoor activity or has enough space for a storage shed or a playground for the kids. This has become increasingly important since the beginning of the pandemic, when many people started spending more time at home. In some areas, a spacious yard is desirable; in other, more densely packed areas, any outdoor space at all is considered valuable. The important thing is for the lot size not to be well below average for the neighborhood.

10. Nearby train tracks, power lines, substations, warehouses or commercial buildings, water treatment plants, etc. These sorts of structures create noise, smells, traffic, and hazards that can make it much harder to sell a home.

11. A death, even of natural causes, that occurred on the property. You are obligated to disclose to potential buyers if there have been any deaths within the past three years. Some buyers, especially if they are superstitious, may be deterred by a recent death on the property.

CASE STUDY – Spanish Flip: Let me tell you about a flip I did that necessitated adding a bedroom and a bath to make the house more like the comparable homes in the area. It was a Spanish-style house, so I call it the Spanish flip.

I had an opportunity to buy the house from an elderly gentleman who wanted to sell and move to a retirement community. The house had been well maintained, but it hadn't been updated for decades and it came with a tiny and dated kitchen, only one bathroom that was unnecessarily large, and a big and beautiful backyard. The deal came with some conditions: there would be no repairs done to the house before it was sold to me, all unwanted personal possessions would be left behind, and the seller wanted a rent-back deal (an agreement for him to rent the property after selling it) until his place in the retirement community became available.

THE NUMBERS

fig. 11

Purchase Price	$1.15 million
Estimated Rehab Cost	$140,000
Final Rehab Cost	$140,000
All Other Costs*	$120,000
Estimated ARV	$1.5 million
Sales Price	$1.675 million
Profit	$265,000

*Other costs include commissions, closing costs, financing costs, insurance, utilities, staging, and miscellaneous costs

Challenges: The house, which was over a century old, consisted of 1,328 square feet, with two bedrooms and one bathroom. Most other homes in the area had three bedrooms and two baths, so I knew that if I didn't make some changes, the house would have limited appeal to buyers. I decided to convert the large dining room into another bedroom, and I used some existing closet space in the larger bedroom to add a bathroom. (See rehab costs in figure 11.) Creating a combined bedroom and bath within the existing footprint wasn't easy, but with some creative planning we were able to pull it off. Removing a wall between the small kitchen and the breakfast nook, and another between the kitchen and the laundry room, increased the size of the kitchen and also created new dining space to replace the old dining room. If you're interested in how I added a bathroom to this flip, see the floor plans in chapter 6.

Takeaways:
» Increasing the functionality of the living space and making it comparable to others in the area added a lot of value to a home that was modest in size.

» Remember that looking at the features of comparable homes (comps) is key to figuring out what a house needs to compete in its neighborhood.

To view before-and-after photos of my Spanish flip, go to the Case Study Library included with your Digital Assets at go.quickstartguides.com/flipping. To watch the video I made about this experience, search for "100-Year-Old House Flip Before and After" on my YouTube channel.

CASE STUDY – Twice Flipped: This story is about a flip in which I nearly ended up losing $80,000 due to a market shift and circumstances in the neighborhood where the house was located. A young man had inherited a house from his parents. His idea was to sell it and make a fresh start someplace else, but he was unsettled regarding his plans. Because of his uncertainty and various other reasons, he preferred to sell the house to an investor instead of putting it on the market, with part of the deal including a three-month free rent-back agreement to give him time to figure out his next steps. I agreed to this, even though it meant I had to pay holding costs until he finally moved out and I could start the renovations.

THE NUMBERS

Purchase Price	$900,000
Estimated Rehab Cost	$80,000
Final Rehab Cost	$80,000
All Other Costs*	$120,000
Estimated ARV	$1.2 million
Sales Price	$1.1 million
Profit	$0

*Other costs include commissions, closing costs, financing costs, insurance, utilities, staging, and miscellaneous costs

fig. 12

Challenges: I didn't realize it when I agreed to buy, but this house came with many challenges in addition to the three-month waiting period before I could start the work. By the time we were ready to begin the renovations, the market had taken a downward shift and the comps had decreased in value, meaning my ARV (after-repair value) would be much lower than anticipated. Fearing the market would continue its downward slide, I downgraded the initial scope of work I'd hoped for in order to turn around the project in less time than I'd planned.

We gave the house a quick cosmetic remodel and got it on the market as soon as possible, but it didn't sell. After letting it sit for a month, I realized that potential buyers were put off by the neighbor's house, which was not well kept and had a boarded-up garage.

Around the same time, I recognized another problem: an elementary school just across the street from my property! When I bought the house, I hadn't realized a school would be a liability; I thought it might even be an asset. It turns out, however, that many people don't want the noise and traffic associated with a school.

And to make matters even worse, potential buyers weren't impressed with the home's kitchen and bathroom. I knew I had to take drastic measures if I wanted to sell this property. I ran the numbers and realized I was in danger of losing $80,000 on the flip—not good! I approached the couple living next door and offered to fix the exterior of their house for free. Fortunately, they accepted the offer, enabling me to solve one problem. Meanwhile, I took the house off the market and updated the kitchen and bathrooms to appeal to a wider pool of buyers. I had better results when the house was put back on the market, but I still had to discount the price because of the school noise. I did not turn a profit on this flip (see figure 12).

Takeaways:
» Conditions surrounding a house affect its desirability and value. Be sure to take note of any possible drawbacks before agreeing to buy.

» You always want to purchase the worst house on the block for your flip, not the property next to the worst house!

» Selling a flip at a desired price is not always easy; sometimes you have to remove obstacles creatively, like remodeling the neighbor's house for free.

» When offering a rent-back deal, keep it short to minimize market risk.

To view before-and-after photos of this flip, go to the Case Study Library included with your Digital Assets at go.quickstartguides.com/flipping. To watch the video I made about this experience, search for "House Flip Before and After – $80K Loss?!" on my YouTube channel.

Looking for Deals That Are for Sale

You've already read that finding deals can be a challenging task. That's primarily because house flipping is a numbers game, and it's difficult to find deals that satisfy the numbers. To increase your chances of finding good deals, you'll want to try several methods of locating them and decide which work the best for you. As I mentioned earlier, I find most of my deals through a network of agents I've worked very hard to build and cultivate. For me, working with agents has been a successful method of finding deals, but it's not the only one. Let's look at some ways of locating deals that are for sale.

Working with Agents

This is my personal favorite. It takes a lot of work to get an agent network established, but once you do, it's completely free, and your up-front efforts can continue generating deals for many years. When I started connecting with agents, I was working a nine-to-five job and my time was limited. I didn't have time for as many in-person meetings as I would have liked, so I often used cold calling to reach as many agents as I could. If I had not been working full time, however, I would have requested in-person meetings instead of relying on cold calling, because agents appreciate investors who make a real effort to connect with them.

To identify agents to call, I looked for those with active listings in the San Francisco Bay Area, where I was interested in buying. You can find agents by looking at properties listed on Zillow or Redfin; the agent information is included on those sites. Once I had identified a list of agents, I began cold calling, using every minute of my coffee and lunch breaks from work.

If you've ever done cold calling before, you know it's nerve-racking to put yourself out there, but, as they say, nothing worth having comes easy. I compiled a script that I used for all the calls, which made me less nervous about making them. It was still pretty scary at first, but the more calls I made, the more comfortable I got. When I got an agent on the phone, I'd introduce myself and right away mention that I was a house flipper in the Bay Area. I'd tell them that they could get both the buying and the selling sides of the commission by working with me, which is double the commission they would make when working with a regular home seller or buyer. I'd also offer to add one percent commission on the relist, in order to make my deals more attractive to them.

If it was obvious that the agent I was speaking with was not interested in working with an investor, I'd thank them for their time and end the conversation. In most cases, however, I could sense an agent starting to become more interested when I mentioned the double commission, the additional one percent on the relist, and my hope for a long-term business relationship.

The cold-call script I used when reaching out to agents is shown in figure 13. It's pretty basic, but it worked!

fig. 13

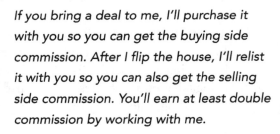

Agent Cold Call Script

Hi, this is Elisa Covington calling, how are you? I'm a house flipper in the Bay Area.

If you bring a deal to me, I'll purchase it with you so you can get the buying side commission. After I flip the house, I'll relist it with you so you can also get the selling side commission. You'll earn at least double commission by working with me.

I am looking for fixer-uppers that I can rehab and resell for a profit.

While going through the script, pause every so often to give the agent time to respond and ask questions. That ensures that the call is an interactive session rather than something like a recorded voicemail. An agent who is interested in working with you is likely to have a lot of questions and want you to clarify some of what you've told them. It took some dedication and perseverance, but after a month of cold calling, I had one hundred agents willing to refer deals to me, which led to my first flip.

During these calls, I'd make it clear from the start that I was looking to build long-term business relationships, and I followed through on that by using these guidelines:

» After making the initial contact, I would follow up every six to eight weeks. This can be done with a phone call, an email, or a text.

» When an agent gave me a lead on a deal, I'd always respond within 24 hours to thank them and let them know whether I thought the deal would work for me. You certainly shouldn't feel you need to take every deal an agent tells you about, but you must let them know you take each one seriously.

» If I rejected a deal an agent brought to me, I'd always make sure to explain why. This helps the agent to better understand your reasoning and also how your numbers work. Once agents are familiar with your financial model, their leads will align with what you're looking for.

» Cultivate long-term relationships by saying what you mean and meaning what you say, respecting others' time, and remembering that trust and relationship are more important than short-term gain.

Agents have access to the *multiple listing services* (MLS), which are databases established by real estate brokers to provide data about properties for sale. Websites like Redfin and Zillow pull information from the MLS directly, and by checking out properties for sale on those websites, you can find houses to flip on your own. However, in some areas, such as the San Francisco Bay Area, the price difference between a fixer-upper listed on the MLS and a remodeled home is usually not significant enough to make the numbers work, so it makes more sense to rely on agents to bring you off-market deals that you can purchase at a discount. Even if deals are available on the MLS in your area, it can still be beneficial to work with agents, as there are a great many houses for sale on the MLS at any given time, and agents can help you sift through them and locate the ones with real potential. Figure 14 is an example of a return on a search query in the MLS.

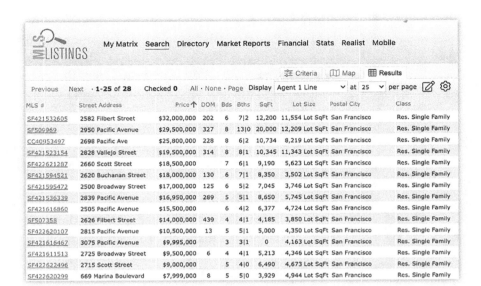

MLS #	Street Address	Price ↑	DOM	Bds	Bths	SqFt	Lot Size	Postal City	Class
SF421532605	2582 Filbert Street	$32,000,000	202	6	7|2	12,200	11,554 Lot SqFt	San Francisco	Res. Single Family
SF509969	2950 Pacific Avenue	$29,500,000	327	8	13|0	20,000	12,209 Lot SqFt	San Francisco	Res. Single Family
CC40953497	2698 Pacific Ave	$25,800,000	228	8	6|2	10,734	8,219 Lot SqFt	San Francisco	Res. Single Family
SF421523154	2828 Vallejo Street	$19,500,000	314	8	8|1	10,345	11,343 Lot SqFt	San Francisco	Res. Single Family
SF422621287	2660 Scott Street	$18,500,000		7	6|1	9,190	5,623 Lot SqFt	San Francisco	Res. Single Family
SF421594521	2620 Buchanan Street	$18,000,000	130	6	7|1	8,350	3,502 Lot SqFt	San Francisco	Res. Single Family
SF421595472	2500 Broadway Street	$17,000,000	125	6	5|2	7,045	3,746 Lot SqFt	San Francisco	Res. Single Family
SF421536339	2839 Pacific Avenue	$16,950,000	289	5	5|1	8,650	5,745 Lot SqFt	San Francisco	Res. Single Family
SF421616860	2505 Pacific Avenue	$15,500,000		6	4|2	6,377	4,724 Lot SqFt	San Francisco	Res. Single Family
SF507358	2626 Filbert Street	$14,000,000	439	4	4|1	4,185	3,850 Lot SqFt	San Francisco	Res. Single Family
SF422620107	2815 Pacific Avenue	$10,500,000	13	5	5|1	5,000	4,350 Lot SqFt	San Francisco	Res. Single Family
SF421616467	3075 Pacific Avenue	$9,995,000		3	3|1	0	4,163 Lot SqFt	San Francisco	Res. Single Family
SF421611513	2725 Broadway Street	$9,500,000	6	4	4|1	5,213	4,346 Lot SqFt	San Francisco	Res. Single Family
SF422622496	2715 Scott Street	$9,000,000		5	4|0	6,490	4,673 Lot SqFt	San Francisco	Res. Single Family
SF422620299	669 Marina Boulevard	$7,999,000	8	5	5|0	3,929	4,944 Lot SqFt	San Francisco	Res. Single Family

fig. 14

Shown here are the results for my queries, which were "Status = active, contingent, pending, sold," "COE (Close of Escrow) Date = 0-360," "Property Type = single family home," and "Map Search = within 0.25 miles of 2505 Pacific Ave, San Francisco." As you can see, my search resulted in numerous listings meeting my criteria.

It would take a lot of work and a lot of money to connect with sellers directly and strike a deal on your own. Working with agents allows you to take advantage of the connection that's already established between the agent and the seller. This could be in the form of a listing agreement that let the agent represent the seller in the sale, or the agent's connection with the listing agent. When a *listing agent* (the agent who represents the seller) brings you a potential deal, they've already earned the trust of the seller, which is a huge step. At that point, all you must do is make an offer that's acceptable to the seller. You'll realize soon enough that homeowners trust agents a lot more than they trust investors. Having your offer presented by the agent with whom a seller has signed a listing agreement will make it a lot easier for a deal to be negotiated than if you made the offer on your own.

Of course you'll pay agents a commission on the resale of your flips, but I think it's totally worth it because of the time and money you save on project acquisition. Through the hundreds of agents in my network, I can depend on a reliable stream of leads that enables me to keep moving forward with new projects.

Foreclosures

A *foreclosure*—the action of a house being repossessed by a lender—can happen for several reasons. One of the most common is when the borrower (the homeowner) doesn't pay their mortgage payments, and the lender (the bank) needs to take the house and sell it to recoup the loaned money. Foreclosures can also occur when a homeowner doesn't pay property taxes or homeowners association fees. When a house goes into foreclosure and back into the lender's ownership, there are several ways it can subsequently be sold. It can be sold by a bank or other lender on the open market (figure 15) or through an auction. If the foreclosed home was purchased using an FHA loan (a mortgage loan that's backed by the US Federal Housing Administration), the Department of Housing and Urban Development (HUD) will take ownership of the house and sell it online at HudHomeStore.gov. If a home is at risk for foreclosure but still in the possession of the owner, it can be sold as a ***pre-foreclosure,*** also known as a ***short sale***. House flippers often look for deals on foreclosed properties, sometimes successfully and sometimes with regret. Let's take a look at some of the ways foreclosures can be sold.

fig. 15

A sign indicating a house is in foreclosure and for sale.

Short Sales

Short sales can be lucrative for a buyer, but they take time and are notoriously difficult to negotiate. A short sale occurs when a homeowner who can't make their mortgage payments sells the property for less than the amount that remains on the mortgage. The sale must be approved by the mortgage lender, and this, of course, is not guaranteed. A lender will sometimes agree to a short sale because it saves on attorney fees, eviction costs, damage to the property, and so forth. If it is approved and the sale occurs, the lender gets all the proceeds and can either choose to forgive the difference between the sales price and the mortgage money owed or require the seller to pay back some or all of that amount.

Short sales typically don't happen quickly, and they normally require a lot of paperwork and negotiating. I purchased my first home through a short sale. I didn't understand at first what my agent meant by "a long and difficult escrow," but I did by the time we finally completed the sale process that took more than six months, requiring in the end for some paperwork to be redone because it had expired! If you're anxious to close a deal and flip a house, you may not have the patience required for a successful short sale. The housing market has been on the rise for almost a decade, and there are not a lot of short sales right now because most homeowners have built up equity in their homes. During a market downturn like the one we saw in the Great Recession of 2008, there were a lot of such opportunities available as homeowners went underwater on their mortgages. If you're interested, you can find short sales in your area on the websites of local real estate agents and in MLS feeds. You might also find them listed on Craigslist or other online resources. If you know a real estate agent who is experienced in short sales, you could ask them to alert you when one comes up. If you get involved with a short sale, be sure to do your homework and learn as much as you can about the process, seeking advice from a lawyer if necessary.

Auctions (Trustee Sales)

A real estate auction involves the sale, by third-party trustees, of homes that are owned by a bank or other lender. I've known house flippers who have found some good deals on auction properties, and others who have gotten burned. Buying a foreclosed house at auction is a risky business that I don't recommend for beginners, but despite the problems associated with auctions, I do think the process is worth a mention.

You can find out about houses to be auctioned by visiting local government websites (look for sheriff's sales) or a site like Auction.com or Bid4Assets. com. These sites will tell you if the auction is in person or online (more and more auctions are moving online), the date on which the auction is scheduled, and some information about the property. A problem with auctions is that they're often canceled or postponed because property owners manage to come up with the money they owe at the last minute or work out some sort of agreement with the lender. If you're interested in participating, you'll have to check back often to see if the auction is still on.

Another problem with auction properties is that home inspections usually are not allowed, and you are often expected to buy sight unseen. You usually have to pay in cash, and not every house sold at auction is cheap. The starting price is typically the amount needed to repay lenders what they are owed, plus interest and attorney fees. If you ever decide to bid on a house that's being auctioned, make sure you understand all the auction rules and have learned as much about the house as possible, including whether there are any liens or claims against it. One final caution: it's not unheard of to buy a house at auction and find out the former owner—or someone else—is still living in it. Buying a house at auction can mean you'll have less competition, and there are deals to be had; however, auction purchases are generally riskier than regular purchases. If you choose this route, be prepared for what you could encounter.

Real Estate Owned Properties

If you're looking through real estate listings and see "REO," it means the property is *real estate owned*. An REO property is one that has gone through a foreclosure and didn't sell at auction. It's owned by a bank or another lender who has placed it for sale on the open market. Normally, the bank will have made any necessary major repairs to the house, cleared any liens on the property, and evicted the previous owner before selling the house—but if you plan to go this route, it's a good idea to make sure all of that has happened. The bank, which wants to sell the house to get back what is still owed on it, usually hires a local real estate agent to list and sell it.

Because the bank has invested in the property, it is likely to list it at a competitive market price. It's in the bank's interests to not have the house remain on the market for a long time, though, so if it doesn't sell in a reasonable amount of time, the price may be lowered. Other sources of REO homes are Fannie Mae and Freddie Mac, companies that issue conventional mortgages that are backed by the federal government. When a conventional loan is foreclosed on, the property reverts back to Fannie Mae or Freddie Mac, often as an REO. While these houses are sold through agents and listed on the MLS, they're also sold on the

Fannie Mae and Freddie Mac websites. Homeowners get first shot at making offers on these houses—investors have to wait 15 days after the house is listed to make an offer. If the house is still listed after 15 days, there might be a deal waiting.

An advantage of buying an REO home is that you can view it before making an offer. While the bank is likely to have taken care of major repairs, don't expect the house to be in tip-top shape—it is, after all, a foreclosure. But if you're looking for a deal, it won't hurt to consider an REO. Just be sure to do your homework and know what you're getting into, because REOs usually don't come with helpful seller disclosures.

Other Sellers

There are a variety of other options for buying homes that aren't necessarily being sold through agents or foreclosures. The following may not be as consistently available as those methods but are well worth looking into.

Wholesalers

As you read in chapter 1, a variation of house flipping is called wholesaling, and wholesalers can be a good resource for rehabbers who are looking for deals. Rehabbers are in the business of buying houses to fix up and sell for a profit, and wholesalers find deals and resell them to fix-and-flip investors without doing the work of rehabbing. You can often meet wholesalers at real estate group meetings and events. Give them your contact information and ask to be included on their buyer list. Most deals from wholesalers probably won't pan out, but if you find a wholesaler or two who are good at what they do and collect a lot of deals, you should get to know them and build a relationship. Because wholesalers must mark up their prices so they can make money on a deal, your rehab profits might not be as high as they would on a deal you find on your own. Still, the time and effort saved on deal acquisition might be worth the profit sacrificed. If you do work with wholesalers, though, never rely on the analysis they give you. It's common for them to underestimate the rehab costs and inflate the after-repair value (ARV), which is what the property will be worth when all the rehab work is done.

Craigslist

Don't discount Craigslist as a source for potential deals. You'll find postings by homeowners looking to sell without enlisting the help of an agent (see figure 16) as well as posts from wholesalers hoping to lure investors into cash deals. Craigslist is easy to use and includes the benefit of allowing you to enter specific words or phrases that help you narrow down your search for deals. Once you click on "real estate for sale" in the housing section, you can enter keywords and terms like "cash sale," "as-is," "REO," "fixer-upper," "must sell," "handyman special," and so forth.

fig. 16

$300,000/1,670 sq ft

Contractor special. Home is gutted. REO sale. Sold as-is. No permits or plans are in seller's possession.

Once you've narrowed your search, you can start a conversation with the seller by replying to the post. While you'll want to find out as much as you can about the property, your initial contact should only let the seller know you are interested, you have cash, and you can close quickly. Ask to set up a meeting to discuss the deal, at which time you can get all the details. If you're replying to a wholesaler, identify yourself as a local cash buyer and ask to be added to the wholesaler's cash buyer email list. You'll know it's a wholesaler's post because it will mention that the seller has many properties available, or it may even state that the seller is a wholesaler. Again, request a time when you can discuss the property in further detail so you can also learn about the wholesaler and share with them your buy criteria.

For Sale by Owner

Most sellers who list their houses "for sale by owner" (FSBO) do so because they want to save on real estate agent commissions. Because they'll be saving on commissions, FSBO sellers are sometimes willing to accept less than their asking price, especially if they've been trying to sell for a while. It's also common for homeowners to have unrealistic expectations about their home's value, so you'll need to be prepared for a drawn-out negotiation.

You can look for FSBO deals on sites like Zillow and Trulia, or check the classified ads in your local paper, as well as Craigslist. Some homeowners post FSBO signs in their yards to get the word out. If the house has been for sale for a long time, be sure to ask why. It could be that the seller is simply asking for too much or that there is something wrong with the house.

Looking for Off-Market Deals

Beyond the arena of houses for sale is another less obvious potential market for deals. If you can tap into a situation where a homeowner's circumstances have suddenly changed and they want to sell but have not yet gotten around to officially putting the house on the market, you have the potential for a great deal.

There are many reasons homeowners find themselves in this situation—and I've seen a lot of them myself. It could be someone who has inherited a house they have no interest in living in or renting. It could be a hoarder who's too embarrassed to put their house on the market and risk people coming in and seeing the mess. Some other reasons houses are "unofficially" for sale include the following:

> » There's a situation in which the homeowner needs cash fast.
> » The owners are aging and can no longer care for the house and property.
> » There's a divorce in progress and neither person can afford to keep the house.
> » There's been a death in the family.
> » A job or relationship is causing a major move that's happening imminently.
> » A landlord is tired of managing tenants and could easily be persuaded to sell the house.
> » The homeowner has had a serious medical diagnosis.

Most of these scenarios are not what I would consider happy or positive reasons for wanting to sell a house. The truth is, there are a lot of people with houses who are in over their heads, or who can feel their circumstances falling in around them and realize they will soon be unable to keep the house. Understanding the seller's motivation can help you craft an offer that meets their needs and creates a win-win scenario.

MY TAKE

If you identify a possible off-market deal and try to get the house, realize there's a balancing act between landing a great deal and treating the seller fairly. No one sets out in life to be a hoarder or wants to admit they're too frail to take care of the house they've lived in for 40 years. Often, sellers are desperate and not sure what to do. These can be very sensitive situations that require the seller to be treated with respect and compassion.

EXAMPLE

CASE STUDY – Awkward Addition Flip: A homeowner was being relocated to another state because of his job, and his employer hired a relocation company to help with the move. The owner needed to move quickly to accommodate his work schedule and didn't want to do any repairs to the house—and believe me when I tell you that it was in desperate need of repairs. I wasn't surprised that the homeowner decided to sell to an investor off-market to avoid having to address all the issues we'd have to face. He originally wanted $1 million for the home. Due to its poor condition, I had to discount the purchase price (see figure 17), but I offered to purchase it as-is and cooperate with the relocation company. The seller liked the convenience of that and happily accepted the terms.

THE NUMBERS

Purchase Price	$950,000
Estimated Rehab Cost	$160,000
Final Rehab Cost	$160,000
All Other Costs*	$102,000
Estimated ARV	$1.4 million
Sales Price	$1.325 million
Profit	$113,000

*Other costs include commissions, closing costs, financing costs, insurance, utilities, staging, and miscellaneous costs

GRAPHIC

fig. 17

Challenges: Nothing had been done to this house for at least 30 years. The roof was at the end of its life, and the house needed new windows and a new HVAC system. The property had a good-sized backyard, but it had not been cared for and the grass was completely dead. It also needed a new deck, as the old one—along with the kitchen countertops—had been ripped out to clear the termite inspection per the relocation company's policy. And besides all the disrepair, there was a really unfortunate 600-square-foot addition that had been awkwardly fused to the rest of the house, creating all kinds of odd, dark, nearly unusable spaces. Our biggest challenge was to open up the space and make it flow smoothly to provide a functional, attractive floor plan.

We did that by taking out some walls between the kitchen and the living room to create a large, open space. We redid the entire kitchen, adding an island to serve as an entertainment center. And because the house didn't have a bedroom with its own bath, we created one by connecting a bedroom with a guest bathroom. By reimagining that awkward addition that had been connected to the living room and kitchen, we were able to create a space that looked great and was fully functional. The backyard was made over by installing sod and rebuilding the deck that had been removed.

This was a substantial and expensive project, costing $160,000, which is on the higher end of all the flips I've done. Even though we managed to completely transform the interior by opening up the floor plan, the sale didn't go as well as expected, possibly due to the flat roof on top of the addition.

Takeaways:

» When selling a home off-market, the seller is usually looking for convenience. That's why I could negotiate a lower sales price in exchange for an as-is sale without any repairs. Lowering your expectations about property conditions and meeting the seller's needs can help you close the deal.

» Be sure to be realistic when calculating a renovation budget for a house that needs as much work as this one did.

» Beware of a poorly planned addition. I wouldn't necessarily avoid a house with an addition like this one had, but it did complicate the project and result in a lower sales price, even after the rehab.

In rare cases, you might hear about someone who is in a situation that may require them to sell their house. If so, you'd better get in touch with the seller and make an offer immediately, because good deals don't wait, and if you don't act quickly, someone else will. In most cases, however, you'll need to put out feelers or conduct an all-out search for these types of properties. Let's look at some ways you might do that.

Use Classified Ad Websites

You can post ads on Craigslist, Facebook Marketplace, For Sale By Owner, or other websites letting people know you buy houses for cash. Appeal to potential sellers by assuring them you can solve their problem by taking the house off their hands fast, without their having to deal with making repairs or hiring an agent.

Reach Out to Landlords

Google "houses for rent" and the name of the location you're interested in, and you'll find a variety of sites listing rental properties. Also keep an eye out for rental signs in the neighborhoods you're looking in. If you've ever been a landlord, you know there can be downsides to renting: the HVAC system breaks down and needs to be replaced; a pipe freezes and bursts; you get a tenant who refuses to turn down the music at two a.m., drawing both the ire of the neighbors and a visit from the police.

Occasionally, a landlord who is tired of renting will consider selling the house if the right offer comes along. It doesn't hurt to reach out to landlords of properties that are for rent and see if they'd be willing to discuss. You probably have a better window of opportunity if you catch them before the house is listed for rent; the chances are lower once it's rented.

Send Out Mailers

Direct mail involves coming up with a letter or postcard and sending it to your target audience. In it, you express your interest in buying houses and ask potential sellers to contact you if they are interested. It is a proven method of marketing for deals, but it can be expensive, as you'll have to send out a lot of mailers to get a few responses, and of those responses, even fewer will result in a deal.

Sometimes investors target certain zip codes and neighborhoods and send out tens of thousands of mailers, followed by another round to the same recipients a couple of months later. After two or three rounds of mailers, they start getting a few calls from potential sellers. According to Millionacres, an online real estate resource associated with The Motley Fool financial brand, direct marketing commonly results in a response rate of between one and five percent (with a two or three percent rate considered successful). Frankly, even that small number sounds high to me, but that may be due to my location; I think Bay Area sellers are particularly savvy and don't tend to respond to direct mail. Also, the house flipping market is extremely competitive, meaning that many investors may be targeting the same homeowners, which drives everyone's response rate lower. I've met investors from other areas who tend to get higher response rates to their direct mail campaigns than we do where I am.

With all of that in mind, we'll assume a two percent response rate for the example in figure 18. But remember, though two percent of 10,000 mailers is 200 leads, only a small percentage of those leads will result in an offer, and only a small percentage of offers will result in a deal. A direct mail campaign involving 10,000 mailers is likely to result in numbers like those shown in the deal funnel in figure 18.

fig. 18

MAIL 10,000 POSTCARDS

GET 200 LEADS

MAKE 50 OFFERS

GET 10 DEALS

If you have the money to go the direct-mail route, your mailer should clearly convey the information you want people to know. Some investors send out a page-long letter containing a lot of detail about how they work, listing the advantages of letting them buy your home, giving a history of other homes they've purchased, and offering lots of other information. But I think the more effective way is to keep the mailer to a few sentences or paragraphs and keep the homeowner's attention on the essential information. You could do something similar to the sample in figure 19.

GRAPHIC

fig. 19

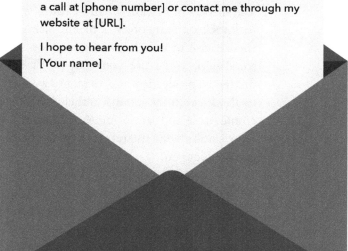

Dear [Name of homeowner]:

I am interested in buying your house at [address].

I can pay all cash for your house and close in one week. You won't have to do any repairs – I'll buy it "as is." If you'd like to hear more about this offer, give me a call at [phone number] or contact me through my website at [URL].

I hope to hear from you!
[Your name]

To target who to send your mailers to, you can ask a title company, which has property details and complete title transfer information, to pull public records to find potential sellers who are experiencing the types of situations that may cause them to be interested in selling off-market, such as no longer being able to maintain the house or needing to sell due to a divorce. Another option is to drive around your target neighborhood and identify properties that are in bad shape, or buy lists of properties that are in foreclosure or pre-foreclosure, etc.

Once you have a target mailing list, get your mailers out, make sure your phone and website are set up to handle responses, and hope you get some replies from people who are interested in selling you their house!

Cold-Calling and Door-Knocking

Using the same list of targeted properties, you can cold-call property owners to see if they might be interested in selling. You can often find phone numbers on a site like Whitepages or Nuwber or obtain them from a title company. There also are skip-tracing services that will provide phone numbers and other information for a fee. As when cold-calling agents, you may want to have a script in place before you start making calls, but be ready to go off-script to answer questions, address concerns, or establish rapport with a prospective seller. It's important to ask questions to understand the seller's situation and what they are looking for. If there is potential, set up a meeting with the seller to check out the house and discuss terms in person.

The in-person version of cold-calling is door-knocking. It takes courage to knock on someone's door and ask if they'd be interested in selling their house to you, but some investors achieve good results from doing so. Again, you'd use your target list of foreclosures, pre-foreclosures, distressed properties, etc., to identify which houses to go to. I'd advise you to think carefully about whether door-knocking is something you'd feel comfortable and safe doing. An alternative would be leaving a note on the door stating your interest in buying the house and how the homeowner can contact you.

The cost of cold-calling or door-knocking is lower than that of sending out mailers, but it's also a lot more time-consuming because it would take you a long time to call ten thousand homeowners or knock on ten thousand doors. Some investors I know achieve great results by hiring virtual assistants to make the phone calls or hiring someone local to knock on doors to reach more homeowners.

Online Options: Social Media and SEO

As more and more business is conducted online, it's helpful to have a handle on your internet-based options. Social media marketing is a great way to reach people who might be looking to sell a home. With more than 70 percent of Americans plugged into Facebook, Twitter, YouTube, LinkedIn, WhatsApp, TikTok, Instagram, or a combination of those platforms, using them to let people know you're interested in buying houses seems like an obvious choice, whether you do it through postings to your friends and followers or running an ad to target potential sellers. When I set up my Instagram account a couple of years ago and started sharing my investing journey with others, it was just for fun. I never thought I would be able to get deals through Instagram—let alone the deal that yielded my largest margin to date! If you have the interest and the time to build a social media account, you might be surprised at the connections you can make with it.

You'll also want to set up a website so it's easy for potential sellers to find you even if they're not plugged into social media. A website also creates credibility and lets people know your business is legitimate. With a website that's optimized to convert potential sellers, **search engine optimization (SEO)** is a powerful tool for driving traffic. It's a subject that's way beyond the scope of this book, but it can be a valuable resource when you're looking for leads. I've gotten many seller leads through organic traffic on my website. Very briefly, SEO includes optimizing website content around specific keywords, creating high-quality content, building backlinks, and using other techniques to get your site listed toward the top of Google's (or another search engine's) search results page. Having your personal site near the top of the page gets you more clicks and more people to your website. If you don't know how to do it or don't have time to set it up, there are many services that can help, some of which charge based on results. You should be able to find SEO consultants on Indeed, Angi, or Craigslist. Be sure to read reviews and find out how they charge for services before you decide who to hire.

CASE STUDY – Care Home Flip: The deal that yielded my highest profit to date was an extensive one: converting a former care home in San Francisco into a modern, luxury residence. I bought the property from owners who had run the care home for many years and were looking to retire. They didn't want to undertake the huge task of clearing out the home and making necessary repairs, so their listing agent decided to search on Google for local investors and ultimately found me through Instagram.

The 2,000-square-foot home had been carved into eight bedrooms, four bathrooms, and some small common spaces on two different levels. The kitchen was very small and dated, and the layout of the house was awkward, having been divided up for a very specific use. An unfortunate feature was that more than three hundred square feet of the lower level didn't meet zoning requirements to be considered living space, which significantly decreased the value of the home.

THE NUMBERS

Purchase Price	$1.4 million
Estimated Rehab Cost	$350,000
Final Rehab Cost	$400,000
All Other Costs*	$275,000
Estimated ARV	$2.5 million
Sales Price	$2.675 million
Profit	$600,000

*Other costs include commissions, closing costs, financing costs, insurance, utilities, staging, and miscellaneous costs

Challenges: I wanted to convert this choppy, largely nonfunctional floor plan into open space designed for entertaining that would be perfect for a young couple working in the tech industry. I also wanted to legalize the three-hundred-plus square feet of living space that was not permitted as living space when I bought the house. I knew that getting all the permits we'd need would be a time-consuming hassle because the permitting process in San Francisco is notoriously complicated and lengthy. But I also knew that legalizing that space would add tremendous value to the property, so I went ahead with it. Permitting was slowed down even further due to the pandemic, which also made it difficult to source some of the materials we needed. I realized early in the process that this flip would take much longer than any I'd done previously, but I didn't anticipate it taking almost two years, resulting in an extra-long hold time. While the total profit was significant, as shown in figure 20, the annualized return was lower because of the much longer hold time compared to my other projects. Still, the end result was very satisfying, and it made me so proud of what I do.

Takeaways:

» Social media can be a powerful tool in deal acquisition.

» When doing analysis, always budget extra time and money for unexpected costs and delays, especially when you are doing a new type of project in a new location. This was my first extensive project in San Francisco, and even though I knew that permitting is a difficult process there, I didn't anticipate that it would be as lengthy as it was. I also didn't foresee the pandemic-related delays, which further increased my hold time of the property.

» The bigger the disaster, the better the makeover. A long, difficult project can create major value and be very satisfying. When we finished the project, what had been an old building in disrepair was a beautiful, modern home that the buyers loved.

To view before-and-after photos of the care home conversion, go to the Case Study Library included with your Digital Assets at go.quickstartguides.com/flipping. To watch the video I made about this experience, go to my YouTube channel and look for "San Francisco High End House Flip Before & After – Luxury Home Remodel, House Renovation."

Bandit Signs

You've seen these signs, I'm sure. They're often in all-capital letters, sometimes even hand-drawn, and contain a lot of exclamation points. They might be on wire frames and stuck into a median strip or in a grassy spot next to the road or tacked onto poles (see figure 21). Basically, they state that the buyer will pay cash for houses and can close quickly, and they list a number to call. If you choose to go this route, it's a good idea to check with the municipality in which you plan to post them; there may be prohibitive ordinances. Also, how well this method works depends on the area—in terms of both competition for buyers and savviness of the sellers. You could definitely test it out anyway, because it doesn't take much money or effort.

fig. 21

WE BUY HOUSES CASH... FAST!!!
777-777-7777
WWW.WEBSITE.COM

Example of a "bandit sign"

Driving for Dollars

Driving around targeted neighborhoods—often referred to as "driving for dollars"—is old school, but it can still be an effective means of scouting out houses that may be poised for sale. Some signs that a property is distressed or vacant include overgrown bushes, an uncut lawn, mailers lying about, boarded-up windows, notices tacked to the front door or other unkempt exterior features, and so forth. You can note the addresses of such properties and then do some research to find a way to contact the seller, usually through mailers, cold-calling, or door-knocking, as mentioned above.

Finding deals is the meat and potatoes of house flipping, because without a deal there is no house to renovate and sell. After trying a variety of methods, you'll find the ones that work best for you. Looking for deals should be an ongoing effort, but as you hone your skills and build your network, it will become easier and more predictable.

Chapter Recap

» Finding deals is the most essential aspect of flipping houses.

» You should identify the areas in which you want to buy before you look for deals.

» Knowing what type of property you're looking for will narrow your search.

» There are many ways to find deals, but they are ultimately in two markets: houses that are for sale and houses that are potentially for sale.

| 3 |

Analyzing a Deal

Chapter Overview
» The All-Important After-Repair Value
» Estimating Rehab Costs
» Other Costs
» Determining Your Desired Profit
» Getting to the Maximum Offer Price

Once you've found a deal, you'll want to do a careful analysis to make sure it will be profitable. A correct analysis is the basis of a flip. If the analysis is not sound, the flip will be like a house built on a poor foundation, and it will become a flop and you'll lose money. I usually like to shoot for a profit of at least 10 or 15 percent. To be confident with my numbers, I analyze potential deals using three important steps:

1. Determine the ARV of the property.
2. Estimate the rehab costs and other costs and deduct them from the ARV.
3. Determine my desired profit and deduct that from the ARV minus costs.

It might seem counterintuitive to start with the ARV and work backward, but that's the only way you can tell if your numbers work and your deal is sound. You can't know what your maximum offer is until you've got the other numbers in place. I like to use a simple tool called a House Flip Deal Analyzer when trying to figure out if the numbers work. I'd like to share this tool with you.

My House Flip Deal Analyzer (pictured in figure 22) is included free of charge with your Digital Assets at go.quickstartguides.com/flipping.

DEAL ANALYZER	
After-Repair Value	**$1,400,000**
Commission	*($70,000)*
Closing Costs - Buy	($5,000)
Closing Costs - Sell	($5,000)
Insurance, Utilities, Staging, Other Misc.	($4,500)
Financing Cost	*($36,000)*
Rehab Cost	**($100,000)**
# Months Purchase to Sell/Close	**4.0**
Purchase Price	**$1,000,000**
(Profit)/Loss	*($179,500)*
Projected Profit %	**15%**

fig. 22

A snippet of the House Flip Deal Analyzer. Deal-specific numbers are added in the right-hand column.

The simplified version of the formula used by the deal analyzer looks like this:

Max Offer Price = ARV – Rehab Cost – Other Costs – Desired Profit

The tool makes it quick and easy, but if you're more comfortable with a scratch pad and calculator, then have at it. Once you've got those numbers in front of you, simply plug them into the formula (or into the Analyzer) to arrive at your maximum offer price. This calculation will help you determine if the deal is one you should pursue.

Determining the After-Repair Value

The after-repair value (ARV) of a property is based on the value of *comparable sales (comps)*. House flippers, as you know, generally look for properties that need some work before they can be put back on the market. This means they're not in the greatest shape when you get them, so you can't do an apples-to-apples comparison with other homes that have been fixed up and are in much better condition. Still, you need to get an idea of what you'll be able to sell the house for once you've finished the rehab work, and you do that by looking at comparable homes, or comps, that are remodeled and in similar condition to what your flip will be like when it's done.

A real estate agent can provide you with a ***comparative market analysis (CMA)***, which is a method of analysis agents use to determine the value of a target property by comparing it to similar ones that were recently sold. A CMA is helpful, but take it a step further and do your own analysis as well, because sometimes agents use comps that are too old, too big, or too far from the house you're considering in order to justify a higher resale value and to sell you the house. Determining the ARV is a key step in your analysis, and you should never trust anyone else to do it without confirming it yourself and trusting your own judgment.

PRO TIP: Generally, only licensed real estate agents have access to the multiple listing service (MLS). If you know an agent, however, you can ask to sign up as their assistant, which would give you access as well. To get my local MLS, I just had to fill out an application and pay $100 a year. Other MLSs may have other rules and fees, but it's worth a try, as there are a lot of advantages to having access to the MLS, and it's well worth a small cost.

If you are able to get access to the MLS, you can use it to run CMAs on your own. If you don't have access to the MLS, you can find comps by looking at the house sale maps on Zillow or Redfin, though that information won't be as complete or up to date as what you get from the MLS. On Zillow, enter the address of your deal in the search box. Photos and information about the house will pop up. Close out of that window and you'll see a map that marks other properties for sale or recently sold, similar to what you see in figure 23. You can zoom in and out to see more or fewer properties, and there are filters to narrow down what you're looking at. Redfin allows you to enter the address of the property, after which you'll scroll down to the Redfin Estimate section of the page. From there you can click on "View comparables on map" to see what nearby properties have sold for.

It's best to find comps that have sold within the past three months; they best reflect the current market condition. If you need to go back further than that, you'll have to adjust your price based on market movements. For example, if you can't find enough recent comps and have to look at houses that were sold six months ago and the market has declined since, you will need to adjust your ARV down based on the percentage of market shift. If you can't find comps in the immediate neighborhood (ideally no more than a half-mile radius), you can expand your search area a little further. But if you do that, you'll need to account for differences in neighborhoods and other conditions, such as the reputation of the school district. Don't ever trust

Zillow's Zestimate or the Redfin Estimate, because Zillow and Redfin don't have any way to account for the conditions of the homes they estimate, and the way they calculate the estimates is hit-or-miss. These sites are useful for providing data on comps, but don't rely solely on the estimates you find there.

IMAGE

fig. 23

A house sale map

MY TAKE

I had several deals underway when the COVID-19 pandemic struck and brought the financial market to a screeching halt. No one could predict what was going to happen or how long we'd have to wait for things to get back to some sort of normalcy. It was impossible to get through to anyone from the city to approve building plans or issue permits because the agencies were shut down and their voicemail boxes were full. California also had a statewide shelter-in-place order, and we had to stop construction for a few weeks until it was again deemed essential work. Plus, no one could look at houses at the beginning of the pandemic, so I didn't even know if I'd be able to sell my flips when they were finished. At the start of the pandemic, the housing market went down by about 10 percent due to uncertainty and buyers' lack of confidence. Therefore, I adjusted my ARV down by 10 percent when evaluating new deals. In the end, a couple of my flips took a few months longer to complete due to delays in permitting, and I had to pay a lot more in holding costs. Fortunately, however, the housing market turned around pretty quickly and has been on the rise since. So the final sales prices of my projects were actually higher than I expected. By being conservative with my ARV, I might have missed out on a few deals, but no one knew what was going to happen in those unprecedented circumstances, and it could easily have gone the other way. I never regret being too strict with underwriting because I would much rather miss out on winning deals than get stuck in losing deals. The experience taught me that it's always better to be conservative with your ARV because many unexpected things can happen—including a pandemic.

In addition to seeking out comps that were sold recently and are nearby and located within the same school district, you'll want to find those that are similar in size and have the same number of bedrooms and bathrooms. Ideally, your comps will be within 10 percent of total square footage and be comparable in age and style to the house you're considering. Preferably, you'll find some comps that have been remodeled in a style that is similar to what your flip will look like; the selling price is likely to be close. If you can't find very similar comps, you might have to adjust your ARV to reflect the differences. If the comparable house contains an additional five hundred square feet, you should adjust your ARV downward to reflect that. On the flip side, if the subject house is bigger than the comp, you can adjust the ARV upward.

Comparable Market Analysis Checklist – What to Look For

» **Distance**. The comps should preferably be within a half-mile radius of the subject house, especially in a populated urban area that contains micro neighborhoods. Prioritize comps that are on the same street, not those on the other side of a main street or freeway overpass. For houses that are further from civilization, it might be difficult to find comps that are close; in that case, you can expand your search area, but make sure the characteristics of the areas are the same and they are in the same school district. In general, the closer a comp is, the more weight should be given to it. Be sure to use at least three comps.

» **Same bedroom/bathroom count**. In houses with between one and four bedrooms, the price and desirability can vary greatly. Once you get to five or more bedrooms, the price difference tends to flatten. In general, additional bathrooms indicate a higher ARV due to added convenience and the presence of one or more master bedrooms.

» **Size.** If the size difference is more than 10 percent, either larger or smaller, you'll want to adjust the price based on the price per square foot that applies to other houses in the neighborhood. Keep in mind that the price per square foot is normally higher in small homes than in those that are much larger.

» **School district.** This is a very important factor that can significantly affect the selling price of a house. Buying a house in a good school district gives parents the potential to save hundreds of thousands of dollars over time by enrolling their children in the local schools instead of private schools. If two comps are in different school districts, you will want to adjust your price based on the price difference between similar homes sold in each district.

» **Year built.** Newer homes are usually worth more than older ones, with new construction bringing a premium. It's hard to define the premium, so I don't recommend using new construction as a comp for older homes. Houses built within 10 years of each other can usually be looked at as equal comps.

» **Lot size.** Bigger is better, but unless the difference is more than 20 percent larger or smaller, you probably won't need to adjust your price.

» **Architectural style, including how many stories.** If the home is of a specific architectural style, you'll want to know whether that style is desirable in the area. As I mentioned, my first flip was a Victorian, and many buyers in the area loved older homes and were willing to pay a premium for it. It would not have worked for me to compare homes that were not of the same style, as the Victorian was clearly worth more. In general, buyers prefer single-level homes to multilevel homes because of the convenience.

» **A lot of noise or other undesirable features.** If your house is on a busy street or backs up to a freeway, use comps that share the same characteristic, or adjust your price down by at least 10 percent.

» **Location.** Proximity to large employers is a plus, but proximity to commercial or apartment buildings is a minus. When the new Apple Spaceship was completed and became the company's headquarters, home prices in the neighborhood skyrocketed by 20 percent in just a few months.

» **Recently remodeled comps.** Using comps that were recently remodeled and have finishes similar to what you'll put in your flip gives you a good idea of what your sales price will be.

» **Comparable selling date.** Ideally, the comp should have been sold within the last three months. If none are available, use comps sold earlier, but adjust for any market condition changes.

PRO TIP: Houses that are "sale pending" make great comps because they've most likely gone under contract within the last 30 days and reflect the most recent market value. You won't be able to see the pending contract price on these properties, but Zillow or Redfin will include the asking price and the name of the listing agent, whom you can call to ask about the pending price.

It's interesting to consider some of the things that affect the value of a particular property. While an elementary school nearby might be a selling point for parents, who like the idea of walking their children to school, a high school tends to be seen as a negative because people worry about noise. Proximity to a large employer can increase the value of a home, but having commercial real estate nearby tends to decrease value. These are all things to consider when working to determine your ARV.

Once you've found a number of suitable comps and know what houses have been selling for, choose an ARV for the subject property. I recommend using the low end of the comp prices to determine your ARV, as the lower price is always easier to achieve, and this gives you a financial buffer.

CASE STUDY – Low-Pitched Roof Flip: This was one of my first projects after starting to flip houses full time, and I was super excited to get started on it. It had taken me a while to find the deal, and my analysis showed it would yield a very nice profit. Due to my lack of experience, however, I failed to pay attention to features of the house that would negatively affect its desirability. Most notably, this mid-century modern home had a low-pitched roof—a roof that slants at a lower angle. If you know anything about roofing, you'll know these types of roofs are constructed cheaply and are much more prone to leaks and damage than steep-pitched roofs.

THE NUMBERS

Purchase Price	$1.25 million
Estimated Rehab Cost	$80,000
Final Rehab Cost	$107,000
All Other Costs*	$123,000
Estimated ARV	$1.6 million
Sales Price	$1.5 million
Profit	$20,000

*Other costs include commissions, closing costs, financing costs,
insurance, utilities, staging, and miscellaneous costs

Challenges: The house had problems in addition to the low-pitched roof, and due to my inexperience, I didn't budget enough to address them properly. About halfway through the project I realized that I needed to greatly increase the scope of work, which blew the project budget. On top of that, because I didn't realize that the low-pitched roof and some other design elements of the mid-century modern house were undesirable features, I overestimated my ARV by six percent. That might not sound like much, but remember, my ARV was $1.6 million (see figure 24), so six percent amounts to $100,000.

Takeaways:

» Always budget for unexpected costs, regardless of how good you think your estimates are.

» Architectural style can mean making a premium or having to offer a discount on a house.

» In addition to using comps for properties that are close by, in the same school district, and in a similar size range, you'll also need to pay attention to comps that are in the same *style* as your house.

To view before-and-after photos of the Low-Pitched Roof flip, go to the Case Study Library included with your Digital Assets at go.quickstartguides.com/flipping.

Estimating Rehab Costs

Trying to figure out the cost of rehabbing a property can be a daunting task for new house flippers. I can assure you, though, that the more houses you flip, the easier estimating these costs will become. And at this point of the process, you're really just looking for an estimate. If you end up buying the property, you'll need to get into much more detail about the cost of renovations and put into place a *scope of work (SOW) document*, which is a detailed outline of all the work that needs to be completed during the rehab. You'll learn more about SOW documents in chapter 6.

For now, you'll want to think about what you would need to do to make the property appealing to potential buyers. Does the house require only cosmetic changes, or will you need to redo the kitchen and move walls to get it ready to sell? Regardless of the condition, you'll need to come up with an estimate at this point as part of your deal analysis. You can find and download checklists of common repairs and their prices online. Labor and material prices can vary significantly in different locations, so it's important to make sure you're looking at costs that apply to your area. HomeAdvisor, a digital marketplace that connects homeowners with local, prescreened service providers, offers a True Cost Guide that enables you to get estimates on costs for a wide variety of projects, based on the area in which you live. The tool contains more than four hundred types of projects and enables you to list specifics regarding what you're planning to do. You can access the guide at homeadvisor.com/cost (full disclosure: I have no business relationship of any kind with HomeAdvisor). For a more accurate estimate, however, you'll need to get contractor bids.

Eventually, you will develop a pretty good sense of the cost of particular repairs and will be able to come up with a fairly accurate estimate of what you'll need to spend. As you are starting out, though, I recommend that you find a good general contractor who will accompany you to look at the property you're considering. We'll discuss the process of finding a contractor in chapter 7. Ideally, the contractor you get will have worked with investors and will have a pretty accurate idea of what work is necessary and how much it will cost. Get the contractor to walk through the property with you, inside and out, and do a basic inspection of what repairs and renovations will be needed.

Discuss concerns and issues and make a list of everything that will need to be done to get the house ready to sell. Remember, at this point you are working to get an estimate of rehab costs—the more detailed work will come later. You'll probably have to pay the general contractor to look at the house and estimate repair costs, but it's usually just a couple hundred dollars and will be money well spent. You'll want to compensate a contractor for their work so they'll agree to come back if you need another estimate later.

Make sure the contractor understands you'll be renovating the house to sell, not to move into yourself. Based on that knowledge, the contractor should provide cost estimates that are investor-friendly, not estimates for work you'd have done if you were renovating your dream home. Generally, contractors charge higher prices for homeowners than for investors, since work for homeowners requires greater detail and more expensive materials.

NOTE

When you're just beginning to work with contractors, ask your mentor or another experienced house flipper to take a look at the breakdown of repairs and rehab costs provided by the contractor, to see if everything looks right.

If it's possible at this point, you could get several contractors to look at the house, discuss repairs, and give you bids. This would be especially helpful if you were looking for a contractor to work with you on the flip project, because you could get to know some contractors and compare bids. This would put you a step ahead in the game if your deal went through and you got the house. It's not always possible, however, because sellers don't always agree to repeated visits to their home.

CAUTION

You'll read much more about finding and hiring contractors, but for now keep in mind that a contractor bid that comes in significantly lower than everyone else's should raise a red flag. Material and labor costs should be similar among contractors who work in the same geographic area. If a bid comes in very low, it's likely that the contractor will include a lot of upcharges during the rehab project to make up the difference, which is not an uncommon tactic among contractors.

You can also get an estimate of rehab costs by bringing in various tradespeople to consult on different aspects of rehab. A roofer would inspect the roof and tell you how much it would cost to repair or replace it. An HVAC specialist would inspect the heating and air conditioning systems, an electrician could tell you how much it would cost to install recessed lighting, and so forth. This would be especially helpful if you were comparing contractor bids and trying to determine whether a general contractor had given you reasonable prices on big-ticket items. But again, the seller might not agree to having numerous people coming in and out of the house, so a general contractor might make more sense at this point. You could bring in additional contractors during the *due diligence period*, a time after the contract is signed during which a buyer can hire someone to inspect the property and make sure there are no problems that would prevent them from wanting to own it. You'll read more about property inspections in chapter 8.

If you need to come up with a rehab estimate in a very short time and aren't able to get contractor bids, you can use the cost-per-square-foot method, which calculates the cost of a rehab based on a broad overview of the work and the square footage of the house. This is not the most accurate method of coming up with an estimate and is subject to the condition of the house, the grade of the materials you need, and the complexity of the rehab. Often, I find the cost per square foot on smaller and older homes to be much higher than that on newer and larger homes. By calculating total renovation costs divided by the square footage of the home, I've determined that the average cost per square foot on my flips is about $80 to $100. Once, however, I got a bid of $130,000 on a 900-square-foot 1940s home, which translates to $144 per square foot! For that reason, I don't recommend using this method unless you don't have other options. An experienced local contractor or house flipper probably could give you an idea of cost per square foot for varying degrees of rehab projects.

Once you've got a ballpark figure for rehab costs, add at least 10 percent for unexpected expenses, particularly if you don't have a reliable contractor yet and you haven't gotten three or more bids. Use that padded number for your deal analysis.

Other Costs to Understand

Before you start plugging numbers into the deal analyzer, think about what other costs you'll encounter when purchasing and reselling a house. There will be closing costs, which cover a range of fees such as recording fees, title search fees, tax status research fees, and *loan origination fees*, also known as *points*, each of which represents one percent of the loan. The origination fees, sometimes called origination points, pay for the evaluation, processing, and approval of mortgage loans. You'll also have expenses such as the transfer tax and title insurance.

You'll need to pay agent commissions when you sell the house after remodeling it, which, as you've already learned, I feel are well worth the cost. As mentioned, I make sure to purchase and relist a home with the same agent in order to encourage good agents to work with me. Commission costs vary depending on the agent and the location, but typically the commission is five to six percent of the home's selling price, with half going to the buyer's agent and half to the seller's agent unless otherwise specified.

Financing costs are another expense to consider, and they can add up fast. You'll have to pay interest payments, typically between six and 15 percent, during the period you own the house. Rates vary depending on the type of financing you get. We'll expand on this in chapter 4.

And then there are miscellaneous costs that include insurance, utilities, permits, inspections, and staging the house. I usually figure about $4,500 for miscellaneous costs, basing that number on costs in my area.

Targeting Your Profit

The next step in analyzing the deal is figuring out how much profit is realistic and worthwhile for the effort you'll need to put into the flip. As mentioned earlier, I always look to make a profit of between 10 and 15 percent. In the Bay Area, where most homes cost at least a million dollars, a 10 percent profit is $100,000, and I believe that's a good starting compensation for all the money and time I invest in a deal. In other areas, 10 percent may not be quite so sustaining. If houses in your area are priced at only $100,000 or $200,000, your profit would be $10,000 or $20,000, assuming you hit the 10 percent margin. If you need three to four months to turn a project around and you do only one project at a time, your profit might be too slim to constitute an income.

A margin of less than $10,000 also makes the deal riskier, because if something goes wrong and you end up having to spend much more than you anticipated for rehab costs, or if the market shifts all of a sudden and your ARV becomes lower, the margin is not a big enough cushion and you could easily end up losing money on the deal. You might want to aim for a margin of at least $15,000 per deal to make it worth your time and minimize your risk of losing money. Your target profit should be big enough to ensure that, even in a worst-case scenario, you at least break even. Your profit margins might not be as high as you'd like at first, but as you gain experience, you'll develop a better deal flow and will be able to afford to be pickier based on potential margin. As a rule of thumb, the more difficult and extensive the renovation is, the more profit you should aim for.

Looking at the Numbers

Once you've got all your numbers figured out, you can come up with a maximum offer price for your deal. As mentioned earlier, the formula is pretty simple. You take the ARV and subtract all the costs you'll encounter, along with your desired profit. What's left is what you can afford to pay for the house. An example is provided in figure 25.

GRAPHIC

fig. 25

| ARV − ALL COSTS − DESIRED PROFIT = **MAX OFFER PRICE** |

$300,000 − $67,000 − $28,000 = **$205,000**

I use the deal analyzer shown in figure 25 to clearly illustrate the numbers I am working with and calculate exactly what my highest offer should be. The agent's commission is calculated as five percent of the ARV. Closing costs on the buy and sell sides will change based on the purchase and selling prices, location, loan size, and local taxes and fees. You should be able to get fairly accurate estimates on insurance, staging, and other miscellaneous costs by getting quotes. The financing cost is based on the hard money and non-hard money interest, points you pay, and the total *hold time* (the time between the close of escrow on the purchase and the close of escrow on the sale). You can play with the rehab cost and purchase price to try out different scenarios with various profit margins to determine what a good purchase price is. Just make sure you've accounted for all the costs you'll encounter, so that your numbers are accurate.

Many house flippers strive to adhere to a 70-percent rule, stating that you shouldn't pay more for a house than 70 percent of its ARV minus the renovation costs. Thus, using the example in figure 25, if you determined that the ARV of a house was $300,000 and the renovation costs would be $30,000, you'd subtract the renovation costs from 70 percent of the ARV, which is $210,000, and your maximum offer for the house would be $180,000.

70% of ARV - Renovations = Maximum Offer Price
$210,000 - $30,000 = $180,000

You'll probably hear about the 70-percent rule if you get into house flipping as a career, but I'm personally not a big fan because you can't use a blanket percentage on deals at various price points. You can see that in the example I just gave you: the maximum offer based on the 70-percent rule is $25,000 lower than the purchase price we got using the deal analyzer. That means if the asking price for the house was $200,000, you'd be likely to miss out on the deal if you used the 70-percent rule rather than plugging the numbers into the deal analyzer.

fig. 26

After-Repair Value	$300,000
Commission	-$15,000
Closing Costs – Buy	-$4,100
Closing Costs – Sell	-$6,000
Insurance, Utilities, Staging, Other Misc.	-$4,500
Financing Cost	-$7,400
Rehab Cost	-$30,000
Desired Profit	-$28,000
Purchase Price	$205,000
Projected Profit %	10%

NOTE

Closing costs typically run between two and six percent. For simplicity, we used two percent in the deal analyzer in figures 26 and 27 to represent the buyer's closing costs, but in the real world, closing costs vary depending on factors including purchase and selling prices, location, loan size, local taxes, and fees.

Also, the higher the price of the property, the more skewed the 70-percent rule becomes. On a house with an ARV of $1.5 million, for instance, a purchase price of $1,100,000 would yield a 10 percent return—one that I'd be happy with (see the deal analyzer in figure 27). But if you used the 70 percent rule, the purchase price would have to be just $950,000 for the numbers to work, a difference of $150,000! Employing the 70-percent rule in this case would likely mean you'd miss out on an amazing deal because your offer was too low.

GRAPHIC

fig. 27

After-Repair Value	$1,500,000
Commission	-$75,000
Closing Costs – Buy	-$22,000
Closing Costs – Sell	-$30,000
Insurance, Utilities, Staging, Other Misc.	-$4,500
Financing Cost	-$37,950
Rehab Cost	-$100,000
Desired Profit	-$130,000
Purchase Price	$1,100,000
Projected Profit %	10%

Especially when you're new to house flipping, each deal should be evaluated on its own merits, not dependent on the 70-percent rule, or any other arbitrary numbers. Once you've gained some experience, if you find yourself working with deals that all have very similar ARVs, you could apply an appropriate percent rule as a preliminary evaluation, based on your experience. I'd still suggest a careful look at all the numbers, though, before coming up with an offer.

Chapter Recap

» Determining the ARV of a house is the first important step in analyzing a deal.

» You'll need to have a good idea—but not an exact number yet—of rehab costs.

» Additional costs include commissions, closing costs, financing costs, insurance, etc.

» Don't underestimate your desired profit, as cutting it too close could lead to losses.

» Plugging all your numbers into a deal analyzer will clearly show what you're working with.

| 4 |

Funding the Flip

Chapter Overview
» The Cost of Flipping a House
» How to Secure Funding
» Funding Sources: Pros and Cons

When you're starting out, funding a deal might seem like a big hurdle; you probably don't have enough money yourself and don't yet know who you can go to. Of course, the ideal situation is to know exactly where your funding will come from before you find a deal, which removes a lot of stress and allows you to concentrate on other aspects of the deal. But it's okay if that's not the case! When you find a great deal, you'll find lots of funding sources, because there are more people with money to lend than there are good deals. But while you don't need to have all the funding ready in your bank account before you start looking for a deal, you *do* need to know who you can turn to before you make an offer. In this chapter, you'll learn about different types of funding, what you'll need money up front for, and how to fund a deal without using a lot—or any—of your own money.

How Much Money Do You Need to Flip a House?

Many beginners have asked me this question, but it doesn't have a simple answer, because it depends on many factors. The amount of money you'll need to flip a house will depend on the property you buy, the extent of renovations needed to prepare it for sale, how you fund your flip, and so forth. The location of the property you buy will affect how much you'll need, because, as you know, property values vary greatly from one location to another.

For example, say you want to buy a house to flip in Pittsburgh, Pennsylvania. The average home price in 2020, according to Zillow, was estimated at just about $180,000. Clearly, the barrier for entry into that market is lower than for the San Francisco Bay Area. The flip side, of course, is that what you get back in profit per deal in the Bay Area far exceeds what you would in Pittsburgh, even though properties in Pittsburgh are probably also generating good profits for the money you would need to invest.

Regardless of the price range in your target area, you don't need all that much of your own money to fund a flip. Similar to the process of buying a primary residence, you can borrow the majority of the purchase price. But you will need money available to cover some costs up front, and you'll need to be able to demonstrate to the seller that you're able to pay for the house before they will consider your offer. Most sellers (but not all) will want to see a ***proof of funds (POF) document***, which states that you have funds available to pay 100 percent of the purchase price of the house. A POF document could be a bank statement, a stock portfolio, a retirement account statement, a letter from a lender, or a combination of these that shows you have money or that you can borrow enough money to cover the cost of the deal. You might use a ***preapproval letter***, which is simply a letter from a lender stating that they are willing to loan you a specific amount of money. If you're working with a conventional mortgage lender, the amount you'll be able to get preapproved for is based on your income as indicated on a W-2 form. If you're working with a hard money lender, the loan you get will be based on the asset, which in this case is the house you're attempting to buy.

If the offer you make on a house is accepted, you'll need to come up with an ***earnest money deposit*** (EMD), sometimes called a good-faith deposit. This money indicates you're serious about buying the home and intend to move forward with the transaction. An EMD is typically between one and five percent of the purchase price and normally must be placed in an ***escrow account***, which is an account temporarily held by a third party until the purchase agreement on the house has been finalized and the settlement made. Once the offer is accepted, the EMD is usually due in three business days.

You can use cash or a credit card for the EMD, or, if you own a primary residence and you have a good amount of equity, get a HELOC (home equity line of credit). You can also get the money from a retirement account or borrow it from family, friends, or a private money lender. There are many lenders who like to put their money in real estate, as it is less risky than having it in the stock market and they can charge interest that is much higher than what they would get from having the money in a savings account. You'll read more about securing financing in the next section.

You'll need a lot of your funding when you close on the house. In addition to money for the purchase price, you'll need to pay closing costs, which, as you read in chapter 3, include recording fees, title search fees, tax status research fees, and points.

fig. 28

A CHECKLIST FOR HOUSE-FLIPPING COSTS

- ❑ **Purchase Price**
  - • **Earnest Money Deposit**
- ❑ **Closing Costs**
  - • **Buy**
  - • **Sell**
- ❑ **Insurance**
- ❑ **Financing Costs**

- ❑ **Rehab Costs**
- ❑ **Property Taxes**
- ❑ **Agent Commission**
- ❑ **Staging**
- ❑ **Utility Costs**
- ❑ **Miscellaneous Costs**

I often get a hard money loan, which is a type of loan commonly used when flipping houses, for 85 to 90 percent of my purchase price. That means I will borrow $900,000 on a property for which I'll pay $1 million, and I'll only need to look for an additional $100,000 as a down payment. For beginners, a hard money lender generally charges one to two points up front, meaning that for a loan of $900,000, you'll need up to $18,000 at closing to cover the points. If the deal was in Pittsburgh and I borrowed 90 percent of the cost of an average home ($180,000), I'd have to come up with only about $18,000 for the down payment and $3,240 to pay two points on the loan.

Also, after closing you'll need to pay the utilities and property taxes on the property until you've resold it, as well as financing costs, which could be in the form of mortgage interest or interest on your hard money loan. As of late, hard money lenders in my area are charging beginners eight to nine percent, but that will be different in other locations. So you can see that costs for the loan will add up quickly.

Once you own the house, you'll need money to fix it up and get it ready to sell. Some lenders will loan you 100 percent of the construction money—if your deal is highly profitable. The lenders I've worked with don't want to lend money in excess of 75 percent of the ARV, so if the purchase price is already at or close to 75 percent of the ARV, then the loan will not cover all of the rehab. Construction loans can be costly, and they're usually held back until a portion of the construction has been completed and inspected, even though points on the loan are charged up front. Also, it's good to have some reserves on hand so you can pay your contractor on time while waiting to get reimbursed by the lender.

The key to getting hard money that will cover both your purchase price and at least some of your rehab costs is to find a really good deal in which the purchase price is way below the ARV. If you get a loan for 90 percent of the purchase price and that amount is close to 75 percent of the ARV, the hard money lender won't lend you more than the difference between those two numbers to use for rehab costs.

If, for instance, your purchase price is $350,000 and your ARV is $400,000, a hard money lender will look at the deal and figure out that 90 percent of the purchase price is $315,000, which exceeds 75 percent of the ARV of $300,000, meaning that you can only get up to $300,000 to cover the purchase price, and there won't be any additional loan money for your rehab.

But if you've paid only $250,000 for the house and the ARV is $400,000, you have a much bigger cushion between 90 percent of the purchase price and 75 percent of the ARV, and a hard money lender would likely be willing to lend you more to cover the rehab costs. In this case, 90 percent of the purchase price is $225,000, and 75 percent of the ARV is $300,000. That $75,000 difference is likely to prompt a lender to loan you up to that amount for your rehab costs on top of the 90 percent of the purchase price of the house.

Let's simplify this. If you've got a good deal, 75 percent of your ARV will be higher than 90 percent of the purchase price of the house. The bigger the difference between your purchase price and your ARV, the better!

I'm sure you've gotten the idea that, depending on where your deal is and other factors, there's a lot of money involved in buying a house and getting it ready to resell. However, I don't want that to discourage you from getting into what can be a very lucrative business. As I'll explain in more detail in the next section, you can use other people's money to cover most of these costs, and there's no shortage of willing financiers when you have a great deal. It's amazing how real estate allows you to profit without having to put up much of your own funds. Also, as you gain experience and build your network, your costs for financing will decrease, and you'll learn how to identify and make offers on the best deals available. I would not be writing this book if I didn't know firsthand how financially rewarding house flipping can be.

How to Secure Financing

When looking to finance a deal, remember that each method has pros and cons. As you gain experience, you'll learn what type of financing works best for you, and as you build your network, you'll find more opportunities for borrowing money. Let's look at some of the possibilities, as listed in figure 29.

fig. 29

WAYS TO FINANCE A HOUSE FLIP

- Savings
- Personal Line of Credit or Personal Loan
- HELOC or Home Equity Loan
- Credit Card
- Private Investor
- Conventional Mortgage
- Hard Money Loan

Savings

If you have significant savings that are accessible, you could use them to fund, or help fund, a house flip. It's unlikely that you'd have a million dollars in a savings account to buy a home in New York or San Francisco, but if you live in a place where home prices are much lower, it's possible that you'd have enough money available.

One of the biggest advantages of financing your house flip with cash, of course, is that you won't have interest payments. This not only saves you money, but it takes off some of the pressure to sell the house very quickly so you don't have to keep making interest payments.

If you decide to use savings to finance a flip, make sure you have money in an emergency fund as a reserve, so you'll have money to cover all the necessities, and, if the flip doesn't go your way, you'll have extra cash to use on the rehab or cover additional interest payments.

Personal Line of Credit or Personal Loan

A *personal line of credit* is a designated amount of money you get from a financial institution over a specified period of time. Many people apply for personal lines of credit and use the money to repay loans that carry higher interest rates. House flippers often use personal lines of credit to fund renovations.

If you are approved for a personal line of credit, you can get money paid out to you in allotments. You are not required to use the full amount for which you were approved, and you'll only pay interest on the money you take. You'll need to pay back the money that's been loaned to you, of course, with interest. There also might be fees to apply for the line of credit or maintenance fees while you hold the loan. Personal lines of credit are typically unsecured, meaning there is no collateral involved. Some lenders allow borrowers to deposit collateral in exchange for better terms, but if your loan is unsecured, you can still expect the interest rates to be higher than on some other types of loans. However, interest rates vary tremendously depending on who the lender is, your credit score, how much you're borrowing, and other factors.

A personal loan is also a designated amount of money you borrow from a financial institution, but it is a closed-end transaction. The lender simply releases the funds along with a timetable for repayment. Interest on personal lines of credit and personal loans is tax-deductible if the money is used for business purposes.

Home Equity Line of Credit (HELOC) or Home Equity Loan

Another option for financing is a HELOC, which, as you read earlier, is a loan that uses some of the equity in your home to provide a revolving line of credit. HELOCs tend to have fairly low interest rates, since the lender holds your home as collateral. As with a personal line of credit, taking a HELOC means you borrow only as much as you need, and you pay interest only on the money you borrow. A home equity loan, in contrast, is a sum of money you receive all at once and pay back at a specified time.

Credit Card

A credit card typically comes with a high interest rate, but sometimes you can open a new card with a low promotional rate, sometimes even zero percent interest for a period of time. The key, of course, is having a plan in place to pay off your credit card balance before the introductory rate ends and your interest rate shoots up to 15, 20, or even 25 percent.

Credit cards can be valuable tools for paying earnest money deposits, buying materials needed for renovations, or covering other costs for which you don't have cash. If you use credit cards, they should be lines of credit designated exclusively for your business—don't mix your personal expenses with business expenses. Also, don't overlook store cards from major lumberyards or big-box stores that sell materials you need for renovations. Like loans, interest you pay on these cards or credit cards may be tax-deductible, if used for business expenses, not personal.

Private Investors

There are a lot of people with a lot of money, and some of them are looking to invest that money in something that carries lower risk and will yield more consistent returns than what they can get from the stock market or other investment opportunities. Nearly anyone who has money and is willing to lend or invest it can be a private investor. It can be a family member, a friend, a business owner in your community, a colleague, or someone else willing to work with you. Private investors use cash, their retirement funds, HELOCs, or other assets to invest in deals.

Private lenders aren't taking great risks when they invest in real estate because, as in the case of a HELOC, the property they're loaning the money for serves as collateral. If you get a private loan and decide to leave town, the lender can get a lien on the property and claim it through the foreclosure process.

The interest rate a private investor charges will almost surely be higher than that of a conventional mortgage (more about those coming up). On the other hand, it's generally a much simpler process with less stress and a lot fewer fees involved. While some private lenders are willing to lend long term, most prefer that borrowers repay the loan as soon as the house has been sold. Interest rates from private lenders usually start out at about seven percent for lower-risk deals, which is typically more than the interest on a mortgage loan but less than what you would pay a hard money lender.

However, if a private money loan is used to fund the portion of a deal that's not covered by a hard money loan—as is often the case—the interest rate on the private loan could go higher than the rate on the hard money loan. That's because when private money loans are used in conjunction with hard money loans, they are in what is known as the second position. If the borrower defaults, the first lien—in this case the hard money loan—gets paid off first, and that could put the private lender in jeopardy. Some private lenders will not agree to loan money if there's already a hard money loan in place.

As its name indicates, a first position loan is the primary loan for a purchase. It usually is most of the money that's needed to buy and flip a house. But in many cases, a first position loan isn't enough to cover all expenses, so the investor looks for another source of funding. That money, usually a significantly smaller amount, is known as a second position loan. If the borrower defaults, the first position loan, or primary creditor, has the right to foreclose on the property and recover all the money that's available. The lender of the second position loan won't get any money back until the first position loan is satisfied.

When you're just starting out in house flipping, you're more likely to be lent money by someone you know, but don't be discouraged from approaching someone you *don't* know if you've heard they may be open to funding a deal in exchange for interest payments. You might be able to find investor leads through real estate investment clubs, by posting online classified ads, or through a real estate agent you know.

It might sound daunting to have to go to strangers to borrow money, and that's how I felt too when I got a few deals all of a sudden and didn't have enough money to close on the purchases. I was also new in the business and didn't think anyone would be willing to lend money to a newbie, but I decided to give it my best shot. I went to a few local real estate meetings and stood up to tell people about my deals, and, to my surprise, a few private investors came to me after the meetings, and I was able to fund three of my projects with private money, by borrowing and partnering. Learning to network can be stressful, but the payoff is well worth the effort. You'll read more about networking in chapter 15.

I recommend putting together a simple brochure or presentation to give to prospective investors. Outline your experience and explain your business philosophy. If you're just starting out, highlight relevant experience you've acquired through other jobs or ventures.

When you find a private investor, it is up to the two of you to work out the terms of your agreement. You'll need to negotiate the amount of money that will be loaned, the interest rate, the length of the loan, how often interest payments must be made, and so forth. Normally, a private investor simply loans you money with the agreement that you will pay it back with interest. If the deal goes well, the cost to you of borrowing the money will be just the interest and the points. If you end up losing money when you sell the flip, however, you'll still need to repay the money you borrowed, along with interest.

While some private lenders insist on monthly interest payments, others are willing to let interest accrue until the house is sold, at which time you pay back the interest in a lump sum. If you're short on funds, being able to wait to repay the interest can be a huge help.

If home prices in your area are low, a private lender might be willing to fund the entire deal. If prices are very high, it's unlikely you'll find someone willing or able to loan you the entire cost of the deal. In that instance, you might be able to use a hard money loan to cover most of the purchase price of the house, and private money to make up the difference if needed. Borrowing from a private lender on top of a hard money loan may allow you to fund a deal without using your own money. If you can borrow 90 percent of the purchase price from a hard money lender and the other 10 percent from a private lender, none of your own money will be needed to buy the house, and the loans will be repaid when the house is flipped.

To learn more about getting deals without using your own money, check out my videos "Flip Houses with No Money" and "Flip Houses with Other People's Money" on my YouTube channel.

PRIVATE LENDER	EQUITY PARTNER
• Charges interest • Charges points • Gets paid no matter what	• Gets paid a percentage of the profit • Isn't paid if deal is unsuccessful

An alternative to private lending is equity sharing—a private investor wants to invest their money to get equity, not interest, usually because they think they'll make more money by getting equity. There are some advantages to having an equity partner, but also some disadvantages; you may not have as much control as you would on your own, and you could end up with a smaller profit.

When you partner with someone on a deal, they put up the money, just as they would if you were borrowing it. A partner does not charge interest, but you share the profits realized when the house is sold. Normally, the partner funds the deal while you do the work of finding a property, analyzing the deal, managing renovations, negotiating the sale, and all the other tasks involved. How the profit is split varies, depending on how the deal is negotiated. Although you lose some of the profit you would have realized, an advantage of having an equity partner is that if you end up losing money on the deal, you're not on the hook for the money that funded it. So, whether you should borrow money or share equity on a deal depends on what the lender wants—and also how confident you are about turning a good profit on the deal. If you have a juicy deal where you anticipate making a large profit, it's probably better to borrow money, as the cost will be lower than if you were to share part of the profit.

CASE STUDY – Smurf Blue Flip: It was my first year of flipping houses full time and I already had four deals in place when another opportunity arose. With so many flips already underway, I didn't have the funds to finance the portion of the purchase price not covered by a hard money loan. I was really disappointed, because I'd run the numbers and the margin was amazing. And then I realized that even though I was reluctant, I had to start raising some money.

THE NUMBERS

Purchase Price	$1.04 million
Estimated Rehab Cost	$100,000
Final Rehab Cost	$100,000
All Other Costs*	$145,000
Estimated ARV	$1.6 million
Sales Price	$1.525 million
Profit	$240,000

*Other costs include commissions, closing costs, financing costs, insurance, utilities, staging, and miscellaneous costs

fig. 31

Challenges: My challenge was to raise the money necessary to get this incredible deal. I was nervous about this because I didn't have a lot of experience yet and I didn't think anyone would be willing to lend money to a beginner like me. Also, the market was in a downward shift at the time, and I thought that might make it even more difficult.

It occurred to me that I'd seen investors get up at local real estate meetings and share numbers on a deal in hopes of getting someone interested in making a loan. I got up, shared my numbers, and, to my surprise, three investors reached out to me after the meeting to express interest in financing the deal. I ended up financing 10 percent of the purchase price through a private lender who charged 10 percent and two points—$4,500. Because the deal had such a good margin, getting a private loan made a lot more sense than bringing in an equity partner, which would have resulted in my having to pay $24,000.

Another unexpected challenge that gives this case study its name: I painted this house a bright, Smurf-like blue. It turned out that several potential buyers didn't like the color. I've stuck with neutral gray exterior paint ever since.

Takeaways:

» Don't shy away from private lenders, even if you are just starting out. You won't get what you don't ask for.

» If you have a choice, get a lender when the potential margin is high, so you'll only have to pay a pre-negotiated interest rate rather than a percentage of the equity, which could be a lot higher than the interest.

» The sales price of the house was lower than I expected because of the declining market (see figure 31). I thought about holding on to the house in hopes that the price would come back up, but it wound up being a good thing I didn't, because the market continued going down for several more months before flattening out and then recovering. I could have lost more money if I had waited.

» Stick to neutral colors when painting houses! Since I switched to neutral gray paint for exteriors, I've had zero complaints.

To view before-and-after photos of the Smurf Blue flip, go to the Case Study Library included with your Digital Assets at go.quickstartguides.com/flipping.

Conventional Mortgage

Conventional mortgages certainly have their place, a fact that most people who buy homes to live in will attest to. They may not, however, be the best choice for an investor who is buying houses to flip.

You can get a conventional mortgage through a bank or mortgage broker. If the deal involves a Fannie Mae or Freddie Mac property, those companies will offer the mortgage. Your ability to get a conventional mortgage is based on your current financial situation, including income, assets, debt, and credit score. If you turn to house flipping because you've lost your full-time job, which is what happened to me, you're not likely to qualify for a traditional mortgage because your W-2 income has stopped, and a conventional mortgage is income-based.

Also, large banks often won't give you a mortgage if the house you want to buy isn't in move-in condition. Since many fixer-uppers are nowhere close to move-in condition when we buy them, that can be a problem.

NOTE

The usual interest rate that a beginner in the Bay Area will need to pay for a hard money loan is eight to nine percent. Compare that to the average interest rate on a 30-year conventional mortgage, which in the first quarter of 2022 was around four percent. Rates from most companies on a 15-year mortgage at that time were between 2.7 and 3.5 percent, obviously less than the rates for a hard money loan.

The benefits of a conventional mortgage are that you get low interest rates, low points, and a long time to pay back your loan. Drawbacks in addition to those already mentioned are that it can take weeks or even months for a mortgage to get approved and a settlement scheduled, removing your ability to impress a seller with the promise of a quick and easy closing.

Despite those drawbacks, sometimes it might still make sense to seek out a conventional mortgage. Lenders may be more willing to work with you if you have significant assets and can come up with collateral or a cash down payment for the house. Successful experience in real estate investment can also improve your chances of getting a conventional mortgage, as can having a good amount of equity in another property.

If you set out to get a conventional mortgage, you may have better luck with smaller banks or credit unions, which are able to establish their own lending rules and don't impose the stringent requirements of larger banks. These types of banks are often called "portfolio lenders" because they issue mortgages and maintain the debt in a portfolio of loans. Portfolio lenders generally have more flexibility than larger banks, but their interest rates and fees are often slightly higher.

PRO TIP: I often get a quote from a big bank first, and then have the smaller bank I want to work with match the rate. With this approach, I get the best of both worlds: the lower rates of big banks and less strict underwriting and better service from smaller banks.

Hard Money Loan

If you're discouraged after reading the section about conventional mortgages, don't be. As I stated, conventional mortgages have their advantages and are necessary for the majority of people wanting to purchase a home. But in my opinion, they are not the best option for house flippers. A better option, which I use to finance nearly all my deals, is hard money loans, a loan type commonly used by flippers. Lenders use personal cash funds to provide loans that are asset-based, meaning they look at the merits of the deal and lend money based on its soundness. If a hard money lender doesn't think you've got a good deal in which you can turn a profit easily, they're not likely to provide funding.

As you've read, an advantage of conventional mortgages is the interest rates, which are almost always significantly lower than those on a hard money loan. Interest rates on a hard money loan vary depending on location, demand, and other factors, but currently in the Bay Area, a house flipper without a lot of experience is charged eight to nine percent interest plus one or two points. As you gain experience, you should be able to negotiate lower interest rates and maybe even get lenders to waive the points.

When I was starting out, financing was a big chunk of the total cost I incurred on a flip. As I gain more experience, my financing cost has gone lower and lower, and now it's less than half of what I used to pay. Now I deal consistently with three lenders who are so anxious to work with me that they undercut each other's rates to get my business. If you must pay high interest rates at first, don't be discouraged. Experience counts!

A hard money loan is different from a conventional mortgage in several ways beyond interest rates. Hard money loans are asset-based, and conventional mortgages are income-based. When you apply for a conventional loan, your income, debt, tax returns, bank statements, and other financial factors are scrutinized, a process that can take weeks or months. A hard money lender, on the other hand, doesn't care about most of those things, including your income or how many loans you have outstanding (which allows you to have a few loans at a time to fund a few flips concurrently). But they will look at your credit score, your experience, and the deal. If you can't pay back the loan, they'll simply take the house you bought with it.

MY TAKE

I've met some people who want to flip houses but have trouble getting financing because their credit scores aren't great. When I moved to the United States over 10 years ago, I had no credit history here. This not only would have made it difficult for me to get a hard money loan or a mortgage, but it made it hard for me to get a car loan or even rent an apartment until I was able to build some credit. You normally need a score of 620 or above to be approved for a mortgage, and hard money lenders are likely to offer better rates to borrowers with credit scores of 720 and above. If your credit score isn't what it should be (see figure 32), I highly recommend that you learn how the credit system works and take steps to improve it.

fig. 32

A huge advantage of hard money loans for house flippers is that the underwriting process is much simpler and faster than that for a conventional loan. When I have to deal with conventional lenders for loans on my primary residence or a rental property, I often get frustrated by the amount of paperwork and general back-and-forth I have to deal with. With a hard money lender, once you've been qualified as a borrower (more about that in a bit), you can close on a loan quickly—it's one week in the Bay Area. This is great news when you're making an offer on a house, because sellers, whether financially distressed or not, love a quick cash deal. It also allows you to start the construction soon, so you minimize any market risk exposure.

Ideally, you'll be able to get one or more hard money lenders to qualify you as a borrower before you start looking for deals. This gives you a big advantage when making an offer on a house, because you don't have to include a loan contingency in the offer. Personally, I've found that being qualified as a borrower and knowing I can get loans quickly and at what cost has been a huge benefit when it comes to closing a deal. Being able to get a hard money loan, which is considered all-cash financing, in just a few days has helped me land deep discounts on off-market deals, sometimes up to 50 percent less than the after-repair value.

As mentioned earlier, another benefit of a hard money loan is that you may qualify for a construction loan that covers 100 percent of your renovations. That money normally is made available through a draw process, which means it is given in allotments. When a certain amount of work on the house is completed, the lender will send an inspector to make sure the work is satisfactory. If it is, the lender will reimburse you the money you've spent on repairs. Conventional lenders normally will not do this. For more on the differences between the two, see figure 33.

GRAPHIC

fig. 33

HARD MONEY LOAN VS. CONVENTIONAL MORTGAGE	
HARD MONEY LOAN	**CONVENTIONAL MORTGAGE**
• Higher interest rate	• Lower interest rate
• Short term	• Long term
• Asset based	• Income based
• Underwriting simple and fast	• Underwriting complex and slow
• Offers construction loan	• No construction loan offered
• Allows multiple loans simultaneously	• Takes into account all outstanding debt

So how do you go about finding a hard money loan and getting approved as a borrower?

A quick internet search will provide contact information for hard money lenders, but I'd suggest that you dig a little deeper and find one that is known to you in some way, or at least comes with references. If you belong to a real estate club, ask other members who they've borrowed from. Hard money lenders often show up at real estate meetings and events to promote their businesses.

It's a good idea to approach several lenders, comparing their rates, how many points they charge, how long it would take for the loan to be processed, what percentage of the ARV they will loan to you, what processing fees are involved, and so forth. Do a careful comparison, remembering that factors other than interest rates are also important. Paying an extra percentage point on interest might be worth a very quick turnaround time if it could mean the difference between getting a deal and not getting it.

In addition to your credit score, hard money lenders will look at your level of experience. Yes, you're likely to pay more for a hard money loan if you're new to house flipping. There is a steep learning curve with flipping houses, and lenders know that you're more likely to make mistakes as a beginner. But rest assured, most lenders offer loans to beginners too. They just charge higher rates/points to offset the additional risk.

A hard money lender will also want to see that you have three to six months' worth of reserves in the bank, ensuring they'll get their interest payments for that time. Many will also want you to be funding part of the deal with your own money—having some skin in the game, as the saying goes. A lender who is considering giving you 90 percent of the cost of the house will look on you more favorably if you're funding the other 10 percent. Also, many lenders will want to make sure that once they loan you money, you are not getting a second lien on the house at the close of the purchase. On the other hand, there are hard money lenders who don't care about a second lien.

PRO TIP: If you do need money from another lender to help fund the deal, you can do it outside of escrow with a promissory note. A promissory note is basically a written promise that you'll repay the loan first, then record the second deed of trust after you close the purchase—so your original lender wouldn't know.

Hard money loans may not be cheap, but they've been the best source of funding for my deals. And, again, once you build relationships with lenders and get more experienced in the business, you'll be able to negotiate better rates on the money you borrow.

Crowdfunding

Crowdfunding, also known as peer-to-peer lending, has increased in popularity among real estate investors, with platforms such as Fund That Flip, Kiavi, EquityDoor, PeerStreet, and Groundfloor garnering attention among investors and borrowers alike. Although crowdfunding is a very small piece of real estate financing, it accounted for more than $5 billion in loans in 2019, according to EquityDoor.

Potential borrowers, both individuals and institutional investors, can apply for loans through a crowdfunding platform, which will review the application and, if approved, underwrite the loan. Loans that are considered low risk will carry a lower interest rate than those thought to pose a higher risk. A downside, however, is that some platforms will only work with borrowers who meet strict income guidelines or can prove high net worth.

For borrowers, the benefits of these types of loans is that they typically close more quickly than a traditional loan and may have lower interest rates. Investors benefit because they can earn a higher return on their investment than they would on some other types of investments, and risk is reduced because the real estate involved serves as collateral on the loan.

Chapter Recap

» The cost of flipping houses varies dramatically from one region to another and from one deal to another.

» There are a number of options for getting financing to purchase properties.

» For house flippers, hard money loans are usually preferable to conventional mortgages, due to the simplicity and speed with which they can be issued.

» It's possible to flip houses without using your own money, but you'll need to carefully structure the deal.

| 5 |

Making an Offer and Buying the House

Chapter Overview
» Know Why a Home Is for Sale
» Build Trust First
» Make a Fair Offer
» Close on a Purchase

The goal of flipping houses, of course, is to make a profit. The offer you make on a house largely determines how much that profit will be. And it's a delicate balance: If the offer is too high, you may not realize the profitability you're looking for. But if it's too low, you risk offending the seller or the representing agent, who may think you are lowballing them and will seek offers from other investors. When I was first starting out in the business, making an offer was really scary for me. There was a lot of money at stake, and I didn't yet have the confidence to be sure of what I was doing. Walking through high-potential deals with my mentor helped keep me calm and reassured me that my offer was appropriate and fair.

Part of my nervousness during the offer process came from wanting the seller to understand that my offer was fair. I knew I would never take advantage of someone who was very anxious to sell a house, and I wanted to be sure the seller knew that as well. I found that the best way to get a seller to feel comfortable with me was simply to be sincere and compassionate regarding their circumstances. People appreciate that and are more likely to accept an offer from someone they feel comfortable with. Now let's talk about how you can build rapport with a seller and reach a fair agreement.

Establishing Trust

Back in chapter 1, we discussed the various reasons that someone might want or need to sell their house. When flipping houses, you tend to come across particular circumstances motivating a homeowner to sell. Knowing the underlying motivations can help you identify potential deals and also come up with creative solutions to win the business. Let's break down some of the most common circumstances we touched on earlier:

» **There was a death in the family, and someone has inherited a house they don't want.** In these cases, the heirs usually don't have a lot of attachment to the house and just want to get rid of it and get the cash, so a quick close is very attractive to them. If there are several heirs, nobody wants to take the lead to fix up the house, because the increase in value is split multiple ways. At the same time, they don't care if the house sells at a slightly lower price, because the price difference is not significant to each of them individually.

One of my earlier flips was right by the new Apple headquarters when it first opened in late 2017, and I purchased the house from six siblings who had inherited it. One of them was actually a developer who built new-construction houses. I thought the chance of getting the house was slim because the developer would probably want to tear it down and rebuild, given the desirable location it's in. But he wanted nothing to do with the house, because he would have to put in the whole investment and then split the profit six ways.

» Upkeep of the house has become too difficult for an elderly owner. Senior owners usually have lived in the house for a long time. They have a lot of possessions accumulated and need time to pack up and move. So a free rent-back deal is usually highly appreciated. This allows them to use the sale proceeds to get their next living situation in order while still living in their home after the sale, so they can take their time moving. You can also offer to help with any personal items they leave behind.

» **A landlord is tired of renting and wants to get rid of the house.** A lot of long-term rental properties are in terrible shape, so you'll want to purchase them as-is to spare the landlords the trouble of fixing them up. Sometimes you'll need to take over the tenants. Be careful in those situations, especially if there are tenant rights in your area that prevent you from evicting a tenant who refuses to move out.

» **Divorce is forcing a couple to sell the house.** A quick close is usually desired so the divorcing individuals can move on with their lives. One of the divorcing couples I purchased from fought so much that the court had ordered them both to move out of the house by the end of the week, so my offer with a one-week close was especially appealing to them.

» **The homeowner is moving out of town.** Helping with personal items left behind and even covering the moving expenses can be good incentives for the sellers to consider your offer.

CASE STUDY – Hoarder House Flip: The seller and her family had been living in the four-bedroom, two-bathroom house for more than 50 years and it was completely filled with stuff, some of which dated back to the owner's childhood. They planned to move to another state but were embarrassed to put the home on the market because of its condition, so their agent contacted me. The first time I went to look at the house I only stayed for 15 minutes because it was impossible to see much or gauge its condition. I liked the deal and thought I could make it work, since the kitchen and bathrooms were in pretty good shape and wouldn't need as extensive a rehab as I had originally planned for. But I had to figure out how to work with the owner.

THE NUMBERS

fig. 34

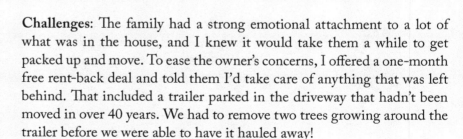

Purchase Price	$1.025 million
Estimated Rehab Cost	$80,000
Final Rehab Cost	$40,000
Estimated ARV	$1.35 million
Sales Price	$1.27 million
Profit	$85,000

Challenges: The family had a strong emotional attachment to a lot of what was in the house, and I knew it would take them a while to get packed up and move. To ease the owner's concerns, I offered a one-month free rent-back deal and told them I'd take care of anything that was left behind. That included a trailer parked in the driveway that hadn't been moved in over 40 years. We had to remove two trees growing around the trailer before we were able to have it hauled away!

Two weeks into the rent-back, I brought my contractor to the house to have another look. Unfortunately, very little progress had been made on clearing it out, and I realized they were going to need more time and some help to get through the packing and moving. I asked my agent to help the seller get movers and storage units and to check in daily on her progress. I also offered another 10 days of free rent-back time. With this help, the family was finally able to move out, and we could get started with the renovations.

Another significant challenge was that the housing market was on a downward shift. It was fortunate that the kitchen and bathrooms didn't need extensive renovations, and we scaled down some other things we'd planned to do to keep the project moving ahead and the renovation cost low (see figure 34). We finished the renovations and got the house on the market in just one month, but the reduced demand made it difficult to sell. I was really worried after three potential buyers backed out one by one, but in the end we were fortunate to find a committed buyer who loved the property.

Takeaways:

» Being sensitive to the needs of the homeowner in this type of situation is crucial. I was reluctant to extend the rent-back at first, but I could see that this was important to them and they needed help. It was the right thing to do and I'm glad that's how we proceeded.

» Factor in extra time in this type of situation, as it's probably going to take the sellers longer than you anticipate to get out of the house.

» If the market is headed downward, consider scaling back the scope of rehab to speed up your work time and lower your budget to secure your return on investment.

To view before-and-after photos of the Hoarder House flip, go to the Case Study Library included with your Digital Assets at go.quickstartguides.com/flipping. To watch the video I made about this experience, go to my YouTube channel and look for "House Flip on a Budget – Hoarder House Renovation Before and After."

If you work with the agent who's also representing the seller, your association with that agent gives you some built-in credibility with the seller. The seller is relying on the agent to sell their house, so you just need to make a reasonable offer and deliver what you promise. If you're dealing directly with a potential seller, it's important that you build rapport with them on your own. You can establish trust and win favor with a seller by letting them know you understand their circumstances and are willing to work with them to make the process of selling and moving easier. If you are already qualified as a borrower and know where your funding is coming from, you can assure the owner that you'll have cash available for a fast closing on the house. If they need the sale proceeds quickly but are not ready to move by the closing date, you can offer a rent-back deal if it's feasible. There are a lot of concessions you can make, but you need to know what's important to the seller and what's motivating them, and be creative. Once you know what a seller's problems are, you can help to fix them.

> One seller I was working with was sick, and he was selling the house to pay for medical expenses. He was staying in the house and didn't want to close quickly, but he needed money right away, so we agreed to release some funds early through escrow to help him out, and that helped us seal the deal.

Some important questions to ask a seller (directly or through an agent):

» Why are you selling?
» How much money do you need to walk away with?
» Other than the price, what terms are important to you?
» Is there anything I can help you with? (rent-back, taking care of junk, quick close, etc.)

Encourage the homeowner to tell you more about their circumstances and the reasons they're interested in selling the house. Be a good listener and let them know you empathize with their situation. As mentioned above, understanding why the homeowner is selling will yield important clues regarding the terms of your offer. Be sure to explain that you are a house flipper who is interested in buying the house to rehab and resell. If the seller's expectation isn't reasonable, take time to explain your financial position, outlining how much you'll need to spend on repairs and other costs to realize a profit when you resell the house. Doing this can help the seller understand that your offer is reasonable and fair. Present your costs to the seller in writing, establishing that you have nothing to hide.

Laying all this groundwork is an honest approach, and it also makes it easier to strike a deal—a seller is far more likely to accept an offer from someone who is transparent and tries to offer a solution to their problems. If the seller is older and mentions adult children, you could offer to meet with them to explain the reasons behind your offer, in an effort to get everyone on the same page and avoid any suspicion that you are trying to take advantage of the seller.

Sometimes sellers pick my offer even if it's not the highest they receive, because they like that I'm honest and that I take the time to listen to them, understand their problems, and offer to help.

Coming Up with a Fair and Acceptable Offer

Before you can make an offer, you need to plug everything into a deal analyzer and study the numbers. As you read in the last chapter, your maximum offer is the ARV of the house minus all your costs and the amount of profit you're looking for. There's nothing magical about that number; it's all based on what you can sell the house for, what you'll need to spend to refurbish and resell the house, and how much profit you want to make.

When you are presented with a potential lead, it's important to run the numbers and come up with an offer quickly, because time is of the essence, especially if you are purchasing a house that's on the MLS. If you think it's a good deal, chances are many other buyers think the same. I always try to act on leads within a few hours, and never more than 24 hours, but I've still had other buyers move ahead of me, causing me to miss out on the deal because I was too slow.

While it's good to know how much the seller expects to make, don't let that number dictate your offer. You know what your numbers are, and they determine how much you are willing to pay for the house. When I was starting out, I tried so hard to meet the seller's expectations that sometimes I had to sacrifice my own margin. It didn't take long for me to realize that it's not worth it. A low-margin deal is not only a waste of time and capital, but it can be very risky because there's not enough buffer to shield you from market exposures (which we'll explain more about in chapter 14). In this business, you'll sometimes feel embarrassed about the difference between the seller's expectations and the amount of your offer. But your numbers don't lie, and if the numbers don't work, there can't be a deal. Don't fall into the trap of improving your offer because you feel sorry for the seller, or you've developed an emotional attachment to the house. You are in business, and if you don't buy the house, someone else will. You need to be fair, but you also need a deal that you're excited about and that will result in a profit.

Once you've determined what your offer will be, if you are working with an agent, your agent will prepare the offer and present it to the seller, using a *residential purchase agreement (RPA)*, which is a legal contract stating your interest in buying the house and what you require for the sale to proceed.

If you're not working with an agent, you'll need to present the offer yourself. If doing so in person, have a signed purchase agreement that's been reviewed by an agent or a real estate attorney, or use a standard state purchase agreement, which you can find online. It should contain all the information that's presented in an RPA, including the following:

» The address of the house

» The price you are offering for the house

» The buyer's name: your personal name or your business entity (refer to chapter 12)

» The amount of earnest money you are willing to offer. I recommend offering as little as possible to lessen the amount you lose if you end up having to back out. But much of the time you'll probably have to put up the percentage that's customary in your area to assure the seller you intend to follow through with the contract. In the Bay Area, it's three percent of the purchase price.

» Anything you'd like the seller to leave in the house, such as appliances. It's usually necessary to replace appliances, but if there's a newer refrigerator or stove, you might want to keep it.

» Who will pay the closing costs. A seller may be more likely to accept your offer if you agree to pay some or all of their closing costs. If you do this, don't forget to figure those costs into your total cost.

» The closing date. If the seller wants to extend the closing date for some reason, you should work with them, but remember that the longer the house stays in escrow, the later it will be when you put it back on the market, thus increasing your market risk exposure.

» Offer expiration date. The seller should have a little time to consider your offer, but not more than a couple of days, because you don't want them to use your offer to shop for a better one.

» In the "other terms" section, I usually add, "Buyer reserves the right to use a combination of cash and private money with no loan or appraisal contingency." This informs the title company that the purchase may be funded by a private money loan, even though

I've indicated the sale is a cash purchase. It ensures that the title company will allow me to fund the deal with a loan. Hard money can fund within one week, and it's considered an all-cash financing, so I check the all-cash box even though I may be using a private money loan.

» Proof-of-funds document as an addendum

Some investors include contingencies with their offers. *Contingencies* allow you to back out of the purchase agreement within certain time frames for specific reasons without any consequences. While contingencies offer some protection for your EMD, they can also make sellers less willing to work with you and can significantly slow down the buying process. Some common contingencies are listed in figure 35.

GRAPHIC

fig. 35

CONTINGENCIES	
TYPE	**DESCRIPTION**
Inspection contingency	Gives the buyer the right to have the home inspected within a specified time frame.
Appraisal contingency	Enables the buyer to cancel the contract if the house is appraised for less than the purchase price.
Loan contingency	Makes the sale contingent on the buyer being able to get a loan.
Title contingency	Protects the buyer if problems arise regarding the ownership of the house.

Hard money lenders usually don't require a formal appraisal, so if you've done your homework and have your preapproval from a hard money lender, the only contingency you will need is the inspection contingency. And you can get around that by bringing a contractor to the house before you make your offer to look things over and make sure there are no structural issues or other serious problems. If you can get that done in advance, you're in a position to make a no-contingency offer, which makes your offer highly competitive and very appealing to sellers.

Many home buyers choose to include a title contingency with their offers, but in my experience with real estate in the Bay Area, I don't feel that it's necessary and I have never used one. It's the title company's job to make sure the title is clear. If it's not, the transaction will not move forward.

Closing on the House

Your offer has been accepted and your earnest money deposited into an escrow account. If you've made a contingent offer, this time period is your opportunity to confirm that your numbers are correct and the deal makes sense. The tasks left to be completed are referred to as *due diligence* and could include having a home inspection, making a scope of work document, finalizing your rehab budget, and making sure your numbers work and you'll be able to realize the profit you're looking for on the sale of the house. If you were able to conduct due diligence before making your offer and you made a non-contingent offer, you're ahead of the game and only need to make sure closing is on schedule; you can get started immediately with preparing and scheduling the renovation work. If you need to conduct due diligence at this point of the buying process, remember that the clock is ticking between the time you sign the contract and the removal of contingencies. Your closing date is a commitment, and it's important to stay on track.

Start the due diligence by reviewing the seller disclosures to make sure there are no major issues. If you haven't already had the house inspected, you may want to get a home inspector or a trusted general contractor who is qualified to conduct an inspection. When you are starting out, without a general contractor you can trust, you may want to do this even if you had some contractors walk through the house for the purpose of establishing a renovation budget. The inspector will identify any and all problems with the house and give you a detailed report about what needs to be done. That report will be the basis for your scope of work (SOW) document. Look for an inspector who is certified by the ***American Society of Home Inspectors (ASHI)***. If the inspector suspects there are structural problems with the house, you may need to set up an inspection by a structural engineer to determine the scope of the issue.

NOTE

PRO TIP: Be sure to accompany the home inspector as they go through the house. Take note of what they look for and what they find out, and don't be afraid to ask questions. You'll want to pay special attention to any safety issues and critical concerns and defects and make sure they are included in your scope of work. The more you understand about home inspections, the better you'll be at identifying issues with future houses.

The inspector will look at the heating and air conditioning systems, the plumbing and electrical systems, the roof, the foundation, the attic, the basement, structural components, walls, floors, windows, doors, and so forth. Basically, the point of the inspection is to identify major problems that will significantly affect the amount of work needed to get the house ready to sell. If you discover you need a new heating system and the entire electrical system needs to be updated, you'll need to get estimates on the work and include them in your budget before considering whether you can make your numbers work or if it makes more sense to pull the plug on the deal.

To help you understand the scope of work necessary and finalize your budget, you'll need to walk through the house with several contractors and get bids. If you find out the renovation costs are skewing your budget and there's no way you'll be able to realize the profit you're looking for, you'll have to either ask the seller to reduce the price of the house or back out of the contract. Don't be tempted to proceed with the project if your numbers don't add up—it's better to stop a project before your flip turns into a flop.

Insurance Considerations

Once you've signed the contract, a title company will conduct a title search to make sure there are no problems with the ownership of the property and no liens or judgments against it. In some cases, you can do a title search on your own by looking at public documents, but for one or two hundred dollars you can have it done and save yourself the time and effort.

To protect yourself from any title issues that may not be recognized until after you close on the house, it's a good idea to buy title insurance, even if it's not required by your lender. If it turns out there are issues with the title, you won't be able to sell the house until they're resolved.

You should also get a title binder policy, or interim binder. A title binder is not a title insurance policy. Rather, it represents an insurance company's intent to issue a policy to a home buyer who resells the same property using the same title company within a certain period of time, usually two years. Having a title binder ensures that the company that issues title insurance when you buy the house will issue a policy of title to the new owner when you sell the house, eliminating the need for another title search. Because a title binder policy costs only about 10 percent more than a standard title insurance policy, it can save you significant costs on the resale of the home—a couple thousand dollars in the Bay Area. You save because the title binder allows you to resell the property and have a policy of title issued to the new buyer at a fraction of what it would cost if you didn't have the title binder.

You'll also want to get property insurance to protect you in the event that someone gets hurt on your property or if there is damage to the house or contents. Make sure that your policy covers the construction process and is based on replacement cost, which is the amount it would take to rebuild the home with similar materials if it was damaged or destroyed. Replacement insurance is based on the square footage of the house times the cost of building per square foot.

As you prepare for closing, it's important to stay in touch with your lender, the title company, and your agent to make sure everything is on track and proceeding smoothly. Your agent will advise you on what you'll need for the closing. Be sure you've got everything you need, and be on time for your closing. Once all the paperwork is signed and you've done a bit of celebrating, you'll get started on the next stage of the project: the rehab. Don't forget to transfer utilities. Ideally, you'll be getting your contractor ready to start the day after closing.

Look for the Prepare for Closing Checklist in your Digital Assets at go.quickstartguides.com/flipping.

A CHECKLIST FOR CLOSING

fig. 36

- ❏ Finalize your scope of work and rehab budget
- ❏ Review all seller disclosures
- ❏ Purchase title insurance and a title binder policy
- ❏ Purchase property insurance
- ❏ Stay in touch with your lender, the title company, and your agent
- ❏ Make sure you have acceptable funding sources for closing
- ❏ Get utility services set up

Chapter Recap

» Understanding the reasons that a house is for sale and working with the seller on a solution to their problems can improve your chances of closing a deal.

» Your offer price is a delicate balance between the seller's expectations and your profitability.

» Due diligence can be completed before or after making an offer; if it's after, you'll need to complete all the necessary tasks prior to removing contingencies.

» Work to stay on track for your closing date, as it's a commitment you've made to the seller.

PART II

TRANSFORMING A HOUSE

| 6 |

Planning the Renovation

Chapter Overview
>> Hiring Professionals vs. DIY
>> Scope of Work
>> Layouts and Finishes
>> The Rehab Budget

In this section of the book, you'll learn about the planning and execution of renovating a home. Some of what we'll cover was briefly mentioned in part I, but we'll get into more detail here about putting together an SOW document, setting your budget, and hiring a contractor.

If you follow the process detailed in part 1, by the time you've closed on a house you should have a rough idea of how much work is going to be necessary to get it ready to sell and how much that rehab will cost. At this point you might already have a contractor who has walked through the house and drawn up an SOW document. This is the information that will serve as the blueprint for your renovation project. If so, congratulations; you're ahead of the game. But you'll still want to double and triple check to make sure the SOW is thorough and complete before you close on the purchase and start with renovations. If you haven't yet accomplished those tasks, it's important to move on them quickly, as the holding cost for the house is expensive and you can't afford to let it add up. You need to determine and finalize the scope of work, hire a general contractor or sub contractors, and lock in a budget. Let's get started.

The Case for Hiring Professionals

Many first-time house flippers think they can save a lot of money on labor costs if they tackle some or all of the rehab work themselves instead of hiring contractors to do it. Unless you're a contractor yourself and have trustworthy subcontractors to call on, I don't recommend that approach. Even if you know how to do the work yourself, chances are that the extra time needed to complete the job on your own without professional proficiency, the tools you'll need to acquire, and other expenses will end up costing more than the price of hiring someone to do the work.

As you read in the introduction, my husband and I once made the mistake of deciding to DIY on a remodel of a small condo we planned to rent out. My husband is very handy and had done a lot of remodeling work on his parents' house. We thought that by leveraging his workmanship we would be able to save a lot of money.

Most of the work we needed to do was cosmetic, but the project still turned out to be very demanding and time consuming. We were both working full time at that point and could only work on the project on weekends. It took us two months to do what professionals could have done in two or three weeks, and we were both exhausted when it was finally completed. Sure, we saved money on the cost of labor, but we had to spend money to buy some expensive tools, and the delay cost us at least a month's rent.

If you're particularly handy or have construction/remodeling experience and the time to do the work, it might be helpful to undertake a small and simple remodeling project early in your flipping career, like painting, flooring, or replacing light fixtures, because it would help you understand what the process entails. Having that understanding can make it easier for you to estimate the scope and cost of repairs in the future. If the work needed involves multiple trades, however, or you're not experienced in construction, or you're working another job and your time is limited, I highly recommend hiring a general contractor. A contractor can not only accomplish the necessary work but can also guide you through the permitting process, hire subcontractors, and shield you from potential liability issues.

You can also hire someone to help you with pre-renovation tasks. For example, if you purchased the house on the MLS, it is usually completely cleaned out before you close on it. But if the deal is off-market, that's usually not the case, particularly if your deal involved a hoarding situation. Cleaning out someone else's house can be unpleasant, time-consuming, backbreaking work. It's another job you can take on yourself if you want to, but it's probably easier and more efficient to hire someone who tackles these situations professionally. Check sites like Yelp, Angi, or Thumbtack for recommendations and ratings. If you hire a contractor, they could begin demolition first and have the trash and construction debris hauled away at the same time, saving you money and time.

It can be dangerous to get into the habit of doing everything yourself. If you plan to flip houses as a career, the value of your time is in deal acquisition, deal analysis, securing funding, project management, and other crucial tasks—not in construction or trash removal. Also, you might eventually want to take on multiple projects at a time. Trying to do everything yourself would definitely slow you down, prevent you from scaling the business, and cost you a lot of money in the end.

If you are new to renovations and don't particularly have an eye for design, you can hire an architect or an interior designer to help you come up with a plan to make the layout more functional and add design elements to your flip. Just keep in mind that these professionals can be a little pricey and probably aren't necessary if you're dealing with a lower-priced home.

Determining the Scope of Work

Understanding the scope of work (SOW) and getting an SOW document in place is imperative for managing your renovation project, keeping the work on track, and staying on budget. As you read in chapter 3, an SOW document is an outline of all the work that needs to be completed for the rehab. It doesn't have to be pages and pages long, but it should include everything that needs to be done, inside and out. The document is an important part of the contract you and your contractor will agree on, as it outlines all the work to be completed within the confines of your budget. If you fail to include certain tasks, you'll need to come up with extra money later to pay for them.

On my first flip, I overlooked the task of installing trim on the second floor of the house, and it wasn't spelled out in the SOW. That mistake put me $8,000 over budget and reduced my profit on the flip.

Having a detailed description of all the necessary work removes the guesswork and enables contractors to give you thorough and accurate bids. It ensures that everyone shares the same expectations regarding the project and the work that you expect to be completed.

When getting a house ready to flip, there are hundreds of potential repairs and upgrades you may be selecting from. You can see a fairly comprehensive list of these by checking out Appendix III, "Renovation Tasks." You can also find the list in your Digital Assets at go.quickstartguides.com/flipping.

You can either compile an SOW on your own or you can walk through the house with a contractor, discuss all the work necessary, and have the contractor put together the SOW. Based on my experience, general contractors are usually good at compiling SOWs, but you want to review it carefully to make sure all the important items are included and the description of the work is accurate. When you are starting out, this is the approach I recommend because you probably won't yet know what to include in an SOW or how to describe the work that's needed. By letting the contractor take the lead, you allow them to use the format they prefer. Most contractors like to be brief on the SOW because they don't like spending a lot of time writing or being on the computer. If they must spend a lot of time writing up a detailed SOW, they'll likely charge you for it by increasing their bid.

Once you've gotten some experience and can easily identify what repairs and renovations are necessary, you can compile your own SOW document, if you prefer to do so. During a walk-through of the house, you'll write down or record everything that needs to be done, after which you'll write up the SOW. You can download a template for an SOW document or make your own. An example is included in Appendix I of this book.

After having flipped many houses, I am fortunate to have a steady contractor whom I trust completely. Our process is to walk through a house together and discuss what needs to be done. I share my vision regarding floor plans and finishes, and the contractor advises me on how we can accomplish those goals cost-effectively. After the walk-through, my reliable contractor compiles a bid/SOW document, listing everything that needs to be done and the prices. Most general contractors will compile an SOW document for you. Remember, though, that it's up to you to review it carefully to make sure it's complete and the bids are reasonable.

PRO TIP: A helpful strategy, especially when you're working with someone new, is to record the walk-through conversation between yourself and the contractor. Then when you review the SOW document, you can make sure everything you discussed is included.

Every SOW document will be different depending on the condition of the home and the level of finishes desired. An entry-level home will require fewer upgrades than a high-end home with a high resale value. An older home will require more updating than a newer one. As you're determining what work must be done, consider how you can achieve the greatest impact for the least cost. You'll want to focus on what will add the most value while enabling you to keep your costs down.

PRO TIP: My rule of thumb is that every dollar invested in rehabbing a property should result in at least two dollars in resale return. If I spend $100,000 on renovations, I want to be able to increase my ARV by $200,000 or more. Apply the 80/20 rule of thinking, which states that 20 percent of the work (usually kitchen and bathrooms) will yield 80 percent of the return. That 20 percent of the work is what you want to focus on, after which you can identify some other important items, such as flooring, lighting, painting, landscaping, etc., to complete the finished product. Never dwell on the tail end of the scope, like trying to achieve perfect wall texture finish or adding an unnecessary surround sound system on an entry- or median-level home. Those are tasks that could cost you a lot of money but generate very little return when done on a flip where they're not needed.

Most work that's needed in a house is included in one of the major categories listed in figure 37. These are just the big categories, but of course under the umbrella of each one are many subcategories. You can refer to the Master List of Renovation Tasks in your Digital Assets for a more detailed list.

fig. 37

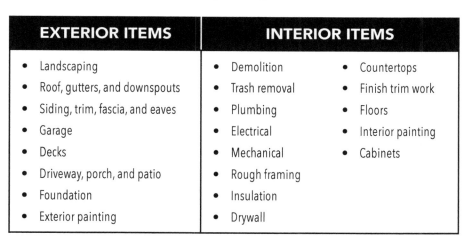

EXTERIOR ITEMS	INTERIOR ITEMS	
• Landscaping	• Demolition	• Countertops
• Roof, gutters, and downspouts	• Trash removal	• Finish trim work
• Siding, trim, fascia, and eaves	• Plumbing	• Floors
• Garage	• Electrical	• Interior painting
• Decks	• Mechanical	• Cabinets
• Driveway, porch, and patio	• Rough framing	
• Foundation	• Insulation	
• Exterior painting	• Drywall	

Keep an Eye on the Comps

Some repairs and upgrades are nonnegotiable and will need to be done in every house you buy, such as interior and exterior painting, new flooring, new light fixtures, etc. Others, however, are case by case and based on the condition, the resale value, and what the comps are telling you.

To fully realize your ARV, you'll want to look carefully at the comps and make sure your upgrades are equal to or slightly better than theirs. You can see what's been done by going to open houses or checking out pictures online. As you observe the comps, look for the layouts and finishes that are popular in the area, and take note of any opportunities for adding value to your property. For example, if comps with a more open floor plan sell at higher prices than those with separate and enclosed living spaces, you'll want to consider opening up your house. If most of the comps feature shaker cabinets and farmhouse sinks, you'll probably want to follow suit. If most comps have garage space converted to living space, you'll want to explore that option as well. Just make sure you use applicable comps, as discussed in chapter 2. Some house flippers renovate based on their personal taste instead of comps or local preferences, and they end up leaving a lot of money on the table.

fig. 38

EXAMPLE

When I was doing research for a flip in San Francisco, I noticed that many comps used modern finishes and attained record sales prices because buyers in San Francisco are mostly young couples who work in tech and love modern design. Other comps had used a modern farmhouse look with shaker cabinets and open shelving, which is similar to what I usually do in the suburbs. (See figure 38 for a comparison.) While it works in the suburbs, the farmhouse look wasn't popular in the city, with sales prices hundreds of thousands less than those of the houses with a modern look.

You want to avoid renovating more than you need to, but you must make sure that any defects in the house are resolved and that it looks appealing to potential buyers. Defects include things that are not functioning properly and will cause inconvenience, such as windows that don't operate smoothly or slow-moving shower drains. Don't be tempted to skimp and take shortcuts with your rehab, as this can turn off buyers, resulting in a lower sales price and some of your money left on the table. Focus on addressing those defects, rather than adding features that are nice to have but not likely to increase the resale value. For example, I've seen entry-level flips with high-end appliances and wine coolers installed. Buyers are going to love those appliances, but are they going to pay much more for the house because of them? I highly doubt it.

NOTE

As you decide on your SOW, a good test is to think as a buyer and ask yourself if you (as the homeowner) would consider the work you're thinking about doing to be worth the extra cost it would add to the house.

EXAMPLE

I once tried to cut costs by having kitchen cabinets repainted rather than replacing them. I had done that at another house and the results were great, but this time I didn't pay attention to the fact that the cabinets were really old. Some of the doors didn't close fully and some drawers were crooked—issues that no amount of painting could resolve. When I saw the result, it was clear that simply painting the cabinets had not been a good idea, and I ended up having them torn out and replaced anyway. Moral of the story: before deciding to salvage some aspect of a home, assess the condition carefully. Otherwise, your attempts to save money may end up costing you more.

Some remodeling techniques are simple and easily accomplished, like refinishing hardwood floors or painting a brick fireplace. Other methods of adding value are more complicated, such as removing a load-bearing wall to add an island to a kitchen, adding a bathroom to create a master bath, or finishing part or all of an unfinished basement or garage. We'll explore those types of changes a little more in the next section.

The finishes you choose should be based on the price point of the home and comparable sales. You don't need high-end materials for entry-level homes, and you also want to be cautious when using less expensive materials for high-end homes. You can definitely do that—I use inexpensive materials in high-end homes all the time and am proud of being able to mix and match to create a luxurious look. But you can't use materials that look cheap. The cheaper materials you use in high-end homes should look stylish and high quality, matching the more expensive materials without seeming out of place. You'll learn more about this a little later.

Three Levels of Rehab

There are three levels of rehab: cosmetic, full-gut, and value-add, with each level done on top of the previous level. Cosmetic rehab work includes the nonnegotiable items I mentioned earlier and is necessary for every house. Occasionally you'll be lucky and find a deal that requires only a cosmetic rehab because the kitchen and bathrooms were recently updated.

A full-gut rehab is the most common level of rehab, and it means you'll need to pretty much gut the interior of the home, including the kitchen and bathrooms being stripped down to the studs. It also entails updating the electric and plumbing according to code and putting in all new finishes.

A value-add rehab is the highest level, and the most expensive and time-consuming. During a value-add rehab you improve the functionality and features of a home through structural changes. It usually requires extensive permitting and plan review processes, so make sure you fully understand what you're doing before taking it on. Let's have a closer look at each level of rehab.

A cosmetic rehab includes the following:

» **Interior Painting:** For walls, I prefer neutral, modern shades such as gray or cream. Some of my favorite gray shades are San Francisco Fog and Feather Stone from Kelly Moore, Harbor Gray from Benjamin Moore, and Ellie Gray from Sherwin-Williams. Cream colors I like are White Dove from Behr and Pueblo White from Dunn-Edwards.

I normally choose off-white when painting ceilings, doors, and trim, often using Swiss Coffee or White Dove from Benjamin Moore. For cabinets, I prefer White Dove for white paint and Silent Night for gray, both from Benjamin Moore.

» **Exterior Painting:** When repainting the body of the house, I usually choose various shades of gray or white. For gray I like Timber Wolf from Benjamin Moore and Westchester Gray from Sherwin-Williams. For white I prefer Simply White from Benjamin Moore or Twinkling Lights from Behr.

For exterior trim, I'll either go lighter than the body paint with the Swiss Coffee shade of off-white, or darker than the body with a shade like Black Horizon from Benjamin Moore.

I think the color of the front door is important, as it can make the house stand out and create nice curb appeal. My door color choices are usually red, blue, yellow, or black, with my preferences right now trending toward Stratford Blue from Sherwin-Williams or Black Horizon from Benjamin Moore.

» **Flooring:** You can repair and refinish existing floors or put in new ones. In the Bay Area, hardwood floors are the most desirable, followed by laminate. In some other parts of the country, tile or another material is preferred. It's important to understand what's popular in your area. Refinishing hardwood floors is a lot cheaper than installing new floors, so that option is my first choice when possible.

» **Lighting:** Lighting is a key component of an updated home, but it's easy for beginners to overlook. I never skimp on lighting and always install a lot of recessed lights in the kitchen, living room, and hallway to make the home bright and inviting. You can also use pendant lights and chandeliers to dress up a kitchen island, dining room, or stairway. In bedrooms, a ceiling light is usually fine. But if you are flipping a higher-end home and you see that the comps have recessed lights, you may want to follow suit.

» **Improving Kitchens and Bathrooms:** As you've read, most of your efforts in a cosmetic rehab should focus on the kitchen and bathrooms. Replacing or painting cabinets, perhaps in colors mentioned earlier, replacing countertops, and upgrading lights and fixtures can greatly enhance these spaces. As mentioned in the example above, painting cabinets can be a good strategy if used appropriately, but don't disregard their condition or what potential buyers are looking for, as it could end up costing you more money and headaches. In the Bay Area, quartz countertops are in and granite is out, but that may not be the case where you are. Always research your comps to figure out what materials to use.

» **Landscaping:** Landscaping work encompasses both the front and back yards. I usually put in sod to enhance curb appeal and make the backyard look pet- and kid-friendly. You can also add plants and mulch for color and diversity. If they're popular and grow well in your area, drought-resistant plants might be an option, because they're cheaper to plant and maintain than some other choices. However, if all your comps have lush lawns, using drought-resistant plants may not be as appealing.

To see examples and before-and-after pictures of cosmetic rehabs, check out the photos from the "Hoarder House" in the Case Study Library included with your Digital Assets: go.quickstartguides.com/flipping.

A full-gut rehab includes some or all of these things:

» **New Kitchens and/or Bathrooms:** This could include replacing cabinets, countertops, tubs, toilets, and other fixtures and appliances; relocating any of those things; and perhaps even expanding the kitchen or bath within the existing footprint. I often remove non-load-bearing walls and relocate fixtures or appliances to make the kitchen or bathroom bigger and the layout more functional. Those aspects of a remodel will be discussed further in the next section, "Designing the Layout and Finishes."

» **Roof:** A roof is a big-ticket item, and it's important to attend to any necessary repairs to make sure it's in good shape. If the roof is at the end of its life, even if it's not actively leaking, it could cause concern for buyers and should probably be replaced.

» **Windows:** Old, single-pane windows are a sign that a home has not been updated. Even if the windows are double-paned, if they don't operate well or have condensation between the panes, it's a good idea to replace them.

» **Electrical and/or Plumbing:** When you put in a new kitchen or bathroom, the plumbing and electrical should always be brought up to code. In some cases, you'll discover that plumbing pipes are corroded everywhere or the electrical is the knob-and-tube wiring of older homes, in which case you will have to replumb or rewire the entire house.

» **HVAC:** If the house has central heating and cooling systems and they still function, I usually don't replace them. But if there is a dated wall heater or a window AC unit, I generally replace them with a central system. You can decide that based on the home's price point and comps. In the Bay Area, most older homes don't have AC installed, so I usually don't put it in unless I'm trying to sell the house in the heat of the summer and it's necessary to keep would-be buyers comfortable.

» **Changing the Floor Plan:** This entails creating an open concept by removing load-bearing or non-load-bearing walls or relocating a kitchen or bathroom to improve the functionality and flow of the house (see figures 39, 40, and 41).

To see examples and before-and-after pictures of full-gut rehabs, refer to "Modern Farmhouse" and "Entry-Level Flip" in the Case Study Library in your Digital Assets at go.quickstartguides.com/flipping.

KEY FOR FLOOR PLANS

▬▬▬ Outer Walls   - - - - Non-Load-Bearing Walls

—— Load-Bearing Walls   ——— Doors

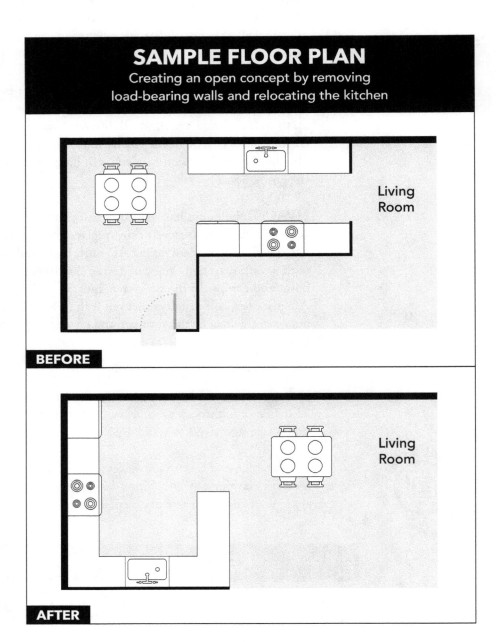

SAMPLE FLOOR PLAN

Creating an open concept by removing
load-bearing walls and relocating the kitchen

Living
Room

BEFORE

Living
Room

AFTER

GRAPHIC

fig. 39

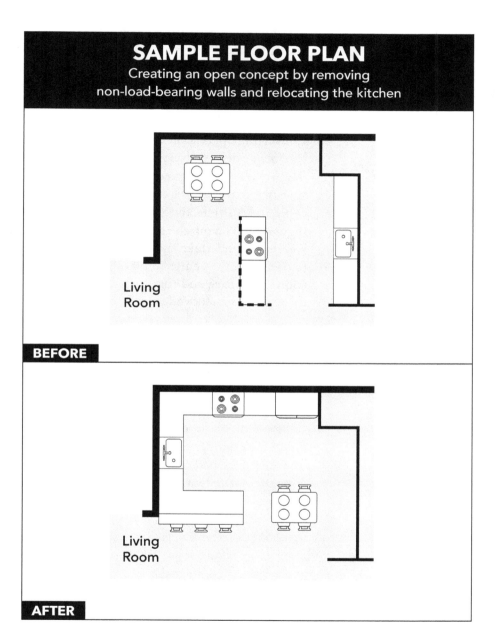

SAMPLE FLOOR PLAN

Creating an open concept by removing
non-load-bearing walls and relocating the kitchen

Living
Room

BEFORE

Living
Room

AFTER

GRAPHIC

fig. 40

A value-add rehab could include one or more of these options:

» **You might add a bathroom, bedroom, or other space,** such as a master bedroom if there is not one, or an additional bedroom or bathroom if the house has too few compared to the comps (figure 41). Doing so within the existing footprint of the home could dramatically increase the house's value.

» **Converting Space:** Sometimes a garage, part of a garage, or a basement can be converted to create alternative living space. In the Bay Area, a two-car garage is pretty standard, but some houses have oversized garages that can be converted to living space easily and cost-effectively while still allowing for a two-car garage (figure 42). Having the space available doesn't necessarily mean you should undertake the conversion; as always, you would want to check out the comps to make sure other houses contain the additional space and that they're sold at prices that can justify the cost of the renovation.

» **Adding Square Footage:** A step up from converting space is to add square footage to the home outside of the existing footprint. This can increase the value significantly but also will result in higher costs and a longer time frame for the renovation. Most house flippers prefer simpler cosmetic or full-gut rehabs over projects that call for additions or other new construction and won't attempt them unless they don't find enough deals that are cosmetic or full-gut. The sales price per square foot has to be a lot higher than building costs per square foot, which is why you usually see these projects in higher-end neighborhoods.

A common misconception is that the more extensive a project is, the more money you can make. I thought this initially, but after completing some complicated and longer projects, I realized that although the bigger projects tend to generate higher total profits due to the increased capital investment and longer hold time, the annualized return is actually lower than that for shorter and simpler cosmetic or full-gut rehabs. When you must hold onto a project for more than six months or even a year, you are also more subject to housing market fluctuations and risks.

To see examples and before-and-after pictures of value-add rehabs, check out the photos from the "Spanish Flip" and the "Knife in the Wall Flip" in the Case Study Library in you Digital Assets at go.quickstartguides.com/flipping.

fig. 41

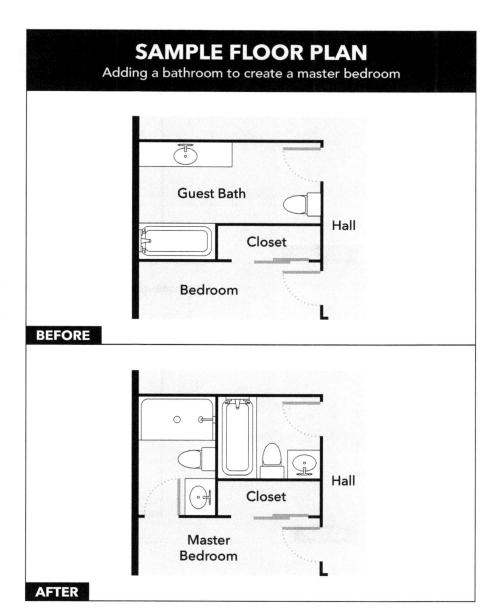

SAMPLE FLOOR PLAN
Adding a bathroom to create a master bedroom

BEFORE

AFTER

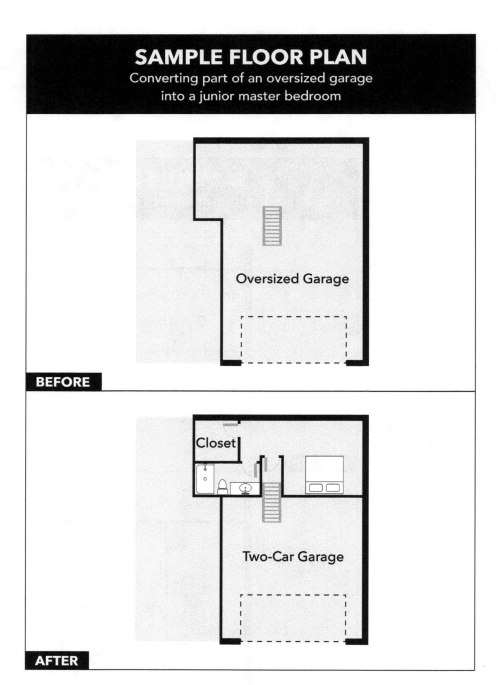

SAMPLE FLOOR PLAN
Converting part of an oversized garage
into a junior master bedroom

GRAPHIC

fig. 42

Oversized Garage

BEFORE

Closet

Two-Car Garage

AFTER

Designing the Layout and Finishes

    Planning a house renovation can seem like a monumental task, but, fortunately, there are guidelines and tools to help. As you determine the level of your rehab—cosmetic, full-gut, or value-add—you'll need to think about what you want the space to look like when the project is finished.

When designing the layout, the kitchen and bathrooms should be your priorities, because updated kitchens and bathrooms usually increase the value a few times more than the money you put in. I generally allocate almost half of my budget to kitchens and bathrooms. I've noticed that older homes tend to have small, enclosed kitchens, as they were mainly designed and used for food preparation and not to be seen by guests. In modern households, though, the kitchen has become the center of entertainment and needs to be appropriate for the size of the house. A large and somewhat open kitchen can be a selling point. When you look at the kitchen in a fixer-upper, compare it to the comps and decide if you need to make it bigger. If that's the case, you can often borrow space from an adjacent dining room, a breakfast nook, or even a laundry room. Adding an island can create additional cabinets and counter space. See figures 43, 44, and 45 for examples of floor plans that enlarge the kitchen.

fig. 43

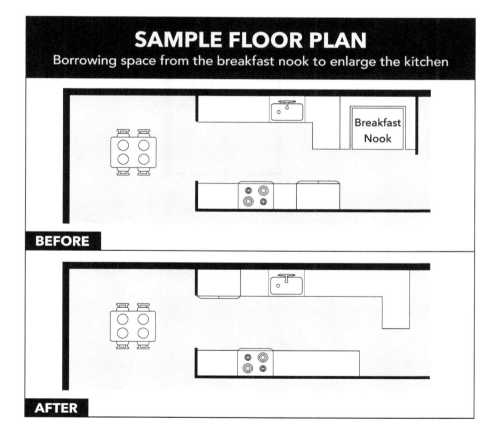

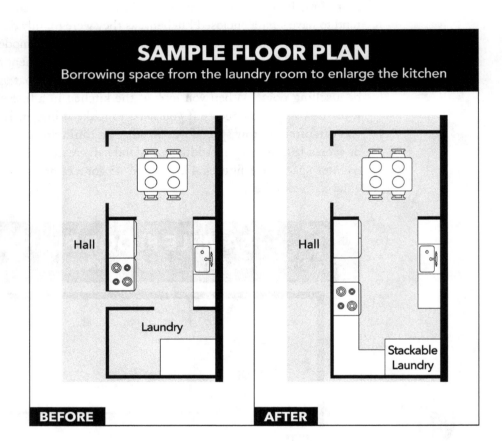

SAMPLE FLOOR PLAN
Borrowing space from the laundry room to enlarge the kitchen

Hall

Laundry

BEFORE

Hall

Stackable
Laundry

AFTER

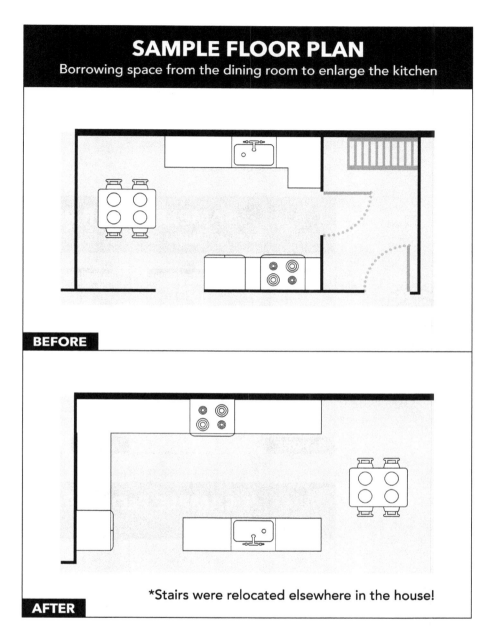

SAMPLE FLOOR PLAN

Borrowing space from the dining room to enlarge the kitchen

BEFORE

Stairs were relocated elsewhere in the house!

AFTER

The kitchen was expanded into the old dining room and the staircase area was converted into the new dining room, with the stairs being removed entirely from that section of the house.

As well as having small kitchens, many older homes have small bathrooms with awkward layouts and tiny shower stalls. Buyers love good-sized bathrooms and functional layouts, especially for master bathrooms. If you are looking to reconfigure the layout, you can usually do it by relocating the fixtures within the bathroom. This will increase your costs but might be worth it, because an awkward bathroom can turn off buyers. You can enlarge small showers by relocating fixtures or borrowing space from a closet on the other side of the wall. For higher-end homes, sometimes it's even worth it to move a few walls to create a master bath retreat with a double vanity and separate shower and tub. This may not be evident in the comps, but when you are selling a high-end home, these added features can really make your flip stand out. See figures 46, 47, and 48 for examples of revised bathroom floor plans.

fig. 46

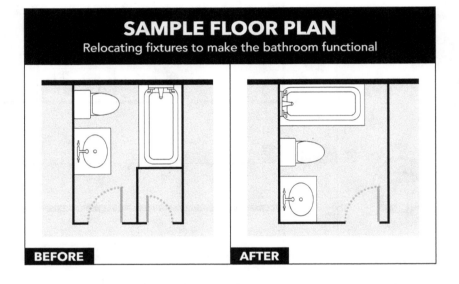

SAMPLE FLOOR PLAN
Relocating fixtures to make the bathroom functional

BEFORE

AFTER

fig. 47

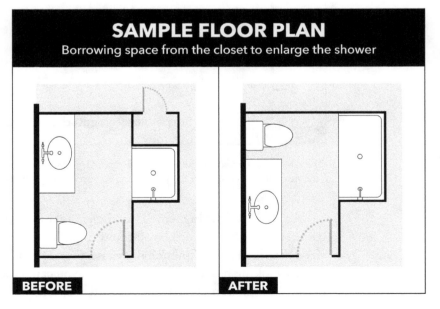

SAMPLE FLOOR PLAN
Borrowing space from the closet to enlarge the shower

BEFORE

AFTER

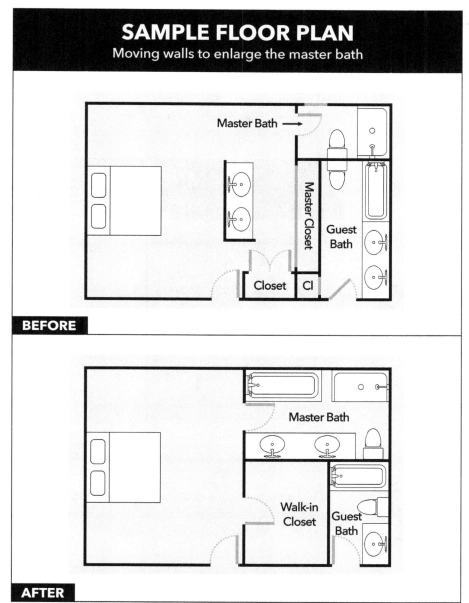

fig. 48

A nice walk-in closet was created as a by-product of the master bath expansion.

Open concept is all the rage right now, but that doesn't mean you should open up the floor plan on every flip. Again, look at the comps to see what's popular in the area. If most of the houses in the neighborhood have open floor plans, or houses with open floor plans are sold at a premium over homes that are enclosed, you'll want to follow that design guide. Remember, however, that different types of buyers tend to prefer different types of layouts. A young couple, for instance, will generally prefer an open floor plan that is ideal for entertaining. A family with two or three teenagers may look for closed rooms that provide privacy. See figure 49 for an example of an open-concept conversion.

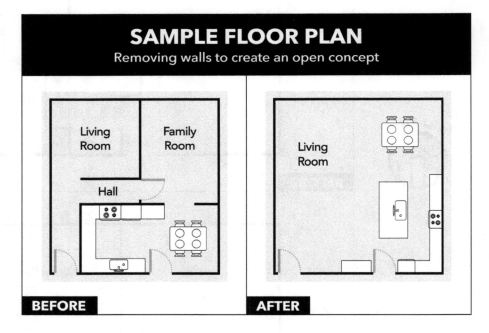

fig. 49

To see examples and before-and-after pictures of layout redesigns, check out the Case Study Library in your Digital Assets at go.quickstartguides.com/flipping.

Remember, though, that while desirability is important, you'll also need to factor in costs and permit requirements. Even though open concept is generally appealing in the Bay Area, I don't always do it because if there are load-bearing walls that need to be removed, you'll have to hire an architect to draw up the plans and a structural engineer to do calculations before you can submit the plans to the city for permit approval. The total cost will be much higher, and the projects will take much longer. The additional work and expense may not be worthwhile in the end.

I have remodeled more than 30 kitchens during my house flipping career. I share all my best tips with you on my video playlist called "Home Remodeling Tips," available on my YouTube channel.

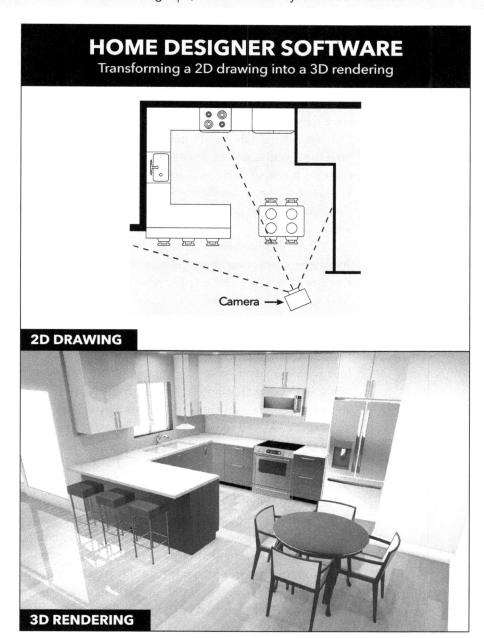

A basic drawing of a home layout that's been converted to a 3D version by a Home Designer software program

When it comes to extensive layout reconfigurations, I depend on Home Designer software, a remodeling and home design program that allows me to draw up the existing floor plan and then play with the wall placements to mock up different layout options. This program was created by Chief Architect, the developer and publisher behind the professional 3D architectural home design software of the same name. It creates a 3D rendering that lets me see what renovations will look like before any physical changes are made. (Full disclosure: I have no business relationship of any kind with Home Designer).

When you're starting out, it might be difficult to figure out how to make an awkward floor plan functional. I've been there. On my first few flips, it took me a long time to decide what changes to make, and it was quite a struggle. But now, as soon as I walk into a house, I can usually envision immediately how the layout could be changed to reach optimum functionality. Just know there's a learning curve and you'll get better with practice. I like the Home Designer software (see figure 50 for an example of what it can look like), but if it seems too complicated, you could hire an architect to help you optimize a floor plan.

When picking out finishing materials for a flip, such as flooring, paint, and countertops, don't base your choices on your personal preferences but on those of potential buyers. If you're wondering what buyers might like, again, refer to the comps. If one or more of the comps was sold at a record price for the neighborhood, its eye-catching designs and finishes were probably what won over the buyers. You may want to do something similar. Remember, though, that using design elements like bright color palettes or bold patterned tiles could win over some buyers but alienate others. I always use neutral and timeless designs that appeal to the majority of buyers. You can learn a lot about home styles, finishes, and decors on websites like Pinterest, Instagram, and Houzz. As you browse, save the ideas you like in one place so you'll have them handy and can refer back to them. You can also get inspiration from visiting local specialty stores, like tile shops that usually have some finished shower tile display. This allows you to see the finished shower walls rather than just a piece of tile.

While you want your design to be attractive and make potential buyers love the house, make sure you use materials appropriate for the home's price point. If you are remodeling an entry-level home, using high-end materials like hardwood floors or marble probably won't get you a good return on your investment. On the other hand, installing vinyl floors in a high-end home is likely to turn off potential buyers. You definitely need to spend more money when outfitting a high-end house, but that doesn't mean you'll need to spend a fortune on everything. I consider the highest level of interior design to be successfully mixing and matching expensive and affordable materials together to achieve a high-end look. To enhance walls, I like to use porcelain tiles with a marble pattern that are less than five dollars per square foot. I find striking light fixtures priced between $100 and $200 on Amazon to hang over kitchen islands. Thoughtful design doesn't need to be overly expensive, but it needs to fit with the overall look of the interior. Great design touches will make your flip stand out from the competition and increase the likelihood of it selling quickly and for top dollar.

The San Francisco Flip mentioned earlier was remodeled as a high-end home and ended up selling for $2.675 million. In it, I used prefabricated cabinets that cost one-third the price of custom cabinets, six-dollar-per-square-foot hardwood floors that looked similar to those priced at $12 per square foot, and tiles priced between two and five dollars per square foot. I mixed those inexpensive materials with glass railings that cost $25,000 and level 5 smooth drywall finishing to create a modern and high-end look, similar to that of a nearby comp. I learned that my total renovation cost was just over half of what had been spent on that comp, but my house sold for almost $200,000 more. You can check out the before-and-after video of this house by searching for "San Francisco High End House Flip Before and After" on my YouTube channel. Also refer to the video "How to Remodel to Make Your Home Look Expensive" for more tips and tricks.

I normally choose specific materials for houses with different price points, as explained in figure 51, but the materials you use can also be determined case by case, based on the comps and the design you are going for.

fig. 51

ENTRY-LEVEL HOME	MEDIUM-LEVEL HOME	HIGH-END HOME
Laminate flooring	A combination of the materials for entry-level and high-end homes	Hardwood flooring
Porcelain/ceramic tiles		Marble tiles
Quartz countertops		Marble countertops
Prefabricated cabinets		Custom cabinets

Materials I use in homes that sell at various price points

It's important to know where to shop for certain materials, as you'll want to look for a large selection and reasonable prices. Materials that cost the most are cabinets, countertops, floors and tiles, interior doors, windows, etc. You can get these from big-box stores like Home Depot or Lowes, but you also want to know about some local specialty stores that can provide more options. I often buy door handles, drawer pulls, mirrors, and lights on Amazon, and sometimes I shop at Wayfair and Lamps Plus.

» **Cabinets and countertops:** Many local specialty stores offer prefabricated cabinets and countertops at much lower prices than custom-made cabinets or countertop slabs. In my market, the most popular kitchen cabinets are Shaker-style cabinets. The look is the same whether you get them custom or prefab, but custom cabinets can cost three times as much. You can save at least a few thousand dollars by using prefab cabinets. Another advantage is that they're readily available at the store and come assembled, while custom cabinets have to be ordered, take a few weeks to arrive, and have to be assembled. When doing a rehab, using prefab cabinets can save you precious time. Countertop slabs look the same as prefab countertops, but they cost three or more times as much. In my mind, prefab cabinets and countertops are an obvious choice.

» **Vanities:** When working on furnishing an entry-level or medium-level home, I'll often shop at a big-box store like Home Depot or Lowes where I can buy prefabricated vanities for small bathrooms for between $200 and $300, which saves at least $500.

» **Flooring:** The price of flooring can vary a lot depending on the manufacturer, material, thickness, width, etc., but most buyers won't pay attention to the subtle details as long as they like the finish and style. You don't have to purchase the most expensive floors, even for high-end houses. Home Depot carries a limited selection of hardwood, laminate, and vinyl floors, so I usually go to local flooring stores for a wider choice.

» **Tiles:** Local tile stores have a lot more options than the big-box stores, but make sure you check the availability before ordering—many stores only carry a few samples and take a couple of weeks to deliver a large quantity. I often shop for tiles that are on sale, sometimes finding stylish ones that are discontinued for a fraction of the original price.

» **Interior doors and windows:** I usually let my contractor purchase these because there aren't that many options. I like one-panel or two-panel doors, which are available at the big-box stores. Because they are custom-sized, windows need to be ordered and take time to be delivered, so make sure your contractor orders them as soon as the project starts.

Specialty stores usually carry products from different manufacturers, meaning that the look, quality, and price can vary significantly from store to store. You'll want to visit at least a few stores before deciding where to purchase from. Examine the quality and selection of the items and make sure they don't look cheap or of poor craftsmanship. You can find such stores by asking contractors or other investors, or simply search online.

The prefab cabinets I use are constructed with plywood frames and maple drawers and doors, which is the same as many custom cabinets. My agents and buyers often compliment me on the quality and style of those cabinets, which can cost 60 to 70 percent less than custom-made ones.

If the house you've purchased is of a certain architectural style that's popular among home shoppers in the area, plan your design around that style. You'll want to complement the style, not compete with it. A rustic design, for instance, would incorporate a lot of wood and stone in cozy rooms, while a modern design would feature expansive interiors, natural light, and clean lines and curves.

The first house I renovated—a 100-plus-year-old Victorian—is in a small pocket neighborhood where there are a lot of older homes of similar style. Buyers in the area share a love for older homes and are willing to pay a premium for those that have been preserved rather than modernized. My flip contained some beautiful features, like ornate wood trim, curved windows, and a marble fireplace. I preserved and restored those features to their full advantage and used finishes and details that complemented the style, such as Victorian-style faucets, a farmhouse sink, a clawfoot tub, and marble and subway tiles. All of these added value to the house, but modern finishes would have been out of place and detracted from its charm. However, if it had been in a different location where potential buyers weren't attracted to older homes, restoring and continuing with the Victorian style may not have been the best idea.

The All-Important Walk-Through

Once you've thought about what upgrades make sense for your property and the level of rehab that's required, walk through the property with one or more contractors to determine exactly what needs to be done. You may have already had contractors in the house, most likely when you were trying to calculate rehab costs before agreeing to purchase it. But if you haven't yet found someone you want to work with, don't despair. Sometimes interacting with multiple contractors has helped me understand how they work and given me different ideas and perspectives, which I appreciate. If you've gotten bids from several contractors before closing, you can compare them and choose someone to work with. If not, continue looking for someone you can trust and work well with. And if for some reason you haven't yet had any contractors come to the house or place bids, now is the time to solicit them. You'll read more about finding and hiring a contractor in the next chapter.

When you're just starting out, you may be surprised at what contractors notice during a walk-through that you don't. They may observe, for example, that the floor slopes or that the electric panel needs an upgrade. As you become more experienced, you'll notice these types of things too, increasing your confidence and making the SOW process easier. The walk-throughs will also help you learn the terms and lingo that contractors use, so you can communicate with them more easily.

During your walk-through, make notes regarding necessary repairs and improvements to the interior and exterior of the home so you'll be able to compare them with the SOW the contractor will prepare. When I have doubts about the SOW, I always ask contractors for their opinions about how we can save money while still making the house look great. Sometimes their suggestions are over the top, but sometimes they offer good ideas. You also can note ideas for optional improvements and decide later whether to execute them, based on cost. Taking photos or videos will help you document the work that needs to be done and remember the condition of the property.

You should be comfortable asking contractors questions because they are your partners in the project and their input is invaluable. During the walk-through, I often ask whether a wall is loadbearing, what they think the optimal layout for the new kitchen should be, or how to update the bathroom for the lowest cost. Contractors probably have a lot more experience with remodels than you do, especially when you're starting out. Asking questions and soliciting their opinions is a great way to learn and to make them feel like they are part of the team.

Usually, the contractor will compile all the information obtained during the walk-through into an SOW document. You'll need to check it carefully to make sure it's complete and accurate before it's finalized as part of the construction contract between you and the contractor you hire. The SOW document will be a valuable tool that you refer to from time to time during the renovation project.

Creating a Budget

Costs vary from house to house, of course, but I've learned that on average, a full house renovation in the Bay Area will cost between $120,000 and $150,000. The cost may be much less where you are, and after you've got a couple of flips under your belt, you'll have a good sense of what your budget will need to be. One thing I can't stress enough is the danger of underestimating your renovation costs. If you underestimate your costs and then run into surprises—as you almost always will—your planned profits will be dramatically reduced. This is especially true if you're flipping older houses, which tend to present more challenges than newer ones. I recommend always adding a buffer of at least 10 to 15 percent of your anticipated costs as a contingency. You don't have to use it, but it's good to have.

fig. 52

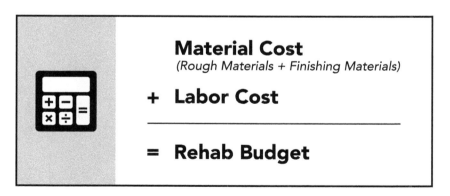

Material Cost
(Rough Materials + Finishing Materials)

+ Labor Cost
_____

= Rehab Budget

To create a budget, you'll need to know the approximate costs of all materials and labor (see figure 52). You'll probably want to use contractor bids to derive the budget, and you'll want to make sure all the bids you get include labor; rough materials such as lumber, drywall, insulation, and piping; and finishing materials such as paint, flooring, and tile. Some contractors quote labor only, and some quotes include only labor and rough materials. Get clarifications and ask them to help you figure out material costs based on the unit price and the quantity needed for your house. In the beginning, you may want to visit the stores or websites to understand the unit price for the specific materials you want to use. It's useful to familiarize yourself with the costs of materials and labor. Being aware of approximate costs can help you catch a contractor who is overcharging.

Once all the bids include labor and materials, you'll be comparing apples to apples. If you get multiple contractor bids, create your budget based on the median price, not the lowest price you can find. You'll learn more about working with contractors in chapter 7.

Once you've gotten prices for everything in your SOW, consider budgeting for some of the optional items you identified—those special touches like a double vanity or a kitchen pantry that will catch the attention of buyers. You can create a spreadsheet to record the estimated cost of each item and keep track of all rehab expenses.

When you've completed your budget, take some time to examine it and make sure the majority of expenditures are for essential improvements and those that will bring you the highest return on investment, such as the kitchen, bathrooms, flooring, paint, landscaping, and any other necessary repairs. Consult your budget frequently during renovations, taking time to make sure the costs seem to be in line and talking with contractors about any changes that need to be made.

Chapter Recap

» Hiring professionals for your rehab work is likely to save you money in the long run.

» Your SOW document will serve as a blueprint for you and contractors during the renovations.

» The ideal layout and look of the flip will vary depending on its style, what's popular among comps, the price point, and other factors.

» Be careful not to underestimate the cost of renovations, always adding money to your budget that can be used as a buffer for unexpected expenses.

| 7 |
Finding a Contractor

Chapter Overview
> » Different Types of Contractors
> » Finding the Right Contractor
> » The Contractor Agreement
> » Managing the Project

Once you've determined the applicable SOW and have a design plan in place, it's time to get started on the renovations. To do that, you'll need a good contractor standing by your side. Ideally, when you're just getting started, you'll be able to have three or more contractors look at the house, help you create an SOW, and give you estimates before you make the offer. As you read in the last chapter, having contractors walk through the house with you is helpful both for determining what the renovations will involve and for giving you a chance to interview and learn more about your possible hires. If you purchased the house without having had a sufficient number of contractors look at it, now is the time to start doing some interviews and finding a contractor to work with as part of your team.

To make reading more manageable, I've written separate sections and chapters on creating an SOW and searching for contractors to accompany you on a walk-through. In reality, though, those are different aspects of the same process, and they occur at around the same time.

This chapter walks you through the basics of choosing and working with a contractor. This is an important step because not having the right contractor can be devastating and discourage you from wanting to do more flips. I've already told you about my unfortunate contractor experience on my very first flip. Believe me, I thought carefully about whether I wanted to undertake a second one after that! While there are good contractors to be found, not all are honest or have a good work ethic or will fulfill their promises at the stated/offered price. I learned from my experience and developed a strategy for locating, screening, and working with contractors, which I want to share with you to help you avoid encountering the same problems. Since employing it myself, I've never been ripped off again. Let's get to it now.

What Type of Contractor Do You Need?

Different states and municipalities enforce different requirements for general contractors. Some states require them to have state-issued licenses and to register with the appropriate authorities before starting work, and others do not. Some states only require licensing or registration for projects that exceed specified costs, while others demand it for every job. Some states defer to municipal regulations, which can vary tremendously. Regulations regarding insurance for contractors and their employees (which in some states includes the subcontractors who work for a contractor) also vary. HomeAdvisor's website offers state-by-state licensing requirements. You simply click on your state to learn what licensing and certifications are needed by contractors there.

PRO TIP: Always ask a contractor for proof of property damage and personal injury insurances before hiring. Failing to do so could result in serious loss and liability issues for you.

If your state requires licensing and registration, you can at least assume general contractors have attained a certain level of competency and are recognized as legitimate by your state or municipality. If your state doesn't have these requirements, you'll have to rely on recommendations and information you've been able to obtain about contractors in your area.

For the purposes of this book, we'll discuss three categories of contractors: general contractors, subcontractors, and handymen.

I highly recommend that beginning house flippers use a licensed general contractor. If your state doesn't require licensure, be sure to get several recommendations before choosing someone. A general contractor has the experience and knowledge needed to manage a construction project, a task that involves finding and hiring subcontractors, overseeing their work, keeping them on track, making sure they are in compliance with all codes, ordering materials, keeping records, maintaining the schedule, writing invoices, and so forth. Having a general contractor is especially important if your house requires full-gut renovations like kitchen and bathroom remodels.

NOTE

An alternative to hiring a general contractor is to hire a project manager to manage multiple subcontractors or handymen. Ideally, the project manager is someone who has knowledge of construction, knows how to manage people, and is trustworthy and easy to work with. A project manager's responsibilities include interviewing contractors, reviewing bids, getting work scheduled, ordering materials, making sure work proceeds on time and on budget, checking the quality of work, and handling payroll. This person's most important task, however, is keeping you informed of everything happening with the project. This requires a high level of trust between the two of you. A project manager could be particularly important if you had several projects going on at once and wanted to avoid hiring a general contractor for each one. To find a project manager, you can post an ad on social media or Craigslist or ask for references from your local real estate clubs.

GENERAL CONTRACTOR

Full-Gut and Value-Add Rehab

- Full-gut kitchen
- Full-gut bath
- Adding sq. footage

SUBCONTRACTOR

Combination of Cosmetic and Full-Gut Rehab

- Roofing
- HVAC
- Plumbing
- Electrical

GRAPHIC

fig. 53

HANDYMAN

Cosmetic Rehab

- Painting
- Flooring
- Landscaping

If your project is less complex, you might be able to hire subcontractors on your own to complete the necessary work while you oversee their various tasks, the way a general contractor would in a more complicated renovation. It's possible to find good roofers, plumbers, HVAC experts, and carpenters on your own, but remember that it takes time and a significant degree of diligence, as licensing and registrations for these trades vary from state to state and municipality to municipality. This would likely save you money because you wouldn't have to pay the general contractor, but it could end up costing you more if you weren't able to manage subcontractors and schedule work as efficiently as a general contractor would.

For a renovation that is cosmetic only (painting, flooring, landscaping, etc.), you might be able to rely on a handyman, who may have plenty of experience and do excellent work but in most cases is not licensed. There are times when a handyman is the perfect fit, but don't make the mistake of hiring one when what you really need is a skilled tradesman. Figure 53 depicts the types of jobs associated with various service providers.

Meeting Contractors

Because you spend time with friends and family and you value and trust their opinions, they can be good resources for referring a contractor who has worked for them. If your cousin's contractor finished the job ahead of schedule and on budget, and your cousin is thrilled with the quality of the work, that's a pretty solid recommendation.

But if you don't have a personal connection to a contractor, don't despair. Other good sources for referrals are real estate agents and other investors— although investors are not always willing to share the contractors they work with. Contractors themselves can sometimes help, too; if a contractor you've worked with in the past is too busy to take on your current project, ask them for recommendations. You can also take note of the names of contractors on trucks you see in your area; if the same ones pop up over and over, they're probably doing something right.

Some investors like to hang out at big-box stores, where contractors pick up materials before starting work in the morning. I personally don't do this, but it can't hurt to hand out some cards and ask contractors to contact you if they're interested. If you see a dumpster in front of a house or notice any signs of construction going on inside, you can ask to talk with the contractors working there. Identify yourself as a house flipper and ask to have a look at the project. If the work is of good quality and everyone is working diligently, ask if the contractor is open to additional work. Again, have cards with your contact information available. You could also post papers on dumpsters outside of construction sites, listing your contact information and saying you're looking for help with renovation.

Online resources like Yelp can be useful, especially when they include reviews from customers. I try to seek out small, family-owned firms when I'm looking for a contractor. Large companies have to pay for multiple general contractors and cover higher overhead costs, which results in higher rates for you. You generally pay much less for contractors who are self-employed or employed by small companies.

NOTE

PRO TIP: When looking for a contractor on Yelp or another website that contains reviews, you might notice that the big contracting companies have many more reviews than the smaller mom-and-pop contractors; that's because they do more projects. Pay attention to the individual person the review is written about. If all the reviews of a contractor mention the same person, it's likely that person is also the principal of the company.

Once you locate contractors, you'll need to screen them to determine if they'd be a good fit for your project. Even with those who come highly recommended, I never skip the screening process, because it's so important to be able to feel as if you can trust and enjoy working with a contractor. I've had experiences in which a contractor who was referred to me turned out to be greedy and untrustworthy.

MY TAKE

Though you may be wary of hiring contractors that don't come from a personal recommendation, it's my feeling that contractors listed on sites like Yelp understand that their reputation is on the line, based on customer reviews. It's in their best interests to provide quality work that merits great reviews rather than having their reputation tarnished by comments from dissatisfied customers.

When looking for a contractor, there's a technical distinction you should understand. Those who work primarily for individual homeowners—often called *retail contractors*—are different from those who work primarily for investors—often called *wholesale contractors*. You can see a list of the differences in figure 54. This is something to keep in mind when getting recommendations, since a contractor who works primarily for homeowners may have an approach to work that isn't a good fit for an investor. Of course, many contractors work for both investors and homeowners, and you should set expectations with them early on about respecting the time frame and budget constraints that come with the business of flipping houses.

RETAIL CONTRACTORS	WHOLESALE CONTRACTORS
• Increased attention to detail	• Limited attention to detail
• No urgency to finish project quickly	• Understand importance of quick turnaround
• Accustomed to using high-quality materials	• Have access to cost effective materials
• Charge higher rates	• Work to keep rates low

fig. 54

Screening Contractors

Once you've identified some contractors you feel might be a good fit for your project, you should interview at least three before hiring anyone. The interview can take place during the walk-through of the property, and it should last for between 30 and 60 minutes. Before meeting, though, make sure each contractor understands that you're a house flipper, and find out if they have experience working with investors. Make it clear that your goal is to make the house look spectacular while staying within your budget, and that if the contractor is chosen and does a good job on this project, there could be many future projects. Indicate your interest in establishing long-term relationships with contractors who understand your goals and can help you meet those goals.

PRO TIP: Good contractors are worth their weight in gold. If you find one you like who invests time walking through a house and provides you with a thorough SOW—but then the deal falls through—offer them a couple hundred dollars in acknowledgment of their time and effort. Letting contractors know you appreciate this will help to ensure that they'll be available when the next deal comes around.

When meeting at the job site, have a clear understanding of your vision for the house. If you already know how to draft an SOW yourself, get it prepared and show it to the contractor. Spend some time discussing the work and how it can be accomplished on time and on budget. If you are unsure about part of the scope, ask questions and see if the contractor takes the time to help you find a satisfying resolution. Pay attention during the interview to whether the contractor offers ideas to save you money or seems anxious to have you spend it. Usually, the higher the cost of a project, the more a general contractor makes, so I respond especially favorably to contractors who come up with creative ideas for saving money on my projects.

> While I was in the process of getting bids for work on a fixer-upper, a couple of contractors listed the task of replacing shower tiles without thinking twice. I had accepted that task as a given, but then I interviewed another contractor who told me the tiles were in good shape and that if I was trying to save money on the project, he knew someone who could reglaze them instead of replacing them, using the same method that's employed to reglaze a tub. The paint lasts a very long time, and the shower surround looks new and refreshed, but the cost is a fraction of that of replacing the tiles. The paint worked as well as he said it would. The bathroom looked like new when it was finished, and I ended up saving thousands of dollars on that room. That contractor turned out to be a keeper, and we've worked together on dozens of projects since.

When talking to the contractors, pay attention to their demeanor. Do they talk a lot and promise you the moon, or do they speak conservatively, laying out all the downsides and risks up front? Remember that contracting is not a sales job and that contractors who talk like salespeople also tend to work like salespeople: they over-promise and under-deliver.

Don't hesitate to ask for references from every contractor you screen. Reputable contractors will be happy to provide them, along with photos of previous work. Some may even offer to show you a recently completed job. Follow up with the references, asking not only about quality of work, but dependability, timeliness, staying on budget, and so forth.

Reviewing Contractor Bids

After you've interviewed the contractors you're interested in working with, ask each to submit a bid. You might be surprised that some contractors will take the time to walk through a job with you but then never submit a bid. That's why it's important to interview a few contractors, so you'll get at least three bids to review and compare. If you have an SOW ready, give each contractor a copy of your SOW to ensure everyone has the same understanding of what needs to be done, and how. As you read in the last chapter, this helps to ensure that the bids will be comparable—apples to apples, so to speak.

When you've got the quotes, compare them for pricing and completeness. Even though you've specified what is to be bid on, you'll sometimes receive, for example, two bids that include labor and materials and a third that includes only labor, or labor and rough materials, with no allowance for finishing materials.

If the bids are priced pretty closely, you can safely assume they're fair. The cost of materials in a particular area normally doesn't vary dramatically, so if one bid is much higher or lower than the others, it should raise some red flags. I recommend considering middle-of-the-road bids, even when you're tempted to go with the lowest bidder in the hope of saving money.

If cost for materials is pretty uniform on all the bids you get, as it should be, variations in the total project cost will probably be due to differences in the cost of labor. Labor costs are the hourly rate times the hours needed to complete the job, as illustrated in figure 55. If one bid is much higher than the others, it's an indication that either the cost for labor per hour is much higher than that of the other bidders, or the contractor is anticipating it's going to take much longer to complete the work. On the flip side, a bid with a much lower price indicates a low hourly labor rate or a much shorter time needed to complete the work. Neither scenario is especially desirable and may be a red flag.

fig. 55

Rate Per Hour x Hours Needed to Complete = **Cost of Labor**

Getting It in Writing

Once you've reviewed contractor bids and selected whom you will hire, you'll want to get an agreement in place detailing what is expected of you and the contractor. This agreement will not only protect your interests but will keep your contractor happy by clearly spelling out your expectations. Many licensed contractors have standard contracts they use for every job and will provide one for you. I've included in appendix II a copy of the agreement my contractor uses. If your contractor doesn't provide one, you can find contractor agreements online from an organization such as the Associated General Contractors of America. Just make sure the contract you use is specific to where your house flip is located, as guidelines vary by state and sometimes even among municipalities. Regardless of the source of the contract, make sure it is complete and easily understandable. It should clearly state the details of the project and outline your relationship with the contractor. The SOW should be included as part of the contractor agreement, but be sure to review it one more time to make sure it's thorough.

An important component of the agreement is how much you will pay the contactor and the terms of the payments. Payments should be based on clearly defined milestones, from the signing of the agreement to a post-inspection payment. My contractor agreements break down payment milestones as seen in figure 56.

PAYMENT MILESTONES

GRAPHIC

fig. 56

1. Starting payment
2. Underground electric and plumbing
3. Foundation and framing
4. Rough electric and plumbing
5. Drywall and siding repair
6. Painting and flooring

7. Electric and plumbing
8. First inspection upon completion of work
9. Punch list items (those that were not completed or were not completed correctly)
10. Final walk-through

Note that there is a starting payment—but that the full amount shouldn't need to be advanced up front. Each step of payment should be appropriate to cover the work done in that phase of the project.

The agreement should make it clear that the general contractor is responsible for hiring and paying all subcontractors, as well as managing any problems with subs. A general contractor is also responsible for making sure all necessary permits are obtained and that insurances are in place to protect anyone brought onto the work site. Ask the contractor to provide a waiver of liability before starting work.

CAUTION

Some contractors may ask you to obtain job permits as an owner-builder. That's not recommended, because as an owner-builder you'd be responsible for the contractor's work, and you'd probably need to sign additional paperwork stating that you were aware of all the risks and liabilities.

You'll want a start date and a completion date specified in the agreement, along with any bonus and/or penalty contingencies to discourage delays. Hard money loans—the most common type of financing for flipping houses—are expensive, costing as much as $50 to $100 a day in financing costs on a $300,000 project. If the renovation took a week longer than expected, it would cost you several hundred dollars extra. When I interview a contractor, I always ask how long the project will take. Hoping to land the job, the contractor will often present a time frame that's, shall we say, slightly optimistic. When putting together the agreement, I'll use the timeline that was mentioned but will add a couple of weeks of buffer as the completion date. Because the contractor came up with the timeline, there is usually no pushback on what you include in the contract. If I'm paying $100 a day in financing costs and the contractor tells me it will take two months to complete a particular job, I ask them to agree to a $100-a-day bonus for each day before two and a half months and a $100-a-day penalty for each day over our agreed-upon completion date.

Your agreement should also specify who purchases the materials, including rough and finishing materials. As mentioned previously, contractor bids vary in this regard, and you need to make it very clear in the contract which materials are included and which are not. If the contractor gives you allowances for finishes, that's usually specified in the contract too. Knowing the allowances for each material can help you shop conservatively without having to increase the budget. Some house flippers like to keep control of their money by choosing and purchasing all necessary materials, while others prefer their contractors to do so.

PRO TIP: Most general contractors will order finishing materials for you, but I like to shop for tiles, countertops, flooring, mirrors, and lights myself so I can design the finished look of the home to appeal to the majority of buyers based on my research. I've gotten to know numerous shopkeepers who carry quality materials and will work with me on pricing. If you want to do some shopping, be sure to communicate clearly with your contractor and make sure your agreement specifies that you will be reimbursed out of the money in your budget for any items you purchase.

Another important part of the agreement is an outline of how change orders will be handled. *Change orders* are basically work added or removed from the original scope of work. These changes can affect the project's timetable and cost, so they should be carefully reviewed and considered.

Either you or the contractor can request a change order. You might change your mind about painting the kitchen cabinets and decide that new ones are necessary. Or your contractor might run into corroded pipes and realize that new piping is required for the entire house.

Change orders are by no means unusual and are one reason you should always include buffer money in your renovation budget. If you request a change order, make sure your contractor understands exactly what you want done. If the contractor requests one, have him explain to you why it is necessary. Always ask how much the change will cost, whether it will add time to the project, and if so, how much. Change orders should always be put in writing and approved by you and the contractor before any previously unspecified work begins.

PRO TIP: Have a mentor or another experienced investor look over your contractor agreement before you use it to make sure it contains all the necessary elements.

At the end of the job, you should ask the contractor to sign a *lien waiver*, a document stating they have received full payment for work completed and they waive their right to file a lien against your property. Having a lien against the property could prevent you from selling it until the matter was resolved.

Hopefully, renovation work can begin as soon as you and the contractor have reviewed and signed the contract. Your job now will be to work with the contractor and make sure the project moves forward in a timely manner. But before we discuss that, I want to deal with the topic of permits and inspections, which are important aspects of remodeling projects.

Permits and Inspections

The need for permits will vary depending on the house's local municipality. If your contractor has done work in the area, they'll know when permits are required and how they can be obtained. But you should also do your own research and find out if anything in your SOW will require a permit. You can often find such information online or by calling your city's building and planning department.

While they're necessary for most remodel jobs, permits take time to get and can be expensive. There have been instances when I decided to modify my SOW because I thought the permits I needed would take too long to get approved. But I always get permits when they're necessary because if you don't obtain them and it's reported to the city, you risk getting a stop-work order or possibly a code violation and a fine. Even if you finish the project without issues, potential buyers could be concerned when you disclose that certain work was not permitted. Not disclosing that fact could result in liability issues and complicate or delay the sale of the house. Permits are a part of doing business.

Most licensed contractors will obtain the permits they need, but be sure that you and your contractor are in agreement about who will do this. Permits are issued by the local municipality, with some more stringent about them than others. A permit will almost always be required for projects such as a full-gut kitchen remodel, taking out load-bearing walls, or legalizing or adding additional living space. Some municipalities offer online permits or over-the-counter permits for kitchen and bathroom remodels. Take advantage of that if it applies to your project, because it can save you a lot of time. If you find yourself in a situation where you should have had a permit but didn't realize you needed it, municipal officials are likely to work with you. But if you're adding a new bathroom or expanding the square footage of the house—projects that clearly call for permitting—you could be fined or even forced to open up walls to have the rough work inspected.

PRO TIP: If your deals tend to be in the same areas, it's helpful to forge relationships with the people who issue permits and perform inspections. Even just having a contact person who can answer permit-related questions is helpful, because otherwise you would have to call a general number and might never hear back. You're likely to get the permits faster and enjoy better working relationships if you take time to get to know municipal officials.

Once permitted work is completed, a municipal inspector will come out to look at it and make sure the work meets all codes and standards. There is usually at least a rough inspection after rough electrical and plumbing work is finished, and then a final inspection when the finish work is done. Your contractor should know when to schedule the inspections so they can get the rough work approved timely before starting with the finishes. Check on the inspection scheduling to make sure they're scheduled ahead of time. In some municipalities it can take a couple of weeks to get an inspection done due to high demand.

When a municipal inspector checks on the house, they'll often look at everything, not just the jobs for which you applied for permits. Once an inspector came to inspect the kitchen remodel on my project and discovered that the water heater had not been installed properly by the previous owner. I had to get a permit for the corrective work, even though it was not my fault.

Contractors should not be paid in full until their work has passed the inspection and a permit is finalized. If the work doesn't pass, the contractor should fix it at no cost to you. Make sure there is a provision in your contractor agreement stipulating that.

Keeping the Project on Track

Ideally, you and your contractor will work together to get the rehab work completed on time and on budget. However, it's ultimately your responsibility to monitor the project's progress on a regular basis and make sure it stays on track.

It's not unusual for contractors to get overbooked with projects, even if they are not the best in terms of quality or price. Many contractors take on as many projects as they can and start on all of them so it's harder for the homeowner or investor to fire them. Then they drag the projects on much longer than promised. You can't afford to have your contractor taking time off from your project to work on another. In addition to implementing bonuses and penalties in the agreement, an effective way to keep that from happening is making surprise visits to the work site. If you stop by unannounced and there are few or no contractors on-site or they aren't working diligently, that's a red flag that you'll need to address.

Set up contractor meetings to review progress, and insist that the contractor inform you immediately of any problems. Expected completion dates for various parts of the project will be included in the agreement and the contractor should be held accountable for them. Don't issue payment on work that hasn't been completed as agreed upon, and enforce the penalty/ reward system to encourage work to stay on time.

Speaking of contractor payments, most contractors expect some money before they start working. The payment might be needed to cover the cost of some materials, or it might be meant as a deposit to reserve their time. Even though it's risky for you to pay money up front, this issue can be a deal breaker for many contractors. Hopefully, with the tips and strategies mentioned in this chapter, you've reduced your risk by finding a contractor that's trustworthy. Even when that's the case, though, it's better to be careful and make small payments up front only when necessary.

If a contractor you don't know and have not worked with before tells you they need money to cover the cost of materials, insist on paying the supplier directly instead of having the contractor act as a go-between. It's certainly not unheard of for a contractor to disappear with money that's been paid out to cover the cost of materials. As you build trust with your contractor this won't be as big of an issue, but be very cautious with contractors you don't know.

Also, when starting out with a contractor, never offer another project until the first one has been successfully completed. It's necessary to work through an entire project before you can assess the competency and reliability of the contractor.

When payments to your contractor are due, make sure they're made on time. Good contractors can be hard to find, and on-time payments go a long way in keeping them happy. If you're using a hard money loan for rehab funds, money is usually not available immediately after specified work has been completed because the lender requires the work to be inspected first. That means you risk delaying payment to your contractor. Therefore, if possible, have some extra funds available to pay the contractor until money from the hard money loan becomes available. Before making the payment, however, make sure all specified work has been successfully completed. And don't pay with cash; always keep a paper trail for tax purposes.

PRO TIP: I make it a point to show contractors that I appreciate them. I often take lunch if I visit the job site in the middle of the day, and I give bonuses at the end of a job well done. This helps to ensure the contractors will be available when I get my next deal.

The goal is to find a contractor who can become a partner in all your deals—someone you know, trust, and can depend on without hesitation. Treating contractors fairly and insisting the same in return is key to building relationships that can turn into partnerships—a worthy goal!

Chapter Recap

» A general contractor is normally a smart choice for beginning house flippers.

» You can find a contractor through a referral, online, or at a job site.

» Get bids from at least three contractors and review them carefully before hiring.

» Obtaining permits is a bothersome but often necessary part of doing business.

» Keeping your renovation project on track is ultimately *your* responsibility.

» Treat a reliable contractor well and make it a point to pay on time.

| 8 |
Getting the House Ready to List

Chapter Overview
» The Essential Cleaning
» Adding Curb Appeal
» Necessary Inspections
» Staging the House

Renovations are finished and it's time to get the house ready to put on the market. This is an exciting stage of flipping a house, and one I find to be busy and rewarding. You'll want to proceed quickly now, as time is money and the sooner the house is sold, the better.

Some house flippers start marketing their houses as soon as they're finished or even before renovations are complete. Others—myself included—take a little extra time to get the property in tip-top shape before putting it on the market. There are pros and cons with each of these approaches. Marketing the house before it's completely finished or before it's cleaned and staged works best when the housing market is tight and there are few properties available for sale. In that scenario, buyers have fewer options to choose from and are likely to overlook the fact that the home is not in its final condition. As a result, you may be able to get the flip under contract while work is still going on and finish the construction while the house is in escrow, saving precious time and holding costs.

The downside to that approach is that, because the renovation is not complete, buyers have a chance to offer their preferences for finishing touches, or even to inspect and question the work being done, which can cause delays and complicate the sale. I usually don't start any marketing until the house looks its very best. I don't let my agent put a sign in front of the house or show it as "coming soon" on MLS because I don't want to risk buyers seeing the house until it's completely ready. This may cost me a few extra days or weeks, but I make sure that when the house is ready to be showcased, buyers see it in its best light and fall in love right away.

Personally, I enjoy the staging process and making a house look like a home for potential buyers. I believe this encourages an emotional attachment the minute viewers walk through the door and enables them to imagine themselves living there. This chapter will give you some ideas for getting your newly renovated house into the best possible condition before listing it.

Improve Your Curb Appeal

The outside of the home is the first impression prospective buyers get, so it's important to have this included in the SOW. If you've overlooked this aspect or you want to do a little extra, now is the time to double-check and make sure the curb appeal is fresh and inviting. See figure 57 for a checklist, which I'll go through in greater detail here.

The yard and the exterior of the house should look neat and updated. If the house has vinyl siding and you are not having it repainted, having it pressure washed will brighten it up and remove any moss or dirt. If you didn't have the whole house repainted, you could at least consider repainting the trim and shutters to brighten things up. Painting the front door a bright color can add a pop of interest at practically no cost. Refer to chapter 6 for exterior paint colors I recommend. If the door is in bad shape, you should replace it.

Take note of the garage door as well, and replace it if it's damaged or dated. A garage door takes up a lot of exterior space, and updating it can significantly improve curb appeal. Doors are available in various materials and many different styles, and those with lights are popular now, so look around before deciding what to buy, and make sure you match the garage door to the front door and the style of the home.

Have repairs made to the driveway and sidewalks if they're cracked or uneven or have pieces missing. Large cracks and uneven surfaces are considered safety hazards and will be called out in a property inspection (more about those in a bit). Pressure washing the driveway and sidewalks will brighten them and make them appear more inviting, and sealcoating the driveway can hide imperfections.

You'll also want to pay attention to the lawn and landscaping. If the lawn is in bad shape, consider reseeding it (in the beginning of the renovation, because of the time it takes). But, depending on where you live, it might not be the right season to do so. If you notice after the renovation is done that the lawn is not looking good, it's probably worth it to have sod installed as a quick fix. Landscaping that has been neglected and overgrown should be replaced, or at least trimmed and shaped. Planting some flowers that are in bloom can add appeal.

fig. 57

CURB APPEAL CHECKLIST

- ☐ Exterior Painting
- ☐ Pressure Washing
- ☐ Front Door
- ☐ Garage Door
- ☐ Driveway
- ☐ Landscaping
- ☐ Outdoor Lighting
- ☐ Mailbox

Outdoor lighting makes a difference, so consider both style and function when addressing it. Lights should be bright enough to illuminate the entryway, driveway, and other exterior areas and should match the style of the home. You can get a good idea of outdoor lighting options by shopping at Home Depot or looking at sites like Amazon, Wayfair, or Overstock.

An inexpensive upgrade to a front yard is to replace the mailbox, especially one that is leaning or has peeling paint. If you're installing a mailbox by the street, check out the US Postal Service website to see what regulations apply. I use mailboxes that can be attached to the house because they are very easy to install.

Cleaner Is Better

Once the renovations are finished, your contractor should clean up all the debris and leave the property empty. Even if the house looks semi-clean, it's probably not ready to be showcased, because construction dust on surfaces, dirty vanity mirrors, or foggy windows can affect potential buyers' interest and cost you money. Before putting the house on the market, you should hire professional cleaners to give it a thorough cleaning.

I recommend hiring cleaners rather than doing the work yourself. The reasons for that are similar to why I think it's preferable to hire contractors for your renovations rather than trying to do them yourself. You can probably clean the house yourself, but it will likely take you longer than it would a professional cleaner, and you have better things to spend your time on, such as making sure the finishing touches are perfect, filling out disclosures and ordering inspections, or starting to look for your next deal.

The cleaning that you have done to get your flip looking its best should be at a higher level than a regular residential cleaning, which doesn't usually include cleaning the windows or the insides of appliances and cabinets. The cleaning you need requires all those areas to be spotless, so make sure your cleaners understand that.

Having given you my opinion on the benefits of hiring cleaners, I understand it might not be possible to find someone to do the work, or you choose to do it yourself to save money. If that's your decision, make sure to allocate enough time—expect it to take you at least a whole day—and try to get a couple of helpers to keep you company and make the job go faster.

Gather all the materials you'll need before you start, using a bucket or caddy to organize everything. I recommend the cleaning products and equipment shown in figure 58.

GRAPHIC

fig. 58

CLEANING PRODUCTS	CLEANING EQUIPMENT	
• An all purpose cleaner in a spray bottle for cleaning dirt, grease, and stains	• Shop vacuum	• Microfiber cloths
• Tile cleaner	• Vacuum cleaner	• Towels
• Glass cleaner/window spray	• Razor blades for scraping paint	• Broom
• Toilet bowl cleaner	• Toilet brush	• Dustpan and brush
	• Rubber gloves	• Sponges
		• Extendable duster

Be systematic as you clean, finishing one room before starting another. Clean from the top down, making sure to dust all vents, fans, and surfaces, including windowsills and baseboards. Wash the windows, using razor blades to scrape off splashed paint or manufacturer stickers. Renovation work stirs up a lot of dust; you may have to wipe down the walls, appliances, and so on. Take all the stickers off appliances and gather all the instruction manuals, warranties, and other paperwork together in a binder or folder. If cabinets are dull, use an oil-based cleaner to shine them up, and make sure all stainless-steel appliances are clean and streak-free. If the range or the refrigerator is not new, make sure it's thoroughly cleaned.

The point is to make the house look spotless, shiny, and welcoming to potential buyers so they feel comfortable calling the home their own. Clean is okay, but sparkling is better.

Package the Listing

Walking through an empty house is simply that—walking through an empty house. Walking through a house that's been furnished and decorated enables prospective buyers to visualize what it would be like to live there, and it evokes emotion. HomeAdvisor reports that staged homes spend 33 to 50 percent less time on the market than homes that were not staged. Having your flip spend less time on the market is especially important when you're paying interest rates on hard money loans and other expenses associated with the house. Staging can also make a house look bigger, and I believe a well-staged and decorated house is likely to fetch a higher price.

Staging a house is the process of making it attractive and appealing to the highest possible number of potential buyers. It highlights the home's best features while deflecting attention from flaws. Staging also improves the appearance of a house in photos, which is where most people will get their first look; see figure 59 for an example. If you're tempted to forgo having the house staged, check to see if local comps are being staged. If they are, not staging your house will put you at a significant disadvantage.

Admittedly, the process is not cheap. HomeAdvisor reports that the average price to stage an empty, three-bedroom, 2,000-square-foot house is about $2,000 a month, which is slightly lower than what I normally pay in the Bay Area. That fee usually includes an initial consultation with the stager, service fees, furnishings, decorating, rental fees for a certain time frame (usually 45 to 60 days), and moving everything in and out. Once the lease is up, you'll need to pay additional fees if you want to keep up the staging. I believe that staging essentially gives that money back, however, by helping you sell a house faster and at a higher price.

I'm lucky to have a wonderful designer to stage my houses. You can see some of her work in the "Staging Examples" file included with your Digital Assets at go.quickstartguides.com/flipping.

You can get recommendations for a house stager from other investors or a real estate agent, or on a site like Yelp. Select a stager by viewing their online portfolio to see if they've done projects that are similar to your house. Make sure you like their work; don't choose a stager only because they're cheaper than others. Before you work together for the first time, meet with the stager to discuss your ideas, making sure to let them know the look and style you'd like for the house. The look of the staging should match the style of the house and complement the colors you've chosen. If you engage a stager before or during the renovation, they may be willing to provide recommendations on tile or paint choices.

Make sure the furniture used to stage the house is appropriate in size, so it doesn't overwhelm the space of the rooms. And leave plenty of room to walk around. Staging is helpful when there are less-than-desirable spaces in a home, such as a super-small or oddly shaped room. Installing a small desk or a table and chair instills the idea that the room has a purpose as an office or a reading nook, instead of leaving potential buyers to regard it as unusable. If your budget doesn't allow a full house staging, you can stage it partially, concentrating on the main living spaces—living room, dining room, kitchen, and master bedroom and bath.

fig. 59

Source: Photos from DeAnda Photography

An example of virtual staging

Some house flippers embrace the notion of staging homes themselves. Again, I don't endorse that idea because I think it's totally worth it to hire someone with access to furnishings and expertise to make a house look beautiful. I do, however, understand that some people do the staging themselves to save money or because they don't know who to hire. I also know several house flippers who do their own staging and have started staging businesses on the side! That transition makes sense, because to do your own staging, you need to have furniture and accessories that can match any style of house. You shouldn't, for instance, use modern, minimalist furnishings in a Victorian-style home. That means you'd need a variety of furniture, and a place to store it in when not in use.

Sure, some stagers use tricks like placing a blow-up mattress on top of a box spring and covering it with a quilt or comforter. Still, it takes a fair amount of furniture and accessories to stage a home, which can entail a hefty investment. And then there's the physical work of loading and moving furniture and getting it into the house and to the rooms where it's needed without damaging the walls or floors. If you have access to household items and want to try your hand at staging, I'd advise you to look at a lot of photos and read about the process before you start. There's a reason that people who commit to doing it themselves sometimes wind up making it a whole separate business.

During the height of the pandemic, when potential buyers were reluctant to visit houses in person, virtual staging increased in popularity. A talented designer can use virtual décor to create a very realistic photograph of every room (figure 59). I think virtual staging is an interesting idea, and it is less expensive than actual home staging. Overall, however, I still prefer potential buyers to come to the home and see it in person; it feels more real and tactile than when viewed through a computer screen.

Whatever form of staging you decide on, you should definitely pay attention to the photos of the house you're putting out there, even if the house is available to be seen in person. It's well worth the money to hire a professional photographer to take pictures of the house for marketing purposes. Making a good first impression is vital, and high-quality photos will ensure that the house is seen to its best advantage. Your real estate agent usually offers to pay for photography as part of their listing service, which is fine. However, never agree to use smartphone photos for your flip, as those are usually taken by an (unprofessional) agent and often feature bad angles and poor lighting. Unprofessional photos can make your house look undesirable and discourage potential buyers from wanting to check it out. I always feel bad for homeowners who trust their agent to market their home and end up selling it for hundreds of thousands of dollars less than comps, due to poor photos. Believe it or not, some of those homeowners are house flippers who should know better! You should insist on hiring a professional to do the job—and be selective, because not all professional real estate photographers are created equal. You can ask your agent for recommendations or look on Yelp. Check out their portfolio before choosing one. I trust only one photographer, and every time I fail to get him, I end up regretting it and sometimes need to have the photos redone. You also might consider having a 3D virtual tour of the house made for marketing purposes if comps are using them. The use of 3D virtual tours have gained in popularity in recent years, especially during the pandemic. They allow buyers to explore the home online before checking it out in person. Apps are available that enable you to do these virtual tours using your smartphone, but, again, I'd recommend that you hire a professional.

Order Inspections and Make Repairs If Necessary

To control the narrative and ensure the sale can proceed quickly, I like to get inspections done before I list the house. This eliminates the need for the buyer to request inspections and ask for contingencies on the sale. I have the inspections done, make whatever repairs are necessary, and show potential buyers the reports with my notes, assuring them that everything is in order.

I recommend that you schedule a home inspection as soon as the renovations are completed, even if you had an inspection done before bidding on the house. This inspection will ensure that any problems identified previously have been resolved, a fact that will be reassuring to prospective buyers. I'd also get a termite inspection, a roof inspection if the roof is not new, and a chimney inspection, when applicable. Get all the repairs done prior to listing the house if you can. If not, get the repairs scheduled and note on the inspection reports that they will be taken care of and that you will pay for them before *close of escrow (COE)*.

NOTE

A standard home inspection covers nearly every part of a property, but depending on your location and the age and condition of the house, you might benefit from additional inspections, the most common of which are termite, roof, chimney, radon, mold, and foundation. It's better to discover and resolve any problems in these areas before your house is listed.

The main purpose of getting the inspections done is to reduce your risk. If you don't have the inspections completed and the reports ready, the buyer can get under contract to purchase your house with an inspection contingency and then order inspections themselves. If they are not satisfied with the reports (there are always going to be items called out in the inspections, because the homes are not new construction), they can try to renegotiate the price with you or back out of the contract, which puts your house back on the market. That's a very tough position to be in, because other interested parties will probably have found something else by that time, and any new buyers would have concerns about your house, since it's showing as "Back on Market" on the MLS. It's likely that new offers you got would be lower than the original offer—and this could even include a lower offer from the original buyer. It's not an uncommon tactic for buyers to tie up a property with contingencies, only to later renegotiate the price down to take advantage of the vulnerable seller. Some house flippers have been known to do this when buying property, too; make sure you don't fall for that trap.

Having inspections done is a little more work and expense for you, but it really does speed up the sale of the house and increase the likelihood of the offers you receive getting to the finish line. I hardly ever need to accept an offer that contains a property inspection contingency, because I've already provided the buyer with the reports.

See figure 60 for a final checklist of everything you need to get done before listing your house.

LISTING PREPARATION CHECKLIST

fig. 60

- ☐ Final Touch-up
- ☐ Enhance Curb Appeal
- ☐ Deep Cleaning
- ☐ Professional Staging
- ☐ Professional Photography

- ☐ Order Inspections
  - ☐ Property Inspection
  - ☐ Termite Inspection
  - ☐ Roof Inspection
  - ☐ Chimney Inspection
  - ☐ Note report items you will fix

Chapter Recap

» Having a house thoroughly cleaned is an important step in getting it ready to list.

» You can improve the curb appeal of a property with simple steps like replacing the mailbox, painting the front door, improving the landscaping, and updating outdoor lighting.

» Staging a house makes it easy for potential buyers to picture themselves living there and evokes an emotional response.

» Having inspections done before putting a house on the market eliminates the need for buyers to request an inspection contingency and speeds up the selling process.

PART III

FINDING A BUYER AND TURNING A PROFIT

| 9 |
Use an Agent or Sell It Yourself?

Chapter Overview
» Real Estate Agent or DIY?
» Flat-Fee Listings
» Hiring an Agent
» Getting a License

After all the rehab work has been completed and your flip is ready to sell, you may feel ready for a vacation—but that will have to wait. As you've read over and over, time is money in the house flipping business. You can't afford to waste any time before putting the house on the market and getting it sold, which raises the question of whether to use a real estate agent or sell the house on your own.

Although I almost always have agents handle my house sales, I understand why many investors do not. You are not legally required to use an agent, and some sellers are certainly successful selling on their own. The standard commission charged by an agent is five to seven percent, a cost that is split between the buyer's agent and the seller's agent. Naturally, it can be enticing to attempt to sell the house yourself and save on some of those fees. After all, five percent commission on a house, that sells for $250,000 would net the agents $12,500. On a house that sold for $500,000, the agents would get $25,000, and on a million-dollar house the commission would be $50,000. Forgoing the seller's agent would mean saving half of those amounts. Looking at those numbers, the argument for selling on your own seems to make sense.

After all, there are a lot of agents out there; membership in the National Association of Realtors (NAR) has increased steadily since 2012, rising from one million at that time to 1.46 million in 2020. Many of those agents do excellent work, but, as in any profession, it's not uniform. Not all agents possess equal skills when it comes to selling homes, and only good listing agents can provide the value that justifies their commissions. If you're thinking about working without an agent, however, you should understand that there are different ways to go about it. You can go the For Sale By Owner (FSBO) route, which I would not recommend for a completely renovated house, as it means your house won't be listed on the MLS and many prospective buyers won't know it's available. Or you can enlist the help of a flat-fee listing service, which means the house will be listed on the MLS but you won't have the benefit of the services an agent offers. The third way to sell on your own is to get your real estate license and become your own agent. You'll learn more about these options a little later in this chapter. But because I almost always work with agents and have experienced how valuable they are, we're going to start by looking at what agents do and how you can hire and work with a good one.

HOW AN AGENT HELPS YOU SELL A HOUSE

GRAPHIC

fig. 61

- **Determines ARV**
- **Suggests SOW**
- **Performs project management**
- **Sets asking price**
- **Lists on MLS**
- **Oversees marketing**
- **Reviews offers**
- **Negotiates with buyer**
- **Oversees sale**

How a Real Estate Agent Helps You Sell a House

Requirements for becoming a real estate agent vary from state to state, but everyone striving to get a license must fulfill pre-licensing education requirements and then apply to take the real estate salesperson exam. A score of at least 70 percent is needed to pass the exam, and not everyone passes on their first try. Once a passing grade has been achieved, the aspiring agent needs to sign on with a real estate broker, which is basically an agent who has achieved a higher level of licensing and is in a position to supervise and assist agents. So, while all licensed real estate agents have met certain standards, their level of experience varies, and some are more successful than others due to personality, drive, and other variables—as in any profession.

When considering experience level, it's important to keep in mind that agents handle a variety of tasks beyond simply finding a buyer and overseeing the sale (see figure 61). In fact, an agent who works with house flippers should be available long before the house gets to the market. If the agent brought the deal to you, they can also provide you with a CMA (comparative market analysis) to help you determine the after-repair value (ARV). See figure 62 for an example of a CMA. Always rely on your own analysis, but if you are working with a good agent and they know the neighborhood well, they can offer insights to help with your analysis and ensure that you make the right offer. For example, an experienced agent can tell me that I'm too conservative with my numbers and prevent me from losing out on a deal. Oftentimes, I walk through a fixer-upper with my contractor and my agent at the same time, and the agent offers helpful suggestions for the SOW (scope of work) based on their knowledge of sales and their understanding of buyers in the area. A good agent is an especially valuable asset when you have doubts about how to make a floor plan more functional or what finishes are the most appealing to local buyers, etc. And if you're planning a renovation that won't increase the value of the house or isn't what buyers are looking for, your agent can alert you to that, saving you the cost of the work.

fig. 62

	1 Green Ct.	108 Plum Rd.	21 Chilly St.	37 Duke Rd.	12 King Rd.
List Price	$445,000	$585,000	$424,900	$457,500	$550,000
List $/sq. ft.	$263	$245	$260	$290	$276
Sold Price	$445,000	$570,000	$403,000	$450,000	$546,000
Sold $/sq. ft.	$263	$238	$251	$285	$274
Subdiv	Kenilworth	Kenilworth	Kenilworth	Kenilworth	Kenilworth
Year Built	1955	1941	1953	1951	1954
Appx Acres	0.28	0.25	0.28	0.16	0.28
Total sq. ft.	1,690	2,391	1,604	1,578	1,990
Type	1 Story Basement	2 Story	1 Story Basement	1 Story	1 Story
Style	Ranch	Cape Cod	Ranch	Cottage, Ranch	Ranch
Bedrooms	3	3	3	2	3
Full Baths	2	2	2	2	2
Half Baths	0	0	0	0	0
Heat/Cool	Central Air	Central Air	Central Air	Gas Hot Air	Central Air
Heat/Cool	Gas Hot Air	Gas Hot Air	Gas Hot Air	Gas Water Heater	Gas Hot Air
Fireplace	Living Room	Gas Logs	Gas Logs	Bonus Room	Living Room
Parking	1 Car Garage	Attached Garage	1 Car Garage	None	None
Driveway	Gravel	Asphalt	Asphalt	Gravel	Gravel
Foundation	Basement Inside	Crawl Space	Basement	Crawl Space	Block
Flooring	Tile	Tile	Tile	Tile	Tile
Flooring	Wood	Wood	Wood	Wood	Wood
Laundry	Basement	Attic Other	Basement Shop	Main	Main
Int Feature	-	Attic Walk-in	Garage Shop	-	-
Ext Feature	Fenced Yard	-	-	Fenced Yard	-

An example of a comparative market analysis

Your agent also should be available to help manage your rehab project as needed, especially if the house under renovation isn't close to where you live. You and your agent would need to discuss the role the agent would take, how much they would be available to do, and if their compensation should exceed the standard commission. They can often help you find contractors to do the work and oversee the project to make sure it's on budget and on schedule, much like a project manager would. But as with everything else, it can be hard to find agents you can completely trust and rely on, so if you have the capacity to manage the project yourself, that's always the best option. But whether the agent manages the project for you or not, it's important that they be fully aware of all repairs and upgrades done to the property and be able to accurately explain that information to potential buyers.

By the time you're ready to put your house on the market, you already have the ARV from your analysis before purchasing the house, but the number may not be valid anymore due to market fluctuations. Your agent, however, can compare the comps and work with you to confirm whether the ARV is still correct. If market conditions have changed, a good agent might recommend increasing the asking price if the market is on an upswing or lowering your price in the event of a downturn. If an agent recommends a price that's much higher than any other house for sale in the neighborhood, be sure to find out why. A higher price may be warranted, but potential buyers could be put off and the sale of the house delayed. The price should be based on comps—both list prices and sales prices—with considerations made for *local market norms*, which are trends within a particular real estate market.

In some markets, for instance, buyers almost always balk at paying more than the list price, or even the full amount of that price. An agent who is familiar with an area will understand those kinds of market norms and can advise you on them. In the case described here, you'd probably want to list the property slightly higher than your desired price, because you're likely to get offers that are lower than the asking price. In other markets, typically competitive markets like the Bay Area, buyers are used to paying well over the asking price on homes. If that's the case, you usually want to list below what you think the home is going to sell for. This causes more buyers to show up at open houses and submit offers, often resulting in a bidding war.

If you're unaware of the norm and merely list the home at the ARV, you may risk scaring off buyers. This sets up a scenario in which your house sits on the market for a while and you ending up having to discount the price. On the other hand, you don't want to list the home too much below the ARV, as that could cause the final sales price to fall short of its potential and result in your leaving money on the table. That's why it's particularly important to know the local market norms or have an experienced agent who can advise you in that regard.

I had determined that the ARV of a flip I sold recently was $1.7 million, because nothing in the neighborhood had ever sold for more than $1.8 million. When my agent suggested we list the house at $1.7 million, I was shocked. Any good agent in my area knows you can't list a house at the price you think it's going to sell for, and I thought the person I was working with was a good agent. I was wondering what to do when she said, "Elisa, trust me on this. I've lived in the area for a long time, and I know the market really well. I believe this house is going to sell for well over $1.7 million, and we are going to do great." I decided to give her the benefit of the doubt, as she had over-delivered the previous time we worked together. It turned out she was right! Even with the high asking price, we had a ton of interest in the home. Two hundred people came through the open houses and many people wanted to make strong *preemptive offers*, which are offers buyers make in advance of a designated offer deadline. She said no to all the preemptive offers, and we ended up selling the house for a whopping $2 million! I'm so glad I listened to her and didn't list the home for a lower price. This proved to me once again the value of a good agent.

Once you've agreed on a price and the house is ready to be listed, it's the responsibility of an agent to get it on the MLS and begin marketing it. An effective agent should have the ability to word your listing in a way that gets potential buyers excited. Wording that describes the house in a particularly compelling manner can help generate traffic and potentially speed up the sale, as can professional photos. If agents offer to take photos themselves, ask if they've had professional training as a real estate photographer, and ask to check their portfolio. It's not common for a real estate agent to have a photography background, but I've worked with one who uses a professional-grade camera and does a fine job, so you never know. Another word of warning about an agent who wants to take photos with a phone to use with your listing: thank them but insist on hiring a professional photographer, even if you have to cover the cost yourself. I don't believe any good agent would think phone photos qualify as listing photos, so I would seriously question the competency of an agent who suggested that. Don't assume that just because they offer to take photos they're especially good at it!

Good agents use multiple marketing avenues, including putting a For Sale sign in front of the house, printing flyers so potential buyers can reference photos and features, sending out postcards to neighbors, using online ads and social media ads, and so forth (see figure 63). This gives you the advantage of having more people hear about the house and drives traffic your way. You'll read more about marketing a house in the next chapter.

AGENT MARKETING AVENUES

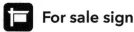 **For sale sign**   **Flyers**   **Postcards**

 Online ads   **Social media ads**

NOTE

PRO TIP: Expect your agent to keep you informed about all showings and open houses, letting you know what the potential buyers like and don't like, how many disclosures packages have been requested, and if there are any indications that some buyers might be interested in making an offer. This is easily accomplished by having your agent consult with the buyer's agent after a showing. The information can provide valuable feedback for you and your agent.

Another important job of an agent is helping you negotiate offers to get the best possible price for your house. This doesn't start after the offers are received but as soon as the house is listed. Interested buyers often have their agents contact the listing agent to ask questions about the house and find out what offer price the seller is expecting. Good agents should know how to answer the questions strategically without giving away your bottom line. It's really an art. You want your agent to inform buyers of other interested parties and encourage them to make competitive offers without scaring them away. After doing 30-plus flips and consciously learning from good agents, I still haven't quite mastered that skill and prefer to have a competent agent handle the sale for me, because each sale is different and various market conditions have to be dealt with case by case.

If you create a desirable flip and receive multiple offers, a good agent may be able to help you use the competition to your advantage and get the offer price up over the highest bid. The strategy for doing this varies according to the market, the price point of the house, and who the potential buyers are, but I've had agents help me increase my sales price by tens of thousands and even hundreds of thousands of dollars. I'd say that makes their work well worth their commissions.

NOTE

Like most people, I used to think offer negotiations started only after the offers were received. During the sale of one of my earlier flips, we received an offer that was $100,000 above the asking price.

Pleasantly surprised, I commented to my agent that he hadn't even had to work his magic to get that great offer. The agent, who has become one of my best agent partners, looked at me and said, "Do you think that additional $100,000 just came out of thin air? I've been working this buyer for a week!" He told me he realized how much the buyer loved the home and how he was able to direct them on the offer price to achieve that amazing sale. That incident really opened my eyes to how much influence agents have on a sale.

Another asset of a good agent is the ability to weed out unqualified buyers. When reviewing offers, experienced agents know to look at a potential buyer's preapproval letter and proof of funds (POF) document carefully. They contact the bank or mortgage broker that issued the preapproval letter to understand the likelihood of the buyer's loan getting final approval. They also make sure the POF is more than enough to cover the down payment and possible appraisal shortage. If the offers you receive have contingencies, your agent can negotiate to shorten or even eliminate them, because the fewer contingencies, the less risky an offer is for you.

Once your property is under contract, there's still one big hurdle to overcome: making sure the sale goes through. A lot can happen between entering into a contract and getting the house through closing. Your agent should make sure the buyer gets the necessary appraisals ordered within as short a time as possible after the contract is signed, because appraisals take time and could delay the closing. The agent should oversee the appraisal process to ensure that the appraised value satisfies the lender's requirement, or find a way to mitigate any issues. If your buyer is getting an inspector to look at the house, the agent should follow up on any concerns and help you address them. And your agent should be the middleman between you, the buyer, and the title company, staying on top of the progress of escrow and alerting you if anything is off track.

I believed my agent when she told me everything was going well with the sale of one of my first projects and that we were on track to close on time. On the day we were supposed to close on the sale, however, I learned that the buyers' lender hadn't even drawn the loan documents yet, which meant the buyers couldn't sign the documents, the lenders couldn't fund the loan, and we couldn't close on the sale. Because my agent hadn't stayed on top of things and had misled me in the process, we missed the opportunity to follow up and stay on schedule, and I had to keep paying the expensive hard money interest for several more days as a result.

Hiring and Working with an Agent

Hopefully you'll establish a network of agents who will supply you with an ongoing stream of deals. I've been lucky enough to do this, and it saves a lot of time and money on deal acquisition. As you read in part I, part of my strategy for finding agents to work with me is to assure them they will represent me on both the purchase and the sale of the property. That has worked out very well, as it benefits both me and the agent.

If you would like to employ the same strategy to find deals, it's important that you fulfill your promises to the agents who bring you deals, even if it means less profit to you due to commission payouts. I've seen many investors make the mistake of bypassing the agent after a flip is done and trying to find a cheaper way to sell the house. This is shortsighted because, though they may save some money on the sale of one property, they lose out on any future deals the agent could have brought them. Believe it or not, agents talk, and a flipper who doesn't keep their word can wind up with a burnt reputation, forcing them to rely on other more expensive and time-consuming ways to find deals.

I was reaching out to an agent for the first time and telling her what my intentions were. She told me that she had been burnt by an investor in the area, and she would never again work with him or anyone related to him. I happened to know that same investor, and I knew his reputation in the business was not great. This told me that the real estate investing circle is very small, and it's crucial to protect your reputation if you want to be in the business for the long term. Safeguard your reputation like your life; it's not worth sacrificing for a short-term gain.

If you have found a deal without the help of an agent, however, or for some reason won't be using the person who brought you the deal (and won't be trying to sell on your own), you'll need to find an agent to help you sell your property. If that's the case, you'll want to choose carefully, with the goal of finding someone you trust and forming a relationship that will be sustained throughout your house flipping career.

Recommendations are important, so don't hesitate to ask other investors for names of agents they've worked with and liked. But don't be tempted or feel pressured to use an agent who's a friend of a friend or a second cousin, unless you're sure their credentials and reputation check out. An agent should be willing to provide references, and you should use them. Ask about the agent's responsiveness, their knowledge of real estate, their negotiation skills, and what kind of assistance and results the seller got.

Also, look for someone who is familiar with the area in which you'll be working and knows what local buyers are looking for and how to position your flip for the best sale. Ask how many sales they've had in your area in the past year. Having someone who knows the area gives you a real head start when you put a house up for sale. You can check previous listings the agent handled, with an eye toward the sales price relative to comps and the listing details, such as photos, house descriptions, and so forth.

Beyond familiarity with your area, you want someone with a good amount of overall experience—I prefer at least five years in the field. And experience isn't just time; you should also find out how many sales the agent does per year. I look for someone who does at least five sales but no more than 40, my reasoning being that someone selling 40-plus houses a year likely relies on other agents or assistants for a lot of the listing-related work and wouldn't be able to handle my sale personally.

AGENT QUALIFICATIONS TO LOOK FOR

fig. 64

1. Familiar with the area

2. Five-plus years of experience

3. 5-40 sales a year

4. High-quality previous listing

5. Most capable, but not cheapest or promising the highest price

Finally, it may sound obvious, but you should hire the most capable agent—in other words, not the cheapest or the one who's going to set the highest list price. I've learned the hard way that not all agents are created equal. Getting a license is fairly easy, so there are a lot of licensed agents out there. But having a license doesn't guarantee that an agent is good at their job. Some agents try to win business by charging a lower listing commission; that can be a savings for you, but if the agent is sloppy at their job, the profit you miss out on could be a lot more than what you're saving. Some agents try to entice you by committing to a higher list price, which does not guarantee a high selling price. As mentioned earlier, if the house is listed at too high a price, it can scare buyers away and cause your house to sit on the market and, ironically, wind up selling for a significantly lower price. Unless otherwise specified in the listing agreement, the agent is going to earn the same percentage of commission whether or not they deliver on getting the set list price. See figure 64 for an overview of the most important qualifications to look for in an agent.

Once you've selected an agent to work with, you'll need to sign a listing agreement. This authorizes the agent to list the house and market it to prospective buyers. Listing agreements vary, but most contain a description of the property, the listing price, responsibilities of the agent and the seller, a termination date, and any other terms and conditions. The agreement will list the agent's commissions and the number of days in which the house is expected to be sold. It may also contain an agreement regarding a bonus if the agent sells the house within or before the specified number of days, or above a certain price. I usually offer a bonus if the agent sells my house for more than my expected ARV, so the agent's interest is aligned with mine on the sale, and they have a good reason to work hard to sell the house at as high a price as possible. Also, consider offering a tiered commission, which can provide additional incentive for the agent to sell the house quickly and at the highest possible price. Start with a five percent commission with the understanding that it will increase by a specified amount if the agent is able to increase the selling price of the house.

Finally, make sure the agreement allows room for you to dissolve your relationship with the agent if things do not go well or proceed as expected.

If You Decide to Sell It Yourself

If, after reading about all the benefits of having an agent, you're still convinced that you want to try to sell a house on your own, read on. There are three major ways to attempt it: For Sale by Owner, using flat-fee listings, and getting a license yourself. While selling it yourself can sometimes work out—and I certainly understand the temptation to give it a try—this does not mean that all three methods are equally effective. I'll walk you through these three methods and explain which ones are better than others.

For Sale by Owner (FSBO)

Unless you have access to a number of potential buyers and have a good understanding of how real estate transactions work, I would recommend steering clear of FSBO. As I've already pointed out, without your house having a listing on the MLS, many potential buyers simply won't know about the property, which limits your audience and your ability to sell your house at fair market value. However, if you have ways to market your house to prospective buyers, don't care about being on the MLS, and are certain you're getting a fair price on the property, I can see the benefit of FSBO. In general, FSBO might make sense when you are selling a fixer-upper, rather than a fully remodeled home, because fixer-uppers mostly attract the interest of other investors, and it's easier to market to investors off MLS than to regular home buyers who are interested in fully renovated homes. Below I'll elaborate on a recommended use case of FSBO.

As mentioned above, FSBO could make sense if you decide to sell your flip to another investor instead of someone who wants the house to live in. As an investor, you know how to run the numbers and how much the house is worth, as will the person you're dealing with. When selling a flip to another investor, there's usually not a lot of margin on the deal, so working directly with another investor could save the commission you'd have to pay the agent, thereby increasing your profit.

WHY SELL TO ANOTHER INVESTOR?

fig. 65

 1
Wholesaling a fixer-upper without doing any work

 2
Selling a flip mid-construction

 3
Getting plans approved and selling the house with the plans

There are several reasons you might sell to another investor (outlined in figure 65). One is if you're wholesaling the house without renovating it, as you read about in chapter 1. You simply locate a discounted property that's for sale, agree to buy it, then find another investor who's looking for a deal and sell it to them at a higher price. Another reason you might sell to another investor is if, for some reason, you have to sell a house in the middle of a renovation project. This could occur if, for instance, you ran out of money, realized you were in over your head, or had a family emergency.

A third reason would be if you bought a house that would benefit from an addition or even from being torn down and replaced by another. Instead of undertaking the work, you plan the project and obtain permits, a process that can take several months. Once the plans and permits are in place, you sell the now-ready-to-renovate property to an investor who will do the necessary work and flip the house.

You already know that investors buy houses for different reasons than would-be homeowners do, but many agents don't understand what is involved with investor purchases or how investors analyze deals. As an investor yourself, you are probably qualified to work with an investor on your own. You, after all, are very familiar with the house and know exactly what's been done to improve and upgrade it.

And while it's almost impossible for you to reach a good number of regular home buyers without listing your house on the MLS, reaching investors is easier. You can go to local real estate meetings, post in real estate groups on Facebook, or market the house on Craigslist. It's also a good habit to collect other investors' contact information when you go to meetings and events. Before long, you may have a long list of investor buyers you can sell houses to when you encounter one of the three circumstances above.

Even when selling to an investor, it's still possible that the extra profit you might realize by avoiding a commission payout may not be as much as you assume. An MLS listing would allow you to reach a lot more investors than you could on your own, and the more investor buyers you reach, the more likely the final sales price will be higher. Research from the National Association of Realtors (NAR) has shown that FSBO homes typically sell for less than comps that are sold by agents. And not just a little bit less. According to the NAR's 2020 FSBO statistics, the typical FSBO home sold for $217,900, compared to $295,000 for a similar home sold by an agent. Obviously, the NAR exists to support and promote real estate agents, but its statistics indicate year after year that agents sell houses for more than owners do. Remember as well that if your buyer is represented by an agent, you as the seller still have to pay commission to the buyer's agent; you only save the listing agent commission, which is normally 2.5 percent.

Other than when selling the house to someone you know or to another investor, I'd stay away from FSBO. You run the risk of leaving money on the table because the house won't be marketed to all potential buyers, and you will not be properly represented. At best, selling on your own is time consuming and difficult. At worst, it can result in legal problems from contracts that were not properly executed, and you can end up making less money than you would have after paying an agent's commission. Also, agents representing potential buyers are sometimes reluctant to involve themselves with FSBO situations, preferring to work with other agents.

About Flat-Fee Listings

A method of selling without a real estate agent that has become increasingly popular in recent years is the use of flat-fee listings. A flat-fee listing service, also known as a discount broker, will get your house listed on the MLS, which is vital to having it sell at a fair market price. Fees for these listings vary from broker to broker. They can start as low as $299, although some offer additional services and charge much more.

Obviously, this flat fee is much less than what you'd pay in agent commissions, but it normally includes only the listing, none of the other services an agent would provide. So if you want a For Sale sign in the yard, a prepared contract, professional photography, a marketing campaign, or help with negotiating a sale, be prepared to pay extra—and understand that these costs can add up quickly. In fact, some sellers find themselves ending up paying more than they would have if they'd paid a commission to an agent!

As in FSBO situations, some agents representing buyers will shy away from showing their clients homes that use a flat-fee listing service. A flat-fee listing might save you the listing commission, but it could end up limiting the buyer pool and slowing down the sale of the house, which could ultimately cause you to lose money.

However, in some cases a flat-fee listing can be a great alternative to hiring an agent, especially in a seller's market. In a market where homes sell like hotcakes, there's more demand than supply, meaning that buyers and buyers' agents have less inventory to choose from. Not having your listing professionally represented and prepared will likely have less of a negative impact on the sale than it would in a buyer's market.

Get a License Yourself

If you don't want to pay agent commissions but are hesitant about FSBO and flat-fee listing, there is another alternative. You could get licensed and become your own agent. That might sound like a lot of work, but I know several house flippers who have done so, much to their advantage. Not only are they able to save thousands and thousands of dollars on commissions, but they enjoy having complete control over every aspect of their deals, and the knowledge they've obtained regarding real estate transaction terminology and processes by preparing for the licensing exam is extremely valuable for their house flipping career.

Becoming your own agent can be especially appealing if you find—or plan to find—deals on your own. But if you think you will rely on agents to bring you deals, like I do, I wouldn't recommend bothering to get licensed. You commit to reselling your flips with the agents who bring you deals. Cutting an agent out of the deal after they've brought you a property is only going to burn bridges for you. Even if you plan to fulfill your commitment of having the agent who brings you the deal serve as your selling agent, the fact that you have a license could cause some agents to worry about getting the listing, since they know you're capable of handling it on your own.

Licensed agents have complete access to the MLS and are able to look at any home for sale, online or in person. That means you could quickly check out a house on the market that you think might be a good deal and pull a CMA yourself to determine the ARV or list price. You'd also be able to list your houses for free on the MLS, which gives you a significant marketing advantage. Although being in control is appealing, be aware that it's also a lot of work, as it includes dealing directly with everyone involved with the purchase and sale of a property. In addition, it would be your responsibility to market the house, set up and conduct showings, schedule closings, and do all the other tasks—including copious amounts of paperwork—that you'd normally rely on an agent for.

Also, to be your own agent, you actually need to get your license. Selling your own flips or even other people's houses would take time away from your house flipping efforts, but it would also give you a backup in the event you reached a point in the future where you no longer wanted to flip. Getting a license and acting as their own agent is a great idea for some investors, but not for all. If you're considering that path, make sure you do your homework and find out what the process involves. In my state, California, the Department of Real Estate (DRE) requires that you complete three college-level courses, each of which takes a minimum of 45 hours. You can do the courses in person or online, and after you complete them, you're eligible to take the DRE's written exam. As you read earlier, the requirements vary from state to state, so you'd need to learn and assess how much time and effort would be involved in getting licensed where you live. Consider carefully whether the effort of getting a license and the continued work of acting as an agent is in your best interests. Keep in mind that if you were selling your own flip as the listing agent, you'd need to disclose that you were representing yourself as the seller.

fig. 66

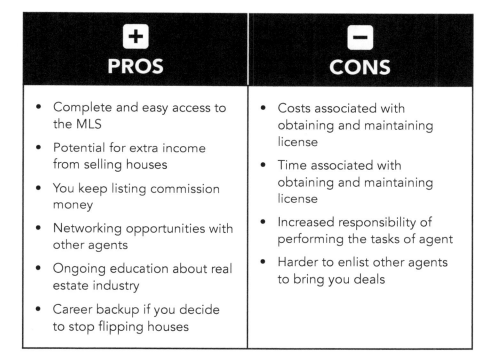

✚ **PROS**	➖ **CONS**
• Complete and easy access to the MLS	• Costs associated with obtaining and maintaining license
• Potential for extra income from selling houses	• Time associated with obtaining and maintaining license
• You keep listing commission money	• Increased responsibility of performing the tasks of agent
• Networking opportunities with other agents	• Harder to enlist other agents to bring you deals
• Ongoing education about real estate industry	
• Career backup if you decide to stop flipping houses	

Unless you're selling a house to another investor or are going to get licensed as an agent to represent yourself, there is no question (in my mind) that hiring an agent is the way to go. An experienced agent understands the market, knows how to package and market your house, and helps you negotiate the sale for top dollar. Having an agent who represents your interests is reassuring and can alleviate much of the stress involved with selling real estate.

Chapter Recap

» There are three ways to sell your flips without using an agent, but each has pros and cons to consider.

» Studies have shown that FSBO houses tend to sell for significantly lower prices than those sold by agents.

» The cost for a flat-fee listing is less than paying commissions but usually doesn't include any of the services offered by an agent.

» An alternative to hiring an agent is to get a real estate license and be your own representative.

| 10 |
Selling the Flip

The period between the time your house is ready for listing and when it sells is exciting, but also potentially stressful. It's easy to second-guess yourself, wondering if the property is priced right, if the photos you had taken do it justice, if someone will make an offer on it soon, whether the offer will be as much as you hope for, and on and on.

My advice during this time is to stay in close contact with your agent if you have one, making it clear that you would like to be kept up to date on any progress and involved in any decisions that must be made. You should be updated on the number of showings and disclosure requests and made aware of every offer, even if it's one your agent doesn't like. If you're not getting offers, work with your agent to figure out why. Is there a problem with the property that you overlooked? Is the asking price too high? Can you make some changes to make the house more appealing?

If you are not working with an agent, all the work of selling the house will fall to you. I'd suggest that you read this chapter carefully to learn more about what selling a house entails and fully consider how you would navigate the process. There are many good resources for learning more about the various tasks discussed in this chapter. Zillow, for instance, offers guides for selling a home, either with an agent or on your own. You can get tips for marketing the house, pricing it, showing it, and other tasks, along with information about closing costs, appraisals, home improvements, and many other topics. Other resources include Bankrate, HomeLight, and U.S. News, all of which offer guides for sellers.

As of this writing, demand for homes is high, so houses are selling quickly and at all-time-high prices. Nationwide, home prices were 17.2 percent higher in June 2021 than they were in June 2020, an increase driven by—among other things—increased demand due to the pandemic and low mortgage rates. As with many markets, however, the housing market experiences high and low points, meaning that sometimes patience is necessary. If you happen to have properties for sale during a down market, you'll need to be prepared for slow sales and have multiple exit strategies in place.

When to List Your House

There are different schools of thought on the ideal time for listing a house. I don't advise that you intentionally delay putting your house on the market once the renovations are completed, but it's helpful (or at least interesting) to know that listing a house at a certain time of the year, or even on a certain day of the week, may increase your chances for a quick sale.

According to Zillow, the best time of the year to list a house is in the spring, specifically the second week of March, and the best day to list is Thursday. I like listing on Thursdays or Fridays, as that's when many serious buyers are looking at what open houses are coming up that weekend, in order to plan their viewing schedule. Your home will show up as a fresh new listing, and even if it doesn't sell after one weekend of open houses, the days on market (DOM) will still be low. It's best to avoid posting a new listing on a long weekend or a holiday, such as Mother's Day, when people are likely to be traveling or celebrating and not paying much attention to the real estate market.

While spring is considered the best time to list a home, summer and early fall are close contenders. Home sales tend to slow down in late fall and winter, although experts are skeptical about whether that will apply in 2022 because of high demand overall. Still, many families with kids wait until school ends to move if it means children won't have to change schools in the middle of the year.

These are things to consider if your house becomes ready very close to an optimal time (if it's ready just before a holiday weekend, hold off until the following week) and to keep in mind if you're feeling rushed to complete your renovations (if it's mid-December, don't sweat it if you won't be ready until January). But there's no need to plan your listing around advantageous dates. Generally speaking, the best time to list your house is as soon as renovations have been completed, regardless of what time of year it is. You don't want to have to continue incurring taxes, financing, utilities, and other costs for longer than necessary, and, as mentioned before, the longer you hold onto a flip, the more unpredictable the market can be.

Filling Out Disclosures

Because your property has probably been remodeled from top to bottom, you shouldn't have much to disclose, as you are obligated by law to do. Disclosure regulations vary from state to state, but it's illegal in every state to intentionally withhold information about major problems that could affect the safety, value, or desirability of a property.

In a normal housing market, most buyers will schedule inspections before they agree to close on a house, unless you, the seller, have already had inspections performed (as suggested in chapter 8). When the market is as competitive as it has been recently, though, some buyers will forgo inspections in order to maximize their chances of getting the house. Regardless of whether the buyer requests an inspection, you should disclose any knowledge you have about problems. Not only is that the right thing to do, but it can help you avoid future liability. Being up-front about any defects also lets prospective buyers know you are being fair with them.

Refer to the disclosures you received from the previous owner when you purchased the house, and give potential buyers a list of upgrades and improvements that have been made. Seeing the improvements that were made in writing provides justification to the buyers for why they will pay a much higher price for the house than what you paid (which is public information) after only a short amount of time. You can't ignore any undesirable features of the property, but you can stress and call attention to all the work you've done. If you work with an agent, they will compile a list of any disclosures available to the buyers.

Listing

Getting the house listed as soon as possible after the renovation is completed is a priority. That said, it's better to be fully prepared before listing. This means preparing your listing in addition to preparing the house itself.

For example, don't list the house before professional photos have been taken and are available to list on the MLS. First impressions are important, and you want prospective buyers to see the house in its very best light. Start out the picture show with the best ones to attract attention and keep viewers intrigued.

302 Target St. Glenville, NY 12302

This lovely 4-bed, 3-bath, 3,100-sq-ft home sits on a three-acre cul-de-sac parcel in the much-coveted Yonda neighborhood. The home was built in 2019, resides in the Yonda school district, and is within walking distance of several local shops.

GOOD LISTING

11 Saint St. Plumotville, NY 12020

2 bedroom, 2 bathroom house for sale in Plumotville.

BAD LISTING

As mentioned earlier, your agent will write a listing description for your house, but this is something you should learn how to do. After all, no one is more familiar with the home than you are or has a bigger stake in the listing. When writing the description, use inviting, exciting language that highlights the best features of the house. And, of course, underline the upgrades you've done, calling attention to features like an open floor plan, high-end appliances, beautiful hardwood floors, and so on. Your description doesn't have to be long but should capture everything that's appealing about the property and the features that differentiate it from the competition. Any popular features that will be attractive to buyers should be mentioned. And be sure to include anything that makes your house stand out, such as a separate living room and family room, an extra-large backyard, good schools, or a great view. See figure 67 for a look at a good listing versus a bad one.

NOTE

Researchers at Zillow analyzed listing descriptions and found some surprising results. Using certain words in your listing can apparently help the house to sell more quickly and result in higher offers. A listing that contained the words "subway tile," for instance, sold for almost 7 percent more and weeks sooner than a comparable home for which the listing did not include that phrase. Mentioning

"Shaker cabinets" resulted in sales that were 9.6 percent higher than expected and more than a month faster. "Farmhouse sink" brought in 8 percent over the expected price, and "quartz" 6 percent over. On the other hand, words like "opportunity," "potential," "cosmetic," and "TLC" tend to be turn-offs for prospective buyers. In my opinion, the first list of words gives evidence that the house has been remodeled, which is probably the reason it's selling more quickly and at a higher price, Shaker cabinets or not. But it's fun to think about these things when you're working on your listing description.

A good agent should be able to write up a description that's appealing, but I usually take matters into my own hands and draft the first version myself, then let the agent edit or add to it. Even a good agent may not put as much thought into the listing as I do, which is understandable since it's not their own house. When I write descriptions, I usually look at comps that were sold for the highest prices in the neighborhood, noting what features were highlighted and what wording was used. It might not be the only factor, but I've noticed that sometimes an agent will be careless when writing a listing description, and the home will tend not to sell as well as homes for which I carefully and passionately drafted the description myself.

Some listings include an *offer deadline*, a stated day and time by which all offers must be received. This gives all interested parties time to view the property, go over disclosures, get inspections if desired, decide what their offers will be, and submit them before the seller begins the review process. Some agents and sellers favor including an offer deadline and others do not. It's considered a valuable tactic in very competitive markets where you can expect multiple offers, because it prevents the seller from having to jump at the first good offer that comes in and can motivate buyers to submit their offers quickly.

From a seller's perspective, an offer deadline can be beneficial in that it tends to increase competition among buyers and drives up the sales price. It pushes buyers that are on the fence to make a decision. It also enables a seller to control the timetable and often results in offers that contain fewer contingencies. If you get a terrific offer prior to the offer deadline, you're free to take it, even though that would mean you'd be accepting an offer before all potential offers had been submitted. If I was in that situation, before taking the offer I would ask my agent to contact everyone else who had shown interest to see if they would be willing to beat the offer that was submitted.

Not only would that be fair to the other buyers, but it could increase the price you got for the house.

There are, however, potential downsides to including offer deadlines with your listings. If the market starts to cool down, buyers may get tired of losing out on bidding wars and choose not to compete when there's an offer deadline. Buyers can feel rushed or pressured to make offers that seem too high just to keep themselves in the game. When this happens, the offer deadline can become a turnoff that sends potential buyers elsewhere.

Whether or not to set an offer deadline can be a tricky decision, as there's always the risk of not receiving any offers by the deadline you choose. Usually, experienced agents gauge buyer interest and make sure there's at least one committed buyer before they set up an offer deadline. In general, if the market is good and you are confident that you'll get at least one offer, an offer deadline is a good idea. Unless my agent's phone is ringing off the hook as soon as the home is listed, I usually wait until after at least one open house before deciding whether to include an offer deadline. If interest seems high, I go ahead and set a deadline. If not, I leave the offer period open-ended.

Marketing the Property

Your agent should handle the majority of tasks necessary for marketing the property, but you can supplement their efforts by taking some steps of your own. Let your social network know the house is for sale, encouraging everyone to spread the news. Email your network of agents, lenders, inspectors, and others who may have leads on potential buyers. In addition to possibly giving you a lead or two, this keeps those in your network updated on your business. On a few occasions, agents in my network responded to my emails and brought potential buyers to my flip. Some of those buyers even made offers.

As you read in the last chapter, tasks your agent should take care of include running online and social media ads, sending postcards to neighbors, and posting your house on their business website and social media. They will schedule and hold open houses to get potential buyers inside and create excitement about the property. Another marketing tool you should ask your agent about is scheduling a *broker tour*, which is an open house for agents. A broker tour gives professionals a chance to look at the house and predict which of their clients will be interested in seeing it. Having 20 or 30 agents view the house is great exposure and is likely to result in many requests for showings.

Your agent will display a For Sale sign prominently in the front yard and arrange for a *Supra box*, which is an electronic lockbox containing house keys that is attached to the door of your house. Be sure that flyers describing the house are placed next to the For Sale sign so that anyone interested can easily grab one. Sometimes my agents invite neighbors to the listed house for wine and appetizers. It's surprising how often a neighbor will know someone who is interested in buying in the same neighborhood and may recommend your house to that person. This also plants a seed in the minds of neighbors who might want to sell their home sometime in the future.

Reviewing and Negotiating Offers

Once your house has been listed and marketed, you can sit back and wait for offers.

If your house is priced right and your rehab done well, you can expect some offers within a reasonable time of listing the house. The time between listing and when you start getting offers will vary depending on the location of the house, whether the market is weak or strong, and the inventory level. If you're not getting any offers or they're coming in very slowly, you should work with your agent to come up with a solution. This will be discussed later in the chapter.

If the house has just been listed, try to resist the temptation to take the first offer you get, even though you want to sell the house quickly. If it has been on the market for weeks without an offer, however, I'd seriously consider the first one that comes in. Remember that the highest offer isn't always the best offer; contingencies and closing time frame and the buyers' financials all play a part. Contingencies make it more likely that something will go wrong and cause the sale to fall through. I've sometimes chosen a lower offer with no contingencies because it's a safer one.

I had an entry-level flip that received multiple offers, the highest of which was $40,000 more than the second-best offer. The highest offer, however, contained both loan and appraisal contingencies. The buyer's loan amount was maxed out based on their income, and they didn't have additional funds in case the appraisal fell short or the loan fell through. The second-best offer refused to match the highest offer, but I decided to go with it because it didn't contain any contingencies and the buyer was in a better financial position.

Take a Close Look at All Offers

It's important that you and your agent review all offers carefully. Obviously, the offer price is the first thing you'll look at, but there are other considerations you'll need to pay attention to.

The ideal scenario, of course, is that the highest offer you get stipulates a cash deal that meets or exceeds your asking price and includes no contingencies. If one of those comes along, schedule the closing immediately and break out the champagne!

Normally, it won't be quite that easy. First, find out what type of financing the buyer has and who is lending them the money. You'll want to deal with a buyer who is preapproved for a loan from a legitimate bank or mortgage broker, as this reduces the risk of the funding falling through.

There are different types of mortgages. You read quite a bit about conventional mortgages in chapter 4. A conventional mortgage is one that's not guaranteed or insured by a government agency. It comes from a private lender or Fannie Mae or Freddie Mac, which are government-sponsored mortgage lenders.

Another type of mortgage is a Federal Housing Administration (FHA) loan, which is insured by the FHA and must be issued by a lender that is FHA-approved. FHA buyers can get approved with lower credit scores than someone would need to get a conventional mortgage. And FHA loans require lower minimum down payments—in 2021 it was just 3.5 percent of the house's asking price. A home appraisal is required for an FHA purchase, and an inspection is highly encouraged but not required. Many FHA buyers ask the seller to pay for some or all of the closing costs, since FHA loans allow the seller to contribute as much as six percent of the value of the home for those fees. The seller may agree to this because they want to sell the home more quickly or get a price closer to the asking price.

A third type of mortgage is a VA loan, for which veterans, military service members, and surviving spouses are eligible. These loans are backed by the US Department of Veterans Affairs and issued by VA-approved lenders. VA loans don't require a down payment and carry lower interest rates than most conventional mortgages. They also have less stringent credit requirements. Like an FHA loan, a VA loan requires an appraisal, but inspections are optional. VA buyers are also likely to ask you to pay some or all closing costs, an expense some sellers are happy to pick up as a means of thanking the buyer for their military service. Figure 68 offers a quick comparison of these three types of mortgages.

	CONVENTIONAL	FHA	VA
Credit Score	620	580	None; unless lender requires
Down Payment	3%	3.5%	N/A
Appraisal	Required	Required	Required
Inspection	Not Required	Not Required	Not Required
Best for	Borrowers with good to excellent credit scores	Borrowers with lower credit scores looking for lower-priced properties	Borrowers who qualify based on military service

GRAPHIC

fig. 68

Most sellers prefer a buyer who has a conventional mortgage, as it usually signifies a down payment of between five and 20 percent, a strong buyer, and a simpler loan approval. I'm not saying every person you sell a house to must have a conventional mortgage; I'm just warning you to consider the implications of an FHA or VA loan.

As you've already read, another consideration when examining an offer is contingencies. Remember, your goal is to make sure the offer you accept will get to the finish line. An offer with contingencies gives buyers opportunities to back out of the contract without any consequences. So the fewer and shorter the contingencies, the better. Sometimes you can try to negotiate the contingencies down or ask the buyers to do their due diligence before making an offer. If you've already had the house inspected, as suggested in chapter 8, the buyer has no reason to get their own inspections or to have an inspection contingency. Having an inspection report available with notes on necessary repairs will assure the buyer that the house is in good shape.

If your buyer is getting a loan, the mortgage lender will order an appraisal of your property to determine its worth in the current market, to justify the loan. The lender's loan amount will be based on the appraised value of the house. So if the appraiser determines the house is worth less than the contract price, the buyer either has to come up with the difference or ask you for a price reduction, if their offer is contingent on an appraisal. They can also dispute a low appraisal or switch lenders, but that takes time, which, as you know, is money. When considering offers, favor buyers who waive their appraisal contingency and have adequate funds available, as this allows the buyer to cover the difference if the appraisal falls short. If your sales price is close to comps, this is unlikely to happen, but you can never be sure. Appraisal shortages often happen when the market is on an upward trajectory. Since a market on the rise is usually a seller's market (meaning there are more buyers than sellers), it's likely you'd be able to get the house under contract with a buyer who did not request an appraisal contingency and had additional funds to cover any appraisal shortage.

Beware of an offer that's contingent on the buyer selling another property, since you can't know how long it will take for the other property to sell or if the deal will go through. If the buyer changes their mind and decides later not to sell the house, they can back out of the contract on your house without consequences.

In a competitive market you can negotiate an EMD (earnest money deposit) timeline, stating that the money needs to be deposited into an escrow account within a short time, usually one business day. Once the EMD is in escrow, it becomes difficult for a buyer whose offer contains no contingencies to back out of the contract without losing their EMD. This protects you in the event the prospective buyer is making offers on several homes and doesn't actually intend to go through with the sale, or if buyers change their minds later in the buying process. For this reason, I feel relieved not after accepting a noncontingent offer, but rather after the EMD is deposited.

Obviously, you'll want an offer that includes as short a window as possible for the closing, preferably within 30 days of signing the contract. Once you've accepted an offer, make sure that everything you've agreed to is in writing, that both parties sign the agreement of sale, and that the buyers sign disclosures, so they can't use that as an excuse to back out of the contract later.

Consider Preemptive Offers

Something else to consider is preemptive offers, which were mentioned in the last chapter. Preemptive offers are made prior to a designated offer deadline, and they include a deadline of their own by which the seller must accept or reject the offer. They're typically used in extremely competitive markets, are often much higher than asking price, and include no contingencies. The catch, of course, is that the seller has a very short window in which to decide whether to accept the offer.

A preemptive offer can be risky for buyers, in that they can end up overpaying for a property they think will be in far greater demand than it really is. Or they may neglect to review disclosures or read reports in their haste to make an offer, discovering later that the house comes with serious flaws.

The problem with a preemptive offer for a seller is that it reduces the number of people who will look at the house and eliminates the possibility of a bidding war. Waiting until the offer date would allow you to receive numerous offers that you could leverage to get the price up even higher, without the pressure of having to make a very quick decision. A preemptive offer might seem reassuring because you know someone wants to buy the house, but it comes before you have an idea of what kind of demand there will be from other buyers. A preemptive offer normally includes a deadline that gives you very little time to consider—from a few hours to one or two days at most. In a hot market, agents sometimes put "no preemptive offers" on the listing to avoid the seller being put on the spot. Remember that buyers who are going to make preemptive offers are likely to make an offer by the deadline anyway. Whether you take a preemptive offer or wait for the deadline should be evaluated on a case-by-case basis. It's not always best to accept this type of offer, but if you get one that's a lot higher than your ARV and doesn't include any contingencies, you'd probably want to take it. You know the saying: a bird in the hand is worth two in the bush.

On a recent flip in San Francisco, I was thrown into a dilemma by a preemptive offer. It came in right at my estimated ARV without any contingencies one day after the home was listed, and it was very tempting. I was happy about the offer, but I also really wanted to see if we might get something better because I had put a lot of work into the home and wanted it to reach its potential. Our strategy was to ask for an extension on the offer expiration date to allow us to hold open houses over the weekend. As expected, we had a huge amount of interest from other buyers at the open houses. We ended up receiving a few more offers in just a couple of days, enabling us to create a bidding war among all of them. We ended up selling the home for almost $200,000 more than the preemptive offer. And the winning offer was from none other than the buyers who had submitted the preemptive offer! They decided to up their offer because they loved the home so much they couldn't stand losing out to the competition.

Can You Get a Better Offer?

If the housing market is hot and you get several offers on your house, you're in a good position to negotiate with potential buyers, either to get a higher price or to sell the house with few or no contingencies. Some strategies to consider in a seller's market are listed in figure 69.

1 Stipulate "no preemptive offers" in your listing to make sure you get as many bids as possible.

2 When prospective buyers request the disclosures, it's an indication they're very interested in the house. If a lot of people are requesting disclosures, make sure your agent lets the buyers' agents know that.

Also let the buyers' agents know when you have other offers on the table or have a few potential offers coming in.

Tell all interested buyers they are to submit their highest and best offer by the offer deadline, and they should not expect a call back or chance to counteroffer. This incentivizes buyers to make their best offer right away.

3 After receiving all offers, return to the highest bidders, tell them about the competition, and ask if they're willing to increase their offers.

4 Have your agent present counteroffers to the second-best and third-best offers, a strategy that creates the potential for raising one or both of those offers higher than the best offer. If that happens, you're in a strong position to negotiate with the person who submitted the original highest offer.

GRAPHIC

fig. 69

When negotiating with buyers, you'll want to gauge their commitment. Try to get a sense of how much the buyer loves your home by noting the number of times they've visited it and how many times their agent has talked to your agent. Prospective buyers who really love a home are more likely to be willing to improve their offer prices and terms.

If there are a lot of offers coming in, it doesn't hurt to play the waiting game. Yes, you want to sell the house as quickly as possible, but in a case where there's a lot of interest, not taking the first good offer you get sometimes pays off handsomely.

I once purchased a house for $700,000 (a steal in the Bay Area) and needed to spend just $80,000 in rehab costs. I listed the house for $899,000 with the purpose of attracting a lot of buyers who would bid up the price. The very first day the house was on the market, I got an offer of $1 million with no contingencies. I was very tempted to take it, but I knew there was a whole lot of interest in the house, so I decided to wait and go ahead with the open houses I had scheduled.

That turned out to be exactly the right decision. More than 500 people attended the open houses and I received eight offers on the house, which ended up selling for $1,085,000. You can hear the entire story of that flip and see before-and-after pictures on my YouTube channel. Just search for "Entry Level House Flip – $220K Profit."

PRO TIP: Gauge the amount of interest in the house. If it's high, be patient, and don't be afraid to negotiate.

Even if you have only one offer, you can still negotiate; it's just a bit riskier. If the price is not what you want or the contingencies are too many or too long, you can try negotiating with the buyer, but aim for small improvements rather than drastic changes. You don't want to risk offending the buyer and losing out on the sale since you don't have a backup plan.

If You Don't Get the Offer You Want

For whatever reason, there may be times when you don't get the offer you're looking for. If this occurs, don't panic. Reassess the situation, remembering that you're bound to experience some of those tough sales in this business. You want to understand the market trend: is it moving upward, downward, or is it stable? The best way to get information on market trending is to talk to your agent and other agents you know. If the market is stable or trending upward and you are not getting the offers you're looking for, it's likely that there's something wrong with the house that's turning buyers off. Ask your agent for an opinion and get feedback from potential buyers. Sometimes buyers will be straightforward with your agent on what they don't like about a house. If it's something specific to your house that you can change, do it immediately. If it's something you can't address easily, like the kitchen being too small, then you may have to consider lowering the price.

I had a flip for sale last summer that I had remodeled from top to bottom, but it sat on the market for almost a month without any offers. That's very unusual where I live, as the market is hot and remodeled homes were selling like hotcakes. I asked my agent if he knew what could have caused it, and he mentioned that the temperature in the home had been very high during the open houses and some buyers may have been turned off by that. I decided to install an air conditioning in the home free of charge before the close of escrow and made sure all the potential buyers were notified. A few days later, we were under contract. Sometimes a solution is straightforward, like installing AC in the heat of summer to appeal to potential buyers. Other times, however, you'll need to get creative, as in the example earlier in the book when I had to offer to remodel the exterior of the neighbor's home so my buyers wouldn't be scared away.

If the market is trending downward and you're not getting the offers you're looking for, the house might be overpriced for the declining market. You'll want to have your agent reach out to active listing agents in the area to get intel. Are there other homes that aren't selling or are selling at less than the asking prices? What condition are they in, and are they priced higher or lower than yours? If other sellers in the area are in the same boat, it might just be that the market is tough. Consider increasing the buyer's agent's commission or offering a bonus to increase their incentive and enthusiasm for selling your house.

If you're getting showings on the house but not offers, don't be too quick to lower the price. If you're not getting any showings, however, you'll likely have to reduce the price. I usually wait at least three weeks before adjusting the price, because once it's lowered it's very unlikely you'll get a good offer—buyers will see that there's been a price reduction and will know the home is not in demand. After three weeks, you can either drop the price just slightly to get the property back on the radar of potential buyers, or drop it significantly to below market price in hopes of attracting a lot of buyers who will bid the price back up. In the Bay Area there's a strong demand for housing, and buyers are used to seeing homes priced below market price and then get bid up. I use that strategy a lot when I have a home that is taking longer than I'd like to sell. I find it more effective than dropping the price a little at a time. However, if demand is not as strong in your area, dropping the price significantly can be risky, and you probably should try the other strategy instead.

If you realize the market has shifted between the time when you purchased the house and when it's ready to sell, it's important to act quickly because the longer you wait, the worse the market could get. You may want to lower your asking price to near the bottom of the range and accept that you might have to take a small loss on the house. Don't hang onto it and hope the market will improve—you'll be losing money every day while risking that the market will go even lower. No one has a crystal ball, of course, and it's possible the market could rebound after some time. But my advice is not to bet on that rebound, because the downside risk outweighs the upside potential.

Closing the Sale

Once you and the buyer have signed an agreement of sale, the closing process begins. This process involves a series of steps leading up to the final closing, at which time the ownership of the house is transferred from you to the buyer. This is an exciting time, but it bears watching. Don't assume everything will proceed as it should and the process will all go smoothly. You'll need to keep tabs on what's happening to make sure everything keeps moving ahead and on time. Here are some points to keep in mind during this process (illustrated in figure 70).

» If you got a title binder policy when you purchased the house, remember that you'll need to use the same title company when you sell the house to avoid having to pay for a second policy.

» Make sure the buyer's EMD is placed into escrow in accordance with the time called for in the contract. As mentioned earlier, the EMD is like an insurance policy that protects the seller, especially with an offer that has no contingencies. If the contract calls for the EMD to be in escrow within one to two business days, you can ask your agent not to update the sale status on the MLS until the money has been deposited. That way, if the EMD isn't made on time, you can continue marketing the home without having to change the status from Pending to Back on Market, which could cast doubt in the minds of future buyers.

PENDING TO CLOSE TIMELINE

GRAPHIC

fig. 70

Escrow and lender receive Purchase & Sale Agreement signed by Buyer and Seller.

Assuming inspection contingency is not waived, buyer orders an inspection of the property.

Appraisal completed and loan approved (hopefully).

Buyer and seller arrange "signing appointments" with title/escrow company.

Seller gets paid and Buyer moves in.

If agreement includes a financing addendum, then the loan application must also be sent to escrow.

Seller may be required to fix items that came up during inspection or provide a credit to buyer accounting for their costs. Assuming the buyer is financing, lender then orders an appraisal of the property.

Seller notifies utility companies that the property will have a new owner (this usually happens 2-3 days prior to closing).

Buyers and sellers sign documents with notaries for closing, and escrow company records the transaction with the county. Key transfer and physical possession of the property has now taken place.

The first box I need to check when I get under contract is making sure the buyer gets their EMD placed in escrow. If it's not there on time, I immediately ask my agent to talk to the buyer's agent and find out if the buyers have changed their minds. If they have, it's better to have them cancel the contract voluntarily rather than my having to send a *notice to perform*, which is a document notifying buyers of the problem with the EMD and giving them 48 hours to resolve it. The problem with the notice to perform, of course, is that it leaves you sitting for two days before you can cancel the contract and get the house back on the market.

NOTE

When the market is shifting downward, you really need to keep an eye out for buyers who don't get their EMD into escrow, because they are likely second-guessing their purchase decision when they hear the market is crumbling. In 2018, the Bay Area market experienced a small but noticeable adjustment when I had just gotten under contract to sell a home. We received three good offers and my agent was able to negotiate the price up. The next day, however, the buyer who offered the highest price decided not to put in the EMD and wanted out of the contract. We had to go to the second buyer, who didn't want the house anymore either. And it was the same with the third buyer. We had to put the house back on the market and start all over again. Thankfully, we were able to find a buyer who offered a fair price, even though it was lower than the first offers we had received. I learned that in such situations it's better to stipulate a fast EMD in the sales contract to allow less time for buyers to change their minds.

» Monitor the appraisal of the house to make sure the result is at least as much as your asking price. If the sales price is close to comps, this shouldn't be a problem. But you still want to closely monitor the appraisal schedule and result, because that determines whether your buyer can successfully get a mortgage; therefore, it's important to facilitate the process so that can happen.

If the market is on an upward trajectory, you might be able to get an offer that breaks the neighborhood sales record. While that's good news for you, it could cause a shortage in the appraised value, because the appraiser won't be able to find any comps to support the sales price. If that happens, in addition to getting the buyer to waive the appraisal contingency and making sure they have extra funds to cover the shortage, get your agent to meet with the appraiser and show them the list of upgrades and before-and-after photos to help justify the high sales price.

» Toward the end of escrow, make sure the buyer's lender has issued final approval of the loan and the loan docs get to escrow. That's an important step in closing, signifying that the buyer's financing is all set and the sale is ready to close. Check in with your agent periodically to make sure they are keeping in touch with the buyer's mortgage agent and everything is proceeding on schedule.

» Don't neglect the condition of the property during this closing period. Keep the yard mowed, shovel the sidewalk if there is snow, and keep up with other necessary maintenance. Remove any staging materials from the house and make any necessary interior touch-ups.

» Keep track of your documentation. I like to get all the closing documents ahead of time so I have a chance to review everything. The escrow officer or notary will go over these documents with you and explain anything you don't understand.

» Right before the final closing, the title agent you're working with will review all paperwork to make sure the numbers are right, get all the necessary signatures, and notarize and issue checks or send out wires. The title company is responsible for recording the deed to the property. Knowing what to expect at closing can help avoid anxiety and ensure that things proceed smoothly.

Chapter Recap

» Knowing the best time to list a home can help you achieve favorable results, even though, in general, listing the house as soon as possible after renovations have been completed is recommended.

» When in doubt, disclose.

» Make sure your agent is using all available strategies to market your house.

» Review all offers carefully, paying attention to all contingencies and conditions in addition to the price.

» It's not the end of the world if you're not getting any showings or offers. Keep calm and figure out the root cause.

» Be sure you understand and pay attention to the closing process to ensure that the sale goes through.

| 11 |

Looking Toward Your Next Flip

Chapter Overview
 » Assessing the Process
 » Building Your Team
 » Real Estate Market Cycles
 » Looking Forward

By the time you leave the closing table, you will have learned things you might never have even thought about. Hard money loans, load-bearing versus non-load-bearing walls, ARVs, curb appeal, and contingencies will be part of your vocabulary and newfound knowledge, all of which will benefit you in your next flip.

I hope you made some money on your first flip, but don't be upset if you didn't. Your first deal is invaluable even if you lose money. The lessons you learn from your first deal can pave the way for a successful career in the future. As I mentioned, I'm extremely grateful that my first deal was not a slam dunk, because I learned so much from it. It wasn't easy or fun while it was in progress, but it served as an important learning experience. Your first few deals are crucial in setting the foundation of your career. Don't expect to make a lot of money right off the bat, but do make sure you learn from each experience.

If you've already completed a flip, I urge you to think about your experience—what went well, what you learned from the process, and what you'll do differently the next time. Think about the people you hired and those you turned to for advice. Will you choose the same team for your next project? Did their values align with yours? Will you look for another deal in the same area, or try someplace different? Was your ARV pretty accurate, or will you need to reassess the way you figured it? If you haven't yet started flipping houses, you'll want to take some time for reflection on those things once you've gotten into the game. In this chapter, we'll explain how to reassess your house flipping process, discuss how to build a team you'll be able to rely on as you move forward, and examine real estate market cycles to help you think more about your future.

Assessing Your Experiences

Self-reflection is a valuable part of almost any work you do, and house flipping is no exception, especially if you're thinking about turning it into your career or livelihood. When looking back on your house flips, particularly your earliest experiences, it can be helpful to examine the specific skills and methods you used before asking yourself what could be done better the next time around from a more holistic perspective. After you complete a house flip, especially early in your career, run through the checklist in figure 71, and be honest about what you've learned to do—and areas where you may have come up short.

ASSESS THE FOUR ASPECTS OF YOUR FIRST FLIP

fig. 71

1

DEAL ACQUISITION

2

DEAL ANALYSIS

3

PROJECT MANAGEMENT

4

SALE

Acquiring Deals

» Review the various methods that house flippers use to acquire deals, and consider which of them you've tried. Would you continue to use the same method(s) or try something different? Which methods do you think would help you maintain a consistent flow of deals?

» What's the hardest part of finding deals? What can you do to improve the process?

» Did you have trouble getting financed? Do you want to keep working with the same lender? How can you improve the financing process if it wasn't as smooth and quick as expected?

PRO TIP: Evaluate the methods you used for finding a deal. Think about what worked and what you'll do differently the next time.

Analyzing Deals

» How did you do when calculating your ARV? Were you too conservative or too optimistic?

» Compare the estimates you came up with for your rehab costs with what the work actually cost. How close did you get? Take note of any areas where your estimates were way off and analyze how that happened.

» Was the profit you targeted high enough to make the project financially feasible? If not, are there ways you can cut costs on your next rehab, or do you need to reduce your offer price?

PRO TIP: Go back and look through all the numbers that apply to your flip. Did everything add up as you thought it would, or will you need to make some adjustments next time?

Managing the Project

» Did you and your contractor come up with a workable SOW with a level of rehab that was appropriate for the house?

» Did you select the right level of finish for the value of the home? What was the feedback you got from potential buyers?

» How well did you work with the contractor? Should you use the same contractor again or look for someone new?

» Did anything unexpected happen during the rehab? How much extra did it cost, and how can you make sure your budget will suffice next time?

» How can you save money on the rehab next time?

» Do you need to hire someone to help with interior design next time?

Selling the House:

» Did you list the house at the right price, or did you have to adjust the price after the house was listed? Were you pleased with the number of offers you received?

» Did you set an offer deadline, and was it the right thing to do? Was your agent able to help you negotiate for a better price or terms?

» What strategies did you learn from your agent?

» How is the market behaving, and what can you do to better prepare yourself for any potential changes?

You may notice that the overriding question about these different assessments is, "What could you have done better?" Regardless of how satisfied you might be with your flipping experience, there are always improvements that can be made. It's important to acknowledge those things and learn from any mistakes that were made during the course of your flip.

If you honestly answered all the questions in the assessment section above, you probably have lots of food for thought regarding improvements that could be made. Should you have set a tighter timetable for the renovations? Did you over-improve for the value of the home? Did you pay too much for the house?

If you worked with a good agent who was able to guide you along the way and assist you in achieving a positive outcome, make sure you take notes, because agents' skills and business acumen can be great assets to your career. If you don't understand a process or the reasoning behind their recommendations, ask questions so you can learn. Keep in touch with other house flippers by maintaining your presence at local real estate events. Even after being in the business for five years, I still get inspired and motivated by other investors when I go to real estate events and meet new investor friends. If you have a mentor, cultivate that relationship and continue to rely on their advice.

Building Your Team

It's not just other investors who can help you on your house flipping journey. Hopefully, you had—or will have—a good experience with the people you worked with when flipping a house. It's really important that your team members' objectives align with yours and that you share the same basic values. When referring to your team, I'm generally talking about agents, lenders, contractors, inspectors, stagers, and photographers (see figure 72). That group of people should serve as your core team, though there may be times when you need others to help. How to go about finding these people has been discussed in earlier chapters, but I want to remind you again of their value and reinforce the importance of building a great team.

TEAM MEMBERS

GRAPHIC

fig. 72

Agents Lenders Contractors

Inspectors Stagers Photographers

You've already read a lot about the value of finding a great agent or, better yet, more than one. After each experience working with an agent, you'll have an idea of their work style, strengths, and weaknesses. If the deal is primarily a positive experience, you'll want to add the agent to your team, and stay in touch so they'll bring more deals your way in the future. If they've done something exceptionally well, you want to learn from them and possibly rely on them for opinions in the future. You'll also want to reflect on any hiccups in the process that may have been caused by the agent and make sure you take notes for future deals. Good agents are great resources for deals, and they can help you achieve incredible sales prices. You really want to take care of the agents on your team, so that you're the first one they call when they have a potential deal.

The best way to make sure the agent's objective aligns with yours is by offering bonus commission when sales prices exceed your expectations. I've noticed that my agents work a lot harder on the sales when there's such an incentive. They also feel better-compensated for their work because when they manage to get me more money on the sale, they earn more as well. A lot of investors I know are stingy about paying commission because it's one of the bigger expenses of a flip, so offering a higher commission sets me apart from the competition and automatically puts me on the top of agents' lists.

Clearly, lenders are vital to your team, since without them there could be no deals. How was your experience funding your first deal? Was your lender able to fund the deal on time? Was the process easy or painful? Even if you were happy with your vendor, you should still seek out others, not only as a backup, but also to compare rates regularly. My experience has taught me that lenders' rates and terms change all the time, and you need to check in with them frequently to make sure you are taking advantage of the best rates available. Leveraging a quote from another lender can usually help you negotiate the rates down with the lender you work with.

We spent a lot of time discussing the best ways to find contractors and other workers for your renovation projects. A good contractor is invaluable, and a bad contractor can make your life miserable. Hopefully your contractor finished your project on budget and on time and provided good quality work. As I shared with you earlier, my first contractor turned my first flip into a nightmare, and I knew midway through the project that I could not work with him again, so he didn't make my team. I started looking for another contractor right away and tried a few different options before finding my current GC.

Inspectors are another important part of your team. Many people don't pay much attention to this part of the process, but an inspector's work cannot be neglected. A good inspector is flexible, consistent, reasonable, and doesn't nitpick. When the market is hot, good inspectors are hard to schedule, meaning you'll want to cultivate a relationship with a few who will answer your calls even when they're busy. I am lucky enough to have worked with a great inspector since my first flip and never have surprises in the reports.

Stagers and photographers are well worth their costs and are valuable to every flipping project I do. I enjoy design and photography, but I don't think I could ever complement a house with staging as well as my stager or take photos of my flips from the right angle with the right lighting like a professional photographer does. If you had good results with your stager and photographer on your first flip, make sure you add them to your team, so you can sit back and relax when they package all your flips to be ready for the market.

Every team member plays an important role in your deals. If you've completed your first flip, spend some time assessing the role each member played and how satisfied you were with their performance. When you're just getting to know someone, a little conflict is not unusual as you come to understand each other's style and learn how the other person works. Small issues can usually be worked out with someone you respect and want to work with. Working with someone who does not share your values and vision, on the other hand, is never a good idea.

There's No Bad Time to Flip Houses

On several occasions, I've talked to people who want to get into the house flipping business but are hesitant because of real estate market conditions. They're worried that housing prices are going to drop and their flips won't turn enough of a profit, or housing inventory is too low and they won't be able to get a good deal. I understand that real estate, like other markets, fluctuates, but I will make the argument that there is no bad time to flip houses, assuming you consider market trends when conducting your analysis. If market values are going up, you'll be able to sell your flips at a good profit. If values are declining, it will be easier to find deals at good prices that enable you to turn a profit. Regardless of whether the market is on the upswing or in decline, house flippers who perform careful and smart analysis can benefit.

While it's certainly important to keep an eye on general economic conditions, which can give you clues regarding where the housing market is headed, there are a couple of reasons why I don't normally worry too much about these things. One is that the point of flipping is to turn over houses quickly. My goal is to flip a house within two to three months from the time I sign the purchase contract. And though the real estate market does go up and down, it's not often subject to wild swings like the stock market or the crypto market, which can lose large amounts of their total values in a matter of days. If my projects stay on track, which I always try to make sure they do, the chances of a huge drop in real estate prices before I get a property on the market are slim. Could it happen? Sure. For example, I could have a house in a neighborhood that's largely destroyed by a tornado or a wildfire—both events that we've recently witnessed in parts of the country. That could drastically affect the value of my property. But those kinds of events are rare and entirely out of my control, and I choose not to dwell on the possibilities.

Another reason I don't worry too much about market conditions is that, despite the real estate market going through cycles, home values tend to rise over the long term. We know that the cost of homes has increased dramatically over the past 50 years, with the median sales price in the US rising from $23,900 in 1970 to $329,000 in 2020, according to the US Census Bureau/Federal Reserve Bank of St. Louis. That's a huge increase in value, even considering inflation and other factors, like the increase in average home size. If you look at figure 73, you'll see some dips when real estate values fell sharply, usually during recessions (indicated by the vertical shading). The most dramatic was in 2008 when the collapse of the housing market resulted in the Great Recession. Generally, however, real estate values tend to move upward.

fig. 73

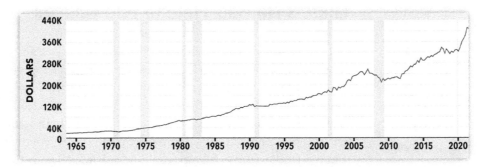

Source: US Census Bureau and Federal Reserve Bank of St. Louis

MY TAKE

I intend to flip houses for a long time. If I hit a point where my profits decrease slightly for a while due to market fluctuations, I won't panic, but will simply make sure I build a buffer into my underwriting to mitigate the risk. Then I'll wait for the market to improve and my profits to go back up. This actually happened in 2018, my first year of flipping houses full time. The housing market in the Bay Area overheated in 2017 and many buyers were priced out of the market, leading to a dip in sales prices by up to 15 percent in some areas. Even though I was new to the business, I quickly learned I had to be conservative with the ARV and have a 15 percent or higher margin on each flip so I could at least break even in a worst-case scenario. Because I was more selective with deal acquisition and underwriting, I cherry-picked the best deals and have managed not to lose any money on flips since then. Once the market stabilized and recovered, my profits on deals normally exceeded my expectations. I know that I'd rather lose out on some thin deals than be stuck in losing flips. I'm confident I can make some profit regardless of market conditions, even if it's perhaps not as much as I'd like for a time.

Annual growth in home prices has averaged 3.9 percent over the past 25 years, according to Black Knight, a leading provider of data pertaining to real estate. While that's lower than the average return of the stock market over the same period, it's fairly steady, solid growth. You'll read more about market risk in chapter 14. It's a real thing, but I advise that you spend your energy fine-tuning your deal acquisition and analysis skills rather than worrying about market conditions and trying to time your entry into the house flipping business.

The real estate industry doesn't exist in a vacuum but is dependent on the general economy, interest rates, and other factors and is affected by events such as the COVID-19 pandemic and the US–China trade war. As of this writing in early 2022, most parts of the country are still in a very hot market, with properties selling quickly and for top dollar. Finding good deals can be more difficult, but profits will be high when you do. When demand inevitably falls off, it will be easier to find deals, but you might not be able to sell at the same high prices. Either of those scenarios is workable, as long as you adjust your analysis numbers to reflect the market condition. If you're going to have to pay more to get a deal, you'll need to sell the house for a price that covers the acquisition and other costs and still leaves room for a profit. If you anticipate you'll need to sell the house at a lower price than you would have previously, make sure you don't overpay to get the deal or overspend on other costs, so that you still end up with a profit.

Understanding Market Cycles

All that said, it helps to be aware of how real estate market cycles work. Generally speaking, real estate regularly cycles through up and down markets. Historically, these cycles have lasted around 18 years and consisted of four phases: recovery, expansion, hyper-supply, and recession. This cycle theory was identified in 1933 by Homer Hoyt, an American economist who specialized in land and real estate economics. It's defined differently by different investment strategists, and the duration of phases varies from cycle to cycle. A recovery phase, for instance, could last less than a year and lead quickly into the expansion phase, or it could drag on for years, depending on a variety of factors such as geography and other economic issues. Generally, however, the patterns have repeated over the past 200 years. Let's take a look at what each of those phases entails, alongside figure 74.

> » **Recovery.** Recovery begins as the economy moves out of a recession. It's defined by limited demand for housing, low numbers of real estate development projects, flat rental rates, and low home

occupancy rates. Prices are typically low during this cycle, and it's a great time for investors who want to buy and hold property—bringing to mind famed investor Warren Buffett's quote, "Be fearful when others are greedy and be greedy when others are fearful." Flippers who can jump in and get some deals at the tail end of the cycle and then sell as we move into the expansion stage will do very well. The trick is to wait until we're far enough into the cycle that house buyers are starting to feel optimistic and get excited about the possibility of buying.

» **Expansion.** Following the recovery phase, expansion includes increased demand for properties, jumps in rental prices, and higher occupancy rates. Employment rates rise along with real estate development starts. People are more confident about the economy and more willing to invest and to purchase homes, which means it will be easier to sell newly renovated homes. Typically, interest rates are low during this phase and low-cost financing is available, which can make it a good time for house flippers to look for deals.

MARKET QUADRANT CYCLE

GRAPHIC

fig. 74

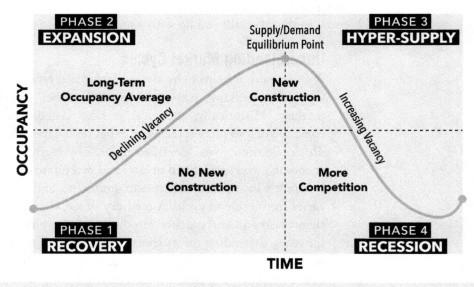

MY TAKE

I believe we're currently near the end of an expansion stage of the real estate cycle and the price of houses will soon start to drop. With that in mind, I am being extremely conservative with analysis on the deals I have coming in, anticipating that prices may fall before I can get the houses ready to sell.

» **Hyper-supply.** At this point, housing supply starts to exceed demand. Construction and redevelopment from the expansion stage have created a glut of housing, and prices start to go down due to lack of demand. Rental rates flatten and vacancy rates increase. Because the hyper-supply stage usually signals that a recession is on the horizon, this is not considered an ideal time to invest, but you can make it work if you keep your analysis very conservative, making sure you have extra profit built in.

» **Recession.** Housing supply exceeds demand, and real estate prices drop. This stage is categorized by a decline in occupancy rates. Unemployment rates increase and new construction drops off. Again, this can be a great time to buy because you're able to acquire properties at good prices, but it's not a great time to sell.

Various factors, including the state of the general economy, government intervention, interest rates, and varying demographics, contribute to how these cycles move. When the overall economy is good, for instance, consumers feel optimistic, and the trend is toward buying houses or moving to bigger houses. The same goes for when interest rates are low, as they have been for several years. Government policies can also affect the real estate cycle, such as the implementation of tax benefits or subsidies for homeowners. And demographics can have an effect, such as the fact that millennials, who long resisted home buying, made up the biggest share of buyers in 2021, purchasing 37 percent of all homes for sale. Having an understanding of the four phases of the real estate cycle and being able to identify each stage will help you to assess the best times to buy and the best times to sell homes. Real estate investment groups often discuss these issues, and there is lots of information available online and from business analysts who appear on radio and TV shows. Keeping an eye on economic indicators such as the stock market, unemployment rate, housing starts, interest rates, the gross domestic product, and others will help you to gauge whether the economy is on the rise, holding steady, or declining. Don't rely on the opinion of one person or group when it comes to real estate cycles or economic conditions in general; there are a range of viewpoints and opinions available. And don't hesitate to conduct your own research by keeping tabs on available housing stock and real estate transactions in your area. If you have an agent or agents, they should be informed about real estate conditions and stages of the cycle.

When working on your analysis, it's important to keep up with real estate trends and cycles in order to understand the market and decide what approach to take. I do not believe, however, that market conditions and real estate cycles should dictate whether or not you begin or continue to flip houses. If you're careful and smart with your analysis, there's always money to be made.

I've found useful information regarding trends and cycles from these sources:

» **The National Association of Realtors.** The NAR's website contains a Research and Statistics section that's loaded with information about market behavior, housing statistics, prices in various areas, and housing indicators.

» **Freddie Mac.** Here you can find quarterly forecasts for the housing market, consumer research information, the latest housing trends, and more.

» **Zillow.** Zillow offers a wealth of information about home values, forecasts, inventory, and other topics in the Research section of its website.

» **Agents.** Many agents regularly send out useful local market updates to those in their network. When you are in their network, you can receive those emails.

Chapter Recap

» Every flip you complete should be reviewed and evaluated.

» Build a team that you can rely on for many deals to come.

» With smart analysis, there is no bad time to flip houses.

» Keep an eye on real estate trends and market conditions when looking for deals; you may have to employ different strategies depending on conditions.

PART IV

LEGAL AND BUSINESS CONSIDERATIONS

| 12 |

Establishing a Business Entity

Chapter Overview
» Sole Proprietorships
» Limited Liability Companies
» Corporations
» Keeping Finances Separate

Getting into the house flipping business is exciting but should be done with a good deal of thought and deliberation. A lot of people take on a flip to see what it's like, end up making some money, and decide to continue with another project. The next thing they know they've got a little business going, without ever having fully considered what that means in terms of liability, taxes, and other potentially thorny issues.

Regardless of how many houses you flip or how you envision growing your business, you should protect yourself by forming a *business entity*, which is simply an organization formed to conduct business. This sounds more complicated than it is; a beginning house flipper can form a simple business structure on their own, although I'd recommend getting some guidance from an attorney or business advisor. A business entity limits your personal liability and can provide some tax advantages. Operating as a *sole proprietor*, which is someone who owns and runs a business on their own, is a common practice, but it comes with risks. Often they're minimal at first but increase as your business grows and you acquire more assets.

The business structure you choose will depend on where you're doing business, the value of your personal assets, how many properties you flip, how you acquire property, and other factors. Requirements vary from state to state, so again, it's a good idea to consult with a business advisor or attorney who could determine what type of entity would be best for you.

In this chapter we'll consider various types of business entities, how they work, and some advantages and disadvantages of each. Most house flippers operate as a limited liability company (LLC) or a corporation, both of which separate the business from its owner and protect the owner's personal assets from liability and debt. A legal expert I have worked with recommends that to protect themselves, house flippers should have either an LLC or a corporation that serves as their primary business, but they should also establish a temporary business entity—usually a type of LLC or a limited partnership—to handle each flip, dissolving it after the flip is completed. If something goes wrong with a flip and the buyer or someone else wants to sue, the entity that handled the sale is no longer in business and there are no assets available. This is how I operate my business, and it has worked well for me. When you're just starting out, however, it's possible that a simpler structure will suffice.

It's important to get an understanding of what types of entities are available and which might be best for you based on the assets you have and the type of business you plan to operate. Your legal needs and considerations will change over time, meaning that the business structure you use when you begin flipping houses might not be the one you'll use in 5 or 10 years. It can be a winding road with many decision points and considerations (figure 75); understanding how the various entity types function in a house flipping business is essential.

fig. 75

Let's start by looking at why a sole proprietorship may not be the best way to go. Then we'll examine some other business structures that can help you protect your personal assets from liability. In most states it's fairly easy and inexpensive to do so, and I highly recommend that you consider it carefully.

Dangers of a Sole Proprietorship

If you start flipping houses under your own name, you're operating a sole proprietorship. You don't have to register with anyone or take any formal action; once you begin flipping houses you've started an unincorporated business of which you are the sole proprietor. You and only you are entitled to all the profits you earn and responsible for all losses, debts, and liabilities.

Although a lot of beginning house flippers go the sole proprietorship route and don't encounter any problems, there are risks involved. The greatest is that a sole proprietorship provides no legal distinction between your personal and business assets, and you can be held personally liable for all debts and obligations the business incurs, as well as for any lawsuits that might be filed against you. If you are sued, your bank account could be at stake, along with your car, house, and any other personal assets.

Regardless of how careful you are to avoid them, lawsuits can occur. A contractor could be injured on your property and file a suit. Someone living next door to the house you're flipping may be frustrated over all the construction noise or unhappy that you've decided to leave some trees in your yard instead of having them cut down (a situation I've encountered more than once) and threaten to take you to court. In some cases, you can even be sued if, for some reason, you're unable to close on the purchase of a property—and your liability can go beyond the earnest money you deposited in escrow. It's upsetting when things like this happen, but knowing that your personal assets are protected can provide some peace of mind.

A real risk for house flippers is having a buyer file a suit because of a problem with the property. A buyer typically has three to six years to bring a lawsuit against a seller for various reasons, such as water damage or a cracked foundation. If you were sued and you had other deals in play, the lawsuit could effectively shut down those other deals, as it's likely you would not be able to sell or refinance them until the suit was resolved. That could leave you in the nightmare situation of sitting with millions of dollars' worth of properties that you are unable to move forward with. If you fully disclose any known defects of a property and any material facts that could affect its value—such as plans for a shopping mall or an expressway to be built nearby—you can greatly reduce the risk of lawsuits, but you can never completely prevent them from happening to you because there are numerous causes that are out of your control. Any material facts you present prior to the sale should be addressed by the buyer before they agree to buy. But if something is not disclosed to them, even unintentionally, you could be at risk for unwanted legal action.

Fortunately, I have never had a suit filed against me, but I've been told that buyers are more likely to resort to lawsuit attempts during market declines when they discover their home values have gone down since purchasing. Making sure that you've had the house inspected, addressed any identified issues, and completed full disclosure before selling can help you avoid this type of situation.

NOTE

On top of filing a lawsuit, a disgruntled buyer can make your life miserable using social media. I heard of a house flipper who was sued because of a problem with a property he'd sold. The home buyer, in addition to filing the lawsuit, threatened a social media smear campaign against the flipper in order to pressure him to settle the suit. Running up against an angry, aggressive buyer is a very unpleasant situation that you should avoid at all costs.

Some people think it's safe to flip houses under their personal name because they don't have a lot of assets accrued. That belief is shortsighted. House flipping can be a highly lucrative business, and even if you don't currently have many assets, it's possible you'll make a good amount of money from your first deal. Without operating as an entity, you'd be risking the money you might earn on your first project.

MY TAKE

Some beginners want to test the water and start flipping houses without forming a business entity because they want to avoid the cost and the hassle and aren't sure if they'll be successful and want to continue. This is naïve, though, because compared to the risks you're exposed to by operating under your personal name, the cost and extra work of setting up an entity is negligible. Remember that you're most likely to make mistakes when you're just starting out in flipping because you haven't yet acquired much experience. Even if you flip only one house, I suggest you set up an entity for doing so. It's the right way to do business and the best way to protect your own interests. You'll learn the benefits of operating as a business entity later in this chapter.

Some house flippers team up and form partnerships, but if you neglect to form a business entity, you're just two sole proprietors who work together.

Naming the business something other than your own name requires you to file a fictitious name or DBA (doing business as), but it does nothing to protect your personal assets.

Operating as a sole proprietor also means any money you make from flipping houses is taxed as income. You'll report it on your personal tax return and be responsible for withholding and paying all income taxes, including self-employment tax. Employees and employers share the cost of payroll taxes to cover Social Security and Medicare, but a self-employed person must cover the complete cost—12.4 percent for Social Security and 2.9 percent for Medicare, for a total of 15.3 percent at the time of this writing.

Another downside of flipping houses under your personal name is that it could cause you to be tagged as a dealer by the IRS, meaning you would not be eligible for 1031 exchanges and some other tax benefits. You'll read more about the distinction between real estate investors and dealers in the next chapter.

Other than the fact that it's quick and easy to establish, I can't see many advantages to a sole proprietorship. It's simply too risky to have your personal and business assets combined and at risk in the event you're found liable. Figure 76 lists some of the expenses and attributes associated with various business entity types, including sole proprietorships.

BUSINESS ENTITY ATTRIBUTES

fig. 76

	SOLE PROPRIETORSHIP	LLC	CORPORATION
Set up cost	Free	Varies by state	Varies by state
Set up difficulty	N/A	◔	◔
Admin difficulty	◔	◔	◔
Protects your personal assets	✕	✓	✓
Your salary is unrestricted	✓	✓	✕
You must pay self-employment tax	✓	✓	✓

The Limited Liability Company Structure

If you decide to establish a business entity, you have some options. As mentioned earlier, one way to go is to set up a *limited liability company*, or LLC, which is a structure that separates the business from its owner, thereby protecting the owner's personal assets from liability and debt. (The owners of LLCs are called members.)

LLC permits are issued according to state laws, meaning that regulations for getting an LLC set up and running vary from state to state. An LLC is normally fairly easy to set up, but you'll need to file formal legal documents with your state and pay formation fees that vary by state. There are also ongoing fees you'll need to pay to keep the LLC in compliance with state and federal laws. These also vary by state but can include an annual franchise tax, business license renewal fees, and fees to file the annual reports that most states require all LLCs to submit. For example, the annual franchise tax for an LLC in California is $800 a year, the highest in the country.

Nolo, a publisher that produces DIY legal books and software to enable people to handle certain legal proceedings on their own, offers its "50-State Guide to Forming an LLC" on its website. You simply click on your state's name to read its requirements, including any fees you'll have to pay. (Full disclosure: I have no business relationship with Nolo).

While it's possible to establish an LLC yourself, I would recommend consulting a business advisor or attorney to make sure it's done properly and within all legal guidelines. I have never formed a business entity on my own, but I know some house flippers who have.

Members of LLCs are responsible for business taxes including federal, state, and local income taxes. The way taxes are paid depends on whether the LLC has one owner or more than one. If you're the sole owner of an LLC, you report income and expenses on Form 1040, Schedule C, as you would if you were a sole proprietor, and you'll owe taxes to the IRS based on your personal income tax rate. The same normally applies to state and local income taxes. Owners of LLCs are usually considered to be self-employed and thus are assessed the taxes for Social Security and Medicare, like sole proprietors.

If you have a multi-member LLC, each member pays income taxes based on how much of the LLC they own, similar to a partnership. If you own two-thirds of the LLC and the other member owns one-third, you'd be responsible for paying taxes on two-thirds of earned income and the other member on one-third. You'd also be able to claim two-thirds of any tax deductions or tax credits the LLC is eligible for.

If you want to, you can have your LLC classified as a corporation for tax purposes. Doing this provides tax advantages without affecting your

LLC's legal status. One benefit is that you don't have to pay tax on all the business income you make on your personal tax return. You also avoid the self-employment tax, as you'd be considered a shareholder of the corporation rather than self-employed. A disadvantage is that in some instances you'd be taxed twice—on the net earnings of the corporation and on the dividends you receive. But you might be able to avoid that problem by forming an S corporation. You'll read more about tax advantages of C corps and S corps in chapter 13, but it would be a smart idea to consult with a tax professional to see if your LLC would benefit.

NOTE

In addition to the $800 yearly tax, California charges an LLC fee based on the revenue of the business, as shown in figure 77. In the Bay Area, where I do business, almost all the houses I've flipped have had resale values of more than $1 million. I flip seven or eight houses a year, giving me revenue of about $7 million. That puts me in the highest bracket of LLC fees and means I would have to pay $11,790 a year in fees—plus the LLC tax—if I used LLCs instead of limited partnerships for each flip I do. A good business advisor should be able to help you avoid these types of fees and decide which entity is best for your business.

CALIFORNIA LLC TAXES AND FEES
(TAX YEARS 2001-PRESENT)

fig. 77

TOTAL INCOME (FISCAL YEAR)	LLC TAX +	LLC FEE =	TOTAL CA TAXES
< $250,000 (including any loss)	$800	$0	$800
$250,000 – $499,999	$800	$900	$1,700
$500,000 – $999,999	$800	$2,500	$3,300
$1,000,000 – $4,999,999	$800	$6,000	$6,800
≥ $5,000,000	$800	$11,790	$12,590

C Corps and S Corps

While many house flippers choose the relative ease of an LLC, some prefer to form a corporation because it offers some tax advantages and can be beneficial in other ways. You'll read more about the tax implications in chapter 13, but here I'd like to briefly explain exactly what a corporation is and how a C corp differs from an S corp.

A corporation, which is called a *C corporation* unless it meets certain qualifications and files as an *S corporation*, is a legal entity that's separate from its owner. An S corp, also a legal entity separate from its owner, varies from a C corp in the way it's taxed. Corporations provide owners with good protection from personal liability, but it costs more to form a corporation than an LLC or a sole proprietorship, and corporations require additional reporting and record keeping. Members of a corporation are called shareholders. C corps are taxed on the income they generate, and shareholders pay tax on the income they receive from dividends paid. C corps are relatively easy to form, with less paperwork required than for an S corp.

Still, some house flippers operate as S corps to avoid the double taxation (having to pay both corporate taxes and personal income taxes) associated with a C corp. For a corporation to be designated as an S corp, it must meet the following criteria:

» Have no more than one hundred shareholders

» All shareholders must be US residents

» Have only one class of stock (unlike C corps, which can have multiple classes)

» Are not owned by another corporation, LLC, or trust

Unlike a C corp, an S corp isn't taxed. Instead, its owners, who are treated as employees and are compensated for the work they do, report company revenue as personal income on which they pay tax.

Each of these types of organizations has advantages and disadvantages that are beyond the scope of this book. The overall point is, establishing a legal entity for flipping houses protects your personal assets. A lot can—and does—happen in the process of buying, renovating, and selling houses. A workplace accident, an unhappy neighbor, or an unsatisfied buyer can be damaging to your business, and to you personally if you're not protected.

Deciding Which Entity Is Best for You

I am not a lawyer or a business advisor, and I cannot tell you which kind of legal entity will best serve you and your business. I can, however, pass along some advice that I've gotten from legal advisors and suggest that you get some help from a qualified person to help you decide how to proceed.

Asset protection is not a one-size-fits-all proposition. As stated earlier, what will work best for you depends on factors including your business location and size, the value of your personal assets, your tax situation, and other factors. Before choosing an entity, take a good look at your overall business plan. Are you thinking you'll flip houses as an occasional project, or are you looking to build a full-time endeavor? How hands-on do you want to be with the business? Will you be overseeing every detail or relying on others to handle the day-to-day operations?

I look at the costs involved with my type of business entity as a form of insurance. I'm a risk-averse person who would rather pay a little than risk a lot. I've worked very hard to grow my business and want to protect it as well as I can. Forming a new limited partnership for every flip protects my LLC from potential liability that could have very negative implications for my business. That gives me peace of mind and is well worth the cost to me.

When you're just starting out in house flipping, you'll probably be fine with a simple LLC. As your business grows and gets more complex, don't be afraid to explore other options. Getting the right structure in place when your business is small can help it grow, because it can minimize your taxes, pave the way for traditional loans if you want them, and give you maximum protection for your assets. Again, I'm not offering any specific advice; I myself rely on advice from experts. I would suggest that you educate yourself so you can understand the different types of entities and which might most benefit your business.

Separating Your Personal and Business Finances

Regardless of what legal entity you choose, it's extremely important to keep your business finances separate from your personal finances. If you are designated as a corporation or LLC, your business is a separate legal entity with its own financial system. But even if you're a sole proprietorship or a partnership, keeping your finances separated should still be a priority. Follow this advice offered by the US Small Business Administration:

» Establish a small business bank account. Having a bank account designated for your business is vital for keeping funds separate and maintaining a clean and efficient bookkeeping system.

» Get a business credit card and use it for everything you charge that's business related. This not only lets you track expenses, analyze your spending, and build your business credit, but it's also helpful when tax season comes around, as you don't need to separate business and personal expenditures.

» Apply for credit in the company's name. If you apply for credit with a supplier or vendor, use your business information on the credit application. Some vendors and suppliers will, as a courtesy, extend their financing terms to those with trade credit, giving you more time to pay for what you need.

» Set up utility accounts in the company's name. Accounts for business phones, cell phone service, internet service, and other utilities used to operate your business should be established in your company's name and kept separate from your personal accounts.

» Apply for a data universal numbering system (DUNS) number. A DUNS number is the most widely used identifying number for businesses in the United States. The system was established by the business data firm Dun & Bradstreet (D&B) in 1963 and is free to US businesses. Those that have a DUNS number are included in a business profile in D&B's database. Having this number allows you to build a business credit identity that's separate from your individual credit history.

Following the advice above, you should use your business accounts for business purposes as much as possible. There may be instances when, for one reason or another, you'll use money from your personal account to pay for business expenses. If that occurs, just make sure the business reimburses your personal account for those costs.

Chapter Recap

» A sole proprietorship is simple but does not offer protection for your personal assets.

» An LLC is a common type of business entity that separates a business from its owner, protecting personal assets from liability and debt.

» Corporations offer some tax advantages but require more reporting and paperwork than LLCs.

» Regardless of what type of business entity you choose, always keep your business finances separate from your personal funds.

| 13 |

Tax Implications

This chapter is near the back of the book for a reason. Taxes are not something you'll need to think too much about when you're just starting out in the house flipping business. But they're likely to become more of an issue as you increase the number of flips you do and the profit you make, particularly if you take your house flipping business to full time. I often talk to beginners who are concerned about the tax implications. My advice to them is to focus on learning the basics of house flipping first and not to worry about taxes until they've started building their business and realizing a significant income. At that point, it's a good idea to consult with someone about minimizing tax implications. Another thing to understand is that with higher income you'll pay more taxes. Still, even if you reach the highest tax bracket, the tax rate is far from 100 percent, meaning that you'll still benefit from your increased net income and be able to employ a lot of the tax advantages that are associated with investing in real estate and owning your own business.

Nevertheless, it's true that if you're not prepared, taxes can seriously impact your profitability. Dealing with taxes can also be confusing, which is why I highly recommend finding a good CPA or tax consultant to work with. Taxes are a part of doing business, but there are ways to minimize their impact. This chapter offers some basic strategies for doing so, in order to maximize the amount of money you keep. A tax professional can further advise you on how to pay the least possible amount of tax.

Real Estate Investor or Dealer?

Whether the IRS considers you a real estate investor or a dealer is an important distinction for house flippers, because it affects your tax rate and can prevent you from taking advantage of certain tax benefits. Basically, the IRS regards a real estate investor as someone who buys property and hangs onto it, such as someone who buys houses to rent out. A dealer, on the other hand, buys and sells properties quickly. That should sound familiar; the goal of a house flipper is to buy properties and then sell them again in the shortest possible amount of time. This tends to put us in the category of real estate dealer, along with wholesalers and developers, who undertake projects with the intent of selling them as soon as they're finished.

If you're considered a dealer by the IRS, the properties you buy are considered inventory, much like the products bought by a grocery store owner to stock the shelves. Property held for more than a year is looked on by the IRS as long term and, as such, a capital asset, but inventory is not. Therefore, inventory is not subject to be taxed at the long-term capital gains tax rate. Dealers must treat gains as ordinary income, which is taxed at higher rates than long-term capital gains. One way to get around this situation is by holding the houses you buy for more than a year. Some flippers buy properties and rent them in order to qualify as a real estate investor rather than a dealer and thereby reduce their tax burden. A problem with that, of course, is that they incur expenses while holding the properties.

So if an investor sells a property they've owned for five years, they'll pay ***long-term capital gains taxes*** of either zero percent, 15 percent, or 20 percent, depending on their income and filing status. If an investor sells a house they've owned for less than a year, they'll pay ***short-term capital gains taxes***, which are the same rate as ordinary income. The ordinary income rate, which in 2022 ranges from 10 percent to 37 percent depending on your income and filing status, would also apply to a dealer who held a property for less than a year. If you're considered a dealer and have not set up a separate business entity to reduce taxes, your ordinary income will be subject to self-employment taxes of 15.3 percent.

NOTE

Once the IRS has decided you're a real estate dealer rather than an investor, it can be difficult for you to sell a property and have it taxed at the long-term capital gains rate even if you've held the property for more than a year. I've heard of this happening to house flippers who also own rental properties and fail to take advantage of the lower tax rate, because once you are a dealer in the IRS's eyes, they tend to categorize all the houses you sell as short-term investments. You can appeal the IRS's decision, but that takes time and is a distraction from your business.

Other disadvantages of dealer status are that you can't take advantage of ***1031 exchanges***, which allow you to exchange one investment property for another and defer capital gains taxes, and you lose access to ***installment sales***, which enable you to defer taxes by selling an investment property and collecting the proceeds in installments instead of all at once.

In addition to the amount of time you've held a property, investor-versus-dealer status depends on factors such as the purpose for which the house was purchased, the extent of improvements made, how many sales you've done in the past, how much advertising was used to sell the property, and the amount of profit realized. See figure 78 for a quick overview.

fig. 78

FACTORS THE IRS CONSIDERS WHEN DETERMINING INVESTOR VS DEALER

- **Number and frequency of sales**
- **Intent when buying the property**
- **How the property was acquired**
- **Extent of improvements made**
- **How long property is held**

- **Amount of profit realized on sale**
- **Number of sales done in the past**
- **Effort involved in the sale**
- **Use of a broker**
- **Nature and extent of your business**

Fortunately, you often can avoid being tagged as a dealer by using an entity like a C corp or an S corp for your real estate activities. Dividing your real estate portfolio into two categories—an active side that consists of flips and wholesaling, and a passive side that holds some rental properties—allows you to realize tax advantages from both types of activity. While the entity that handles the active side is considered a dealer and not able to take advantage of 1031 exchanges, installment sales, and other tax breaks, the entity on the passive side would be designated as an investor. Establishing yourself as an S corp or C corp allows you to avoid having to report income on a Schedule C tax form as a sole proprietor. Using corporations also comes with other advantages, which were discussed in chapter 12.

The subject of investor versus dealer is a complicated one that I strongly suggest you do not attempt to navigate on your own. A business consulting firm or tax expert who specializes in real estate will be able to help you understand how you'll be treated by the IRS, how much tax you'll have to pay, and how you can access available tax advantages.

The Importance of Deductions

At the end of the day, you'll have to pay taxes on the profits you make from flipping houses. Notice, however, that I said the *profits* you make, not the *income* you make. Profit is determined by subtracting expenses, including the purchase price, from the price at which you ultimately sell the house. Some flippers include the points, closing costs, and commissions as part of the purchase price, but many tax professionals suggest counting those as expenses—not part of the actual purchase—so they can qualify as deductions.

In addition to the purchase price of the property, you can typically deduct these expenses (figure 79):

fig. 79

EXPENSE DEDUCTIONS

 Renovation Labor　　 **Insurance**

 Renovation Materials　 **Office Expenses**

 Real Estate Taxes　　 **Marketing**

 Points, Closing Costs, and Commissions　 **Travel Expenses**

 Mortgage Interest　　**Meals / Entertainment**

» Cost of renovation labor, which would include all tasks such as carpentry, plumbing, electrical work, interior and exterior painting, landscaping, HVAC work, flooring work, and others. Any expenses that went into improving the property for resale are deductible.

» Cost of renovation materials, including paint, lumber, flooring, carpet, appliances, cabinets and countertops, lighting and plumbing fixtures, etc.

» Real estate taxes, from the date you purchase the property to the date you close on the sale.

» Points, closing costs, and commissions.

» Mortgage interest accrued during the time you held the property, if you funded your deal by taking out a mortgage, getting hard money loans, or borrowing from another funding source.

» Insurance costs incurred during the time you owned the property.

» Office expenses, including rent if your office space is outside of your home. If you operate out of a home office, you won't have rent to deduct, but be sure to include expenses such as utilities, phone bills, paper, ink, and other supplies.

» Marketing and advertising purchased in order to sell the house.

» Travel expenses, including fuel costs and wear and tear on the vehicle incurred when traveling to and from the property. You can also deduct mileage as it applies to conducting business.

» Meals and entertainment in some cases, but check with your accountant, as changes were made to these deductions in 2017 and again in the COVID-19 economic relief bill of 2020.

Once you've added up your expenses, including the purchase price of the property, simply subtract that number from the selling price of the house to determine your profit (see figure 80). As you can see, this greatly reduces your tax liability.

fig. 80

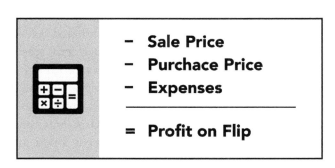

Let's say you paid $200,000 for a house and later sold it for $340,000. Based solely on those numbers, you would have realized a gain of $140,000. However, after subtracting from that amount the $60,000 you incurred in expenses, your profit for tax purposes is just $80,000—a far more favorable tax situation.

Other Ways to Save on Taxes

In addition to deductions, there are some other methods you can use to reduce your tax bill. Again, I do not advise that you undertake these strategies on your own, but they may be topics you'll want to discuss with your CPA or business consultant. You've already read a little about the advantages of S corps and C corps, but let's look more closely at how they can be used as tools for reducing taxes.

Potential Tax Benefits of an S Corp

As you read in the last chapter, an S corp is taxed differently than a C corp. While C corps are taxed on the income they generate, all of an S corp's income, loss, credits, and deductions are "passed through" to shareholders for tax purposes. If you're the only shareholder, any income gets passed through, reported on Form 1040 of your personal tax return, and taxed as regular income. If there is more than one shareholder, income is split up, with each shareholder reporting it on their own personal tax return.

If you're paying self-employment taxes, you could benefit from organizing your business as an S corp, as doing so would allow you to divide the money you make into two categories: salary and shareholder distribution. You'd pay self-employment taxes on the salary portion of your earnings, but not on the money designated as distribution.

While this could save you money, especially if you have high earnings and are paying the self-employment tax on all of it, be aware that the IRS tends to keep a close watch on S corps, as it considers the potential for abuse to be high. The IRS stipulates that a "reasonable" amount of your earnings be designated as wages but provides no specific percentage. It may seem perfectly reasonable to you to declare only 25 percent of your earnings as salary, but doing so could raise red flags with the IRS, perhaps triggering an audit. It's best to pay yourself a salary that's comparable to what a similar business would pay an employee for the same type of work. Also, organizing an S corp involves fees, and in some states you have to pay a percentage of your income in order for your business to remain an S corp.

Some tax experts advise against establishing an S corp because of the fact that income is reported on your Form 1040 instead of a W-2. A 1040 contains a lot more information than a W-2 form, and if you ever wanted to get a traditional loan, like a mortgage to buy a new home for yourself, some of that personal information could ring alarm bells in the ears of lenders. Let's say that one year you decide to take some time off for personal reasons, and you only flip a couple of houses instead of a dozen. The reduced income you experience as a result would be reported on your 1040 as an adjustment to income and could discourage a traditional lender from wanting to give you a loan. Also, banks tend to have long institutional memories, which often include the real estate fiasco of the Great Recession when many house flippers, along with other homeowners, lost a great deal of money when the market tanked. Knowing that you're in the house flipping business could discourage a traditional lender from giving you a mortgage, or you might have to pay more to get it. This may sound complicated, but I know advisors who discourage clients from using S corps and just wanted you to understand their reasoning.

Potential Tax Benefits of a C Corp

A C corp is an entity that separates the owner's income from that of the corporation. It's taxed at a flat rate of 21 percent, although that amount may be subject to change if the Biden administration's American Families Plan or other legislation is approved.

While 21 percent is much lower than the income tax rate many people pay, C corps are subject to double taxation, meaning the owner of the C corp may still have to pay personal income tax after the corporation has paid the flat fee of 21 percent. A tax expert might be able to guide you in avoiding double taxation through deductions and other techniques, but it's a complicated topic about which you should seek advice. Nonetheless, there are other advantages of establishing a C corp, as you read in chapter 12.

Make a Property Your Primary Residence

It was mentioned earlier that some flippers will hang onto a property for a year in order to take advantage of the long-term capital gains tax rate, but there's another reason you might want to consider doing so. If you stand to make a lot of money on a flip and are looking to reduce your taxable income, you could—if your personal circumstances enabled it—move into the house and live there for at least two years before selling it. Why? There is an IRS rule that allows you to deduct a significant amount of profit if the house is a primary residence. As long as you've lived in the house for at least two of the past five years, you can quality for a $250,000 deduction if you're single and a $500,000 deduction if you're a married couple filing jointly. That can help you avoid a lot of tax on a property that you're going to sell for a lot more than you paid for it.

Maybe you don't want to live in the house and have it considered your primary residence. Another strategy is to rent it for a period of time and then conduct a 1031 exchange, a process that allows you to exchange one investment property for a similar property while deferring capital gains taxes. There are many rules that apply to 1031 exchanges, so be sure to do your homework before considering it. Again, I'd advise that you consult a tax expert.

Use Losses to Offset Gains

No one wants to lose money on a flip, but if it happens, there's at least a little bit of a silver lining. You can use any losses to offset gains in the current tax year, which enables you to remove some income from your tax return.

Tax Issues with Independent Contractors

During the course of flipping houses, you're likely to work with a number of independent contractors. How you pay contractors and report that pay is important and can lead to problems if not done correctly. For the purposes of the IRS, an independent contractor does not have taxes withheld and is responsible for paying the 15.3 percent self-employment tax. In other words, an independent contractor is not an employee whose employer withholds payroll taxes from their pay.

When hiring an independent contractor, you'll need to collect some paperwork. It's not a lot, but it's important. The contractor must provide a signed W-9 form, which includes their contact information and taxpayer ID number. You'll want to have some sort of résumé that indicates how the contractor is qualified to do the work you're hiring them for, and a written contract outlining the details of your agreement.

When tax time rolls around, make sure you have a W-9 on file for each independent contractor you've hired so that you don't need to withhold income tax for them. If you've paid any contractor more than $600 in one year, you'll need to provide them with a 1099-NEC form by January 31 of the following year. This is the form used to report nonemployee compensation. You can download the 1099 form for the specific tax year from the IRS website.

If you have employees, either instead of or in addition to independent contractors, you'll need to send a W-2 form to each one—and to the IRS—at the end of the year. The form, sometimes called the Wage and Tax Statement, reports the annual wages and amount of taxes withheld from each employee's paychecks.

A strong word of caution about dealing with independent contractors or employees: It is the job of the IRS and your state's department of labor to seek out people who appear to be operating outside of tax laws. Failing to fill out and submit required information can land you in trouble and subject you to significant fines. If you have employees, you'll have to complete a Form I-9, Employment Eligibility Verification, for each one. Managed by the US Citizenship and Immigration Services, this form is intended to verify the employee's identity and employment authorization.

Also, do not be tempted to pay anyone "under the table" or "off the books." First, you set yourself up for trouble with the IRS or state regulatory agencies, which tend to view cash payments with suspicion as far as taxes are concerned. In addition, you open yourself to potential problems such as a contractor taking your cash and disappearing, leaving you to find out that suppliers haven't been paid for the materials used. If that happened, you could find yourself with a lien against your house. It can be tempting when a contractor offers you a discount for cash, and it's not illegal to pay in cash. It's much safer and cleaner, however, to pay with a check, wire transfer, or other means that allows you to track and have proof of payment and records for when it's time to pay taxes.

Finding Experts to Help

As I've pointed out numerous times, there's no need to try to navigate taxes on your own. Having a good CPA on your team who's familiar with real estate investing provides peace of mind while greatly reducing your chances of running afoul with the IRS or your state tax agency. I don't recommend figuring out your taxes and filing them on your own, because the small savings you'll realize will definitely be outweighed by not taking advantage of business and investing-friendly tax codes and deductions. You also increase the likelihood of being audited if your taxes are not filed properly.

The taxes you'll have to pay are not something you should focus on before you establish a profitable business. Once you start making a good income with your flips, however, I highly recommend that you meet with your tax advisor early in a tax year to discuss your estimated income and your business plan for the year. A CPA can advise you on structuring your business to save what you can in taxes. Tax planning should be done early in the tax year to make sure your business is set up to operate in your best interests. If you wait until the end of the year or the following year just before taxes are due, you'll have to scramble, and even the best CPA will be challenged in helping you.

If you do run into trouble or have an overly complicated tax situation, it might be a good idea to consult a tax attorney, which is a lawyer who specializes in tax law. Hopefully you'll never need one, but if you find yourself having to settle back taxes, explaining why you didn't file returns, or facing another sort of legal problem, a tax attorney could be useful.

Keeping clear and thorough records during the year can make preparing for taxes much easier. Once you flip houses on a regular basis, you may need to invest in accounting software or perhaps hire a bookkeeper to help keep everything in order. Always make sure to get and save receipts for all materials and labor.

As mentioned in chapter 12, don't underestimate the importance of keeping your personal and business accounts separate. This is necessary for protecting your personal assets and credit, and it's also a good practice for tax purposes.

Chapter Recap

» Whether you're considered a real estate investor or a dealer is an important distinction because it affects your tax rate and can limit tax strategies you're eligible to employ.

» Claiming deductions you're entitled to can reduce your tax bill.

» Setting up a corporation can provide tax advantages.

» Pay attention to tax regulations when working with independent contractors.

» Rely on professionals for help with your taxes.

| 14 |

Risks of House Flipping
and How to Mitigate Them

Chapter Overview
»   Worries of Aspiring House Flippers
»   Potential Risks
»   House Flipping Is Less Risky Than You Think

I've met plenty of people who are interested in flipping houses but hesitant to get started because they believe it's too risky. I addressed this issue a bit in the introduction but wanted to delve into it a little deeper and end the book on an encouraging note for anyone who is under this impression.

Sure, there are risks associated with house flipping, but there are risks associated with every business. And I am convinced that for investors who use common sense, act with integrity, and build on their experiences, flipping houses is no riskier than any other business venture. In fact, I'd say that the potential for gain in house flipping far outweighs the risks.

As I mentioned earlier, I am not a big risk-taker; I refer to myself as risk-averse. And yet I make my living flipping houses. I'll tell you the truth: before I got started, I was concerned about the same things you might be worried about. You need a lot of money to flip houses, especially in the Bay Area, where it's common for a run-down starter house to cost more than $1 million. I didn't know if there were lenders who would provide financing for flipping houses. I wondered how I would ever be able to find a good deal or good contractors to work with me. And I worried that if I couldn't sell the houses at projected resale prices, I wouldn't be able to repay my loans. I fretted about all those things and then talked them over with my mentor, who reassured me as I'd like to reassure you.

If you do the necessary work up front, you'll mitigate most of what could be perceived as the risks of flipping houses. For me, that work involved lining up agents who would bring me deals and handle details surrounding buying and selling houses, learning the process of properly analyzing deals, finding lenders to finance my deals, gaining an understanding of SOW (scope of work), and learning how to find and hire contractors. Once I had those pieces in place, all I had to do was start, learning as I gained experience and confidence. I acted cautiously, consulting with my mentor and other experienced investors on a regular basis and relying on my agents and others who had more extensive experience in real estate than I did. Yes, I made mistakes, some of which I've shared in earlier chapters. But I continued to learn as I went and the process has become increasingly easy, with my business running smoothly—on most days, anyway!

Let's go through some common fears shared by would-be house flippers. I hope that after reading this chapter you'll feel much more confident that any risks associated with the business can be mitigated or avoided altogether if you're willing to put in the time to learn what you need to know and find the people you need to help you.

Market Risk

Although it's not common, the housing market can drop precipitously, as it did in 2008. If you were a house flipper back then and had two or three deals in play, it would have been very bad news. But as you probably know, there were specific reasons for that housing market crash. Extremely low interest rates and loose lending requirements meant that borrowers with low credit scores and high risk of defaulting on loans were given mortgages, often by predatory lenders, without having the means to repay them. It seemed that nearly anyone who wanted a home could get one, and with so many people wanting them, home prices soared. When the housing bubble burst in 2008 and home prices posted record losses, many homeowners found they owed more on their mortgages than their homes were worth. That meant that even if they were able to sell their homes, they wouldn't be able to pay off their mortgages, and millions of Americans defaulted on their debt and lost their homes to foreclosure. Those factors, along with others, affected the entire economy and resulted in the Great Recession, one of the worst economic declines in US history.

In that case, the real estate market was the cause of a recession, but interestingly, recessions do not always negatively affect the real estate market—and when they do, it's generally not severe. As you can see in figure 81, in most of the recessions between the early 1960s and 2022, housing prices were barely dented, and the downturns quickly resolved. And following the 2020 recession brought on by the pandemic, which turned out to be one of the shortest recessions in history, the housing market boomed.

fig. 81

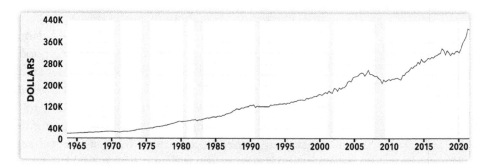

Source: US Census Bureau and Federal Reserve Bank of St. Louis

Economists point out that during a recession, steps are often taken to boost the economy, including the lowering of mortgage rates. This encourages home sales and results in the housing market going up in spite of a decline in the general economy, something we've seen in several recessions between 1980 and today. Some people still point to the housing collapse of the Great Recession as a reason to stay out of house flipping. But regulations have been put in place that tighten up lending practices to ensure that a situation like the one that caused the 2008 recession will not recur. Yes, the real estate market can decline for other reasons, like rising interest rates, a slowing in demand, or a downturn in the general economy (it's possible, but, as the graph in figure 81 shows, only two of the last eight economic downturns caused a clear housing market decline). But when the housing market does decline, it normally happens slowly, giving you time to assemble a coping strategy. Rarely does the bottom suddenly fall out; the market changes gradually over months or years, because buying and selling real estate takes time. Even during the 2008 housing crisis, the market took three years to hit rock bottom. Real estate is less liquid than most other investments—you can't buy and sell it in seconds like you can with stock. According to the National Association of Realtors, the median duration of home ownership is 13 years.

Another reason I consider real estate to be a relatively safe investment is that, although there is a limited supply of housing, demand continues to increase. The balance between supply and demand shifts due to factors such as interest rates, age demographics, new housing starts, and others, but demand tends to rise as long as the economy is stable. Millennials are an age group that many predicted would forgo home ownership in large numbers; but as millennials have entered their 30s, there's been a flurry of home buying among that population that's put a strain on demand and caused many economists to predict that demand will remain strong for years.

Still, market risk is real, and you should have a plan in place to address it if it becomes a concern. When home prices and demand for housing are high, house flippers may have a harder time finding good deals but can count on selling renovated homes at top prices. When demand and housing prices decline, flippers will be able to get deals easily and at good prices but will have to adjust their SOW and rehab costs to accommodate for lower selling prices. Always consider market conditions when working on your analysis for a deal, and adjust your numbers accordingly. Markets normally take months to move as much as 10 percent up or down, which enables you to figure out how to balance your maximum offer price, cost of renovations, financing costs, and all other expenses with your ARV, which should always be based on the worst possible scenario. If you work in a timely manner and are conservative about your ARV and realistic about your expenses, market risk shouldn't dissuade you from making deals and flipping houses.

Contractor Problems

Encountering problems with contractors is a legitimate concern, especially for beginners who haven't yet been able to find contractors they trust and can call on for every flip. Contractors can cause issues and even break a deal in various ways, including what I've outlined in figure 82:

fig. 82

POTENTIAL CONTRACTOR PROBLEMS	
OVERCHARGING YOU	This happens more frequently to house flippers who haven't yet learned the going rates for contracting work.
DELAYING THE PROJECT	As mentioned in chapter 7, it's not uncommon for contractors to take on as many projects as possible without the ability to finish them all on schedule, inevitably resulting in gross delays.
GOING OVER BUDGET	Even if your analysis is spot on, a contractor who upcharges during the project can skew your numbers and prevent you from having enough money for all the rehab.
TAKING YOUR MONEY AND DISAPPEARING	This happens more frequently than you might think, and it can be a real hassle to try to track down the contractor and recover your funds.

Contractors can cause these problems, but choosing wisely and managing them properly can minimize the risk. You read a lot about choosing contractors earlier in the book, so I'll just reiterate a few key points that can help you minimize your risk. First of all, references are important. Getting a contractor referral through someone you trust is generally the best way to avoid problems. If you don't know anyone who can refer a good contractor, talk to someone who has worked with the contractor you are considering. Ask whether work was completed on time and on budget, if they were pleased with the quality, and if the contractor kept them informed and updated on progress.

Spend some time with a contractor before hiring. The best way to do this is to walk through the project together and discuss the SOW. This will reveal whether the contractor is willing to share ideas about how you might save money on your renovations. Don't hesitate to ask about other projects the contractor has completed, and consider asking for references. Be wary of a contractor who asks for payment up front. Understanding that a small amount of money might be necessary to get started, make milestone payments as the contractor completes specific steps of the project. Setting up a reward system for finishing ahead of schedule or a daily penalty for finishing behind schedule can provide incentives for completing work on time. Taking these steps can help you feel confident about your contractors and minimize the risk of problems.

Legal Issues

You read quite a bit about legal issues in chapter 12, but I'd like to raise the subject again, as these issues are a potential risk for house flippers. The stakes can be particularly high when buying and selling real estate and it's important that you be aware of how liability can be assumed, as this can help you reduce such risk. When in doubt, err on the side of caution and seek legal advice to avoid problems.

I've spoken to many real estate attorneys, all of whom tell me the biggest legal risk regarding house flipping is with the disclosures you must provide when selling a completed flip. Filling out disclosures properly is an important step before putting a house on the market, because it's your legal obligation to inform potential buyers of any issues or problems with the property. Make sure you disclose everything that could potentially affect the safety, value, or desirability of the property. This can sometimes be a dilemma, as when you call attention to a material defect or undesirable feature, you risk losing some buyers. Not doing so, however, can cause problems and invite lawsuits even years after a project has been sold. I'll say it again: when in doubt, disclose.

Another way to steer clear of legal issues is to take some time to research the property you're interested in buying before entering a deal. Ask your title company for a two-year property history, including mortgages, and read it carefully. Check to see if there are any liens on the property. Know the zoning that applies, as that will affect what you'll be able to do with the house. Learn what permits were issued for the property, when they were issued, and if they are finalized. An increasing number of municipalities are making this type of information available online, or you can visit the local government's administration building for help. And always buy title insurance to protect yourself against any claims that could occur in the future.

I purchased a fixer-upper where the previous owner had hired a contractor to remodel the home—but the contractor took the money and disappeared, leaving the kitchen torn down to the studs. The owner sold the house to me as-is and told me that her contractor had applied for permits for the kitchen and bathroom remodel. I took her word for it and proceeded to close on the house. After the closing, I went to the city building department trying to get the existing permits transferred, only to learn that permits were never issued, the illegal work done was reported to code enforcement, and the house now had a code violation. In this particular town, to resolve a code violation, you have to go through a lengthy process and pay a fine. In this case, the alteration involved structural changes, and I had to hire a structural engineer and an architect. Unfortunately, the project budget and timeline both had to be adjusted upward. Though the owner might have been kept in the dark about work being done without permits, I could have taken her to court for not properly disclosing the information (though I chose not to, as she was a victim in this case). After this deal, I learned my lesson that doing due diligence includes checking on permit status.

You should also make sure you have what you need to protect yourself. There are all kinds of policies out there, and some insurers urge you to go beyond your homeowner's insurance and buy a builder's risk policy, which covers the property and building materials during construction; a construction general liability policy, which protects you if someone is injured on the property; vacant home insurance; and others. I purchase a policy that is specially designed for house flippers and covers builder's risk, general liability, dwelling coverage, medical payments, and other risks. Seek out a specialized insurance agent who can advise you on the types of insurance you need to protect yourself from liability or loss.

Having the proper business entity in place also helps you mitigate legal risks. It's important to discuss your options with a lawyer or business advisor to make sure you have the protections you need.

Project Management Risk

Until you've gotten some experience, there's also the possibility of risk due to improper management of a flip. This can occur during any stage of the process, from estimating the ARV, rehab, and other costs to making sure the project finishes on time. Underestimating your costs and expenses or overestimating the value of the property can lead to problems, but that type of risk can largely be avoided with smart and conservative analysis and realistic expectations about what a flip will cost in time and money. Getting your numbers right will keep your project on track and alleviate a lot of stress.

Some project management risks include:

» Overestimating ARV
» Underestimating rehab cost
» Underestimating project time
» Underestimating Stress

A common mistake new house flippers make is overestimating a property's ARV. If the ARV is inflated, you won't realize your expected profit because you won't be able to get your asking price for the house. You can avoid this risk by paying careful attention to comps, which basically offer free and clear market information keyed directly to your geographical area, if you're careful about your research. Refer back to chapter 3, "Analyzing a Deal," to review the specifics of using comps to determine your ARV.

Another common mistake is underestimating project costs. In fact, this is probably the most common pitfall of house flipping. It's so easy to underestimate costs when flipping a house because it's almost a given that you'll run into unanticipated expenses at some point. Setting these costs can be an even bigger challenge for beginners, who most likely don't have a good idea of how to budget for a project and are working with a contractor for the first time and have no track record to refer to. Underestimating costs is a serious risk because it can cut into your profits or even result in a loss. Once you've flipped a few houses it will be easier to accurately predict your costs, although it's always good to overestimate renovation costs. Be sure you have a budget for all costs involved with flipping, including insurance, utilities, taxes, permit fees, and so forth, and always add a buffer for unexpected costs to help mitigate this risk.

Sometimes renovation costs get skewed because of bad information from contractors. If you rely on a contractor's opinion of how much renovations will cost and it turns out they grossly underestimated, you're in a no-win situation. That happened to me on my very first flip and caused me a great deal of stress. I realized later that the contractor had committed to a lower renovation cost at the beginning just to get me to sign a contract and was relying on upcharges later in the project to make a profit on the construction. That kind of scam can blow up your rehab budget and leave you making a lot less than anticipated or even losing money on the deal. The best way to avoid such situations is to follow the steps for finding a reliable contractor that were outlined in chapter 7 and to compare at least three bids before awarding a contract.

Let me say it one last time: when you're flipping houses, time is money. Having a contractor who doesn't stay on schedule or thinking you can do the work yourself and finding out it takes much longer than you thought can shrink your profits significantly, because you'll need to keep paying interest on your loans and incurring other expenses that minimize your gains.

Holding costs can be negligible, however, when compared to the additional market risk you're exposed to when a project takes much longer than anticipated. The housing market isn't as vulnerable to wild swings as the stock market, which reduces your market risk if you can turn a flip around within a couple of months. Chances are that the market will be stable and there won't be any drastic changes in supply and demand. If your project takes a lot longer than anticipated, though, say five or six months instead of two, it's possible for the market to experience big changes. The Bay Area real estate market generally doesn't drop by more than 10 percent over a two-month period, but it's possible that in five or six months it could decline by 20 percent or more, exceeding the anticipated profit on your flip and resulting in a loss.

There are a lot of scenarios that can throw off your timetable, so try to be proactive when addressing any potential problems. As much as possible, have an accurate idea of your scope of work in order to avoid surprises once renovations are underway. Don't wait until you close on a purchase to start planning the rehab. And, if you need permits, apply for them as early in the renovation process as you can, since they sometimes take a while to get. Try to get over-the-counter permits, which are reviewed the same day in most cases and are much faster than regular plan reviews, or use online permitting when possible. Throughout the renovation, you'll need to check in with your contractor frequently and drop in on-site to make sure the project is progressing as planned. The contractor reward system suggested earlier can also help ensure that the contractor's goals align with yours and the project is completed as quickly as possible.

Not all risks associated with flipping houses are financial. An important consideration when you're getting into this business is how much stress you're comfortable with. Be assured there will be plenty of it, especially during your early deals. Flipping houses comes with a lot of uncertainties. You'll need to be resourceful and resilient to cope with unanticipated problems and figure out how to move forward. Being able to prioritize and focus on tasks based on their importance and urgency is crucial. To run a house flipping business, you need to wear a lot of hats. You're the acquisition manager, project manager, interior designer, and the CMO, COO, and CEO—all at the same time. You are the person who's ultimately responsible for the whole operation and strategy of the business, and if something goes wrong, you'll need to figure out a way to fix it. Someone who cannot handle stress may want to think carefully before taking on a house flipping project.

Even though you are the head of the business, don't try to go it alone and make all the decisions by yourself. Rely on those you trust—your contractor, agent, mentor, and other investor friends—to help you decide how best to tackle problems. Pay attention to your personal relationships. Particularly if you're working another job and flipping houses on the side, it can become an all-consuming task that negatively affects your relationships with others.

Chapter Recap

» Potential risks associated with flipping houses include market risk, problems with contractors, legal issues, and underestimating time, cost, and stress levels.

» When done properly, flipping houses is less risky than you think.

| 15 |
Prepare for a Career in House Flipping

Chapter Overview
- » Education Is Key
- » Build Your Network
- » Immerse Yourself in Real Estate
- » Practice Makes Perfect
- » Get to Know the Market
- » Find Inspiration from TV

Now that you've learned about nearly every aspect of house flipping, I'm wondering about your state of mind. I hope you're feeling better informed about the process, encouraged that you'll be able to start building a house flipping career, and excited to get started. But if you're feeling overwhelmed and not sure you're ready to jump in right away, that's okay, too. I was in the same position, and I understand. There are steps you can take that will benefit you and keep you moving forward as you prepare to start your career. We'll take a look at those steps in this chapter, which is dedicated to helping you reach the starting point.

In this last chapter, I want to share with you some tips that were crucial in getting me prepared for a successful house flipping career. If they put their mind to it, nearly anyone can find some funding and a deal. But strong preparation will greatly increase your chances of a successful first flip, which hopefully will encourage you to try a second and a third flip and eventually get into flipping full time. If you've read the entire book up to this point, some of the content of this chapter will sound familiar. Think of it as a review—especially if you don't have any real estate experience and you're still not feeling quite confident enough to get started. By the end of this chapter and this book, I hope you'll feel eminently prepared to take on your first flip.

Educate Yourself

There's an incredible amount of information available about flipping houses, and much of it is free. There are blogs and webinars, YouTube videos, books, podcasts, courses, live speaker events, and more—all intended to prepare you to flip houses (figure 83). House flipping isn't rocket science, but the more you know about it before you start, the better prepared you'll be and the less likely to make serious mistakes.

fig. 83

RESOURCES FOR EDUCATION

 YouTube Videos   Books   Courses

 Online Forums    Websites   Podcasts

I told you in the introduction of this book that I spent $25,000 on a course about flipping houses. I also told you that, while I did receive lot of information from the course, I realize now I could have saved my money and gotten that information for free from other sources. There are a lot of YouTube videos you can watch, including those posted on my channel, Transform Real Estate. Like mine, many of these videos contain the advice of experienced house flippers who are willing to share their knowledge and expertise at no cost to you. Some take you through the entire flip process, from finding a deal to getting the house ready to sell. On my channel you can find videos that teach you how to flip houses with no money of your own, how to analyze a flip, how to come up with a scope of work, how to sell a house for top dollar, and many before-and-after videos.

Once you've watched some videos, look for an online course. There are plenty of offerings out there, ranging in cost from free to thousands of dollars. Major players in e-learning and finance, including Udemy, MarketWatch, BiggerPockets, Freedom Mentor, and Harvard Extension School, have courses in this space. Figure out the price point you're comfortable with, look over course reviews, and choose your tutor!

Listening to podcasts is another great way to educate yourself. There are dozens of podcasts available from sources such as Real Estate Disruptors, Flipping Junkie, Real Estate Lab, The Real Estate InvestHER, BiggerPockets, and REtipster. Whether you listen when you're in the car or on the treadmill, you'll be able to learn a lot from these experienced flippers. Even though I'm an experienced investor myself now, I still listen to podcasts whenever I have time, and I always learn something new. There are also many good books on house flipping, so get online or go to the bookstore, and don't forget about the many websites and online forums that offer information on nearly everything related to flipping houses. You won't become an expert on your own, but you can certainly give yourself a good start.

Your Network Is Your Net Worth

While you can learn a lot from books and online resources, there's nothing like connecting with others who can share their firsthand knowledge and experience. I firmly believe in the power of networking and strongly encourage you to exercise that power whenever possible, even if you don't consider it your strong suit. Why? Because networking exposes you to people who can help you learn, serve as mentors, and introduce you to others. Networking with experienced house flippers when you're just getting started can help you understand how the business works and who you need on your team. You'll learn about reliable funding sources, local market trends, and where to get discounted kitchen counters. Connecting with people who are willing to share knowledge and resources is invaluable.

So how do you meet people who can help you along in your house flipping career? A good way to start is to look for meetings of like-minded folks. There are plenty of real estate clubs and associations across the country, many of which are always open to new members. While a lot of these groups went virtual at the start of the pandemic, many are back to meeting in person. In-person meetings come with some advantages, but virtual meetings offer safety and convenience, and some have small group breakout sessions that provide opportunities for networking. Find out what's available in your area and reach out for more information. These groups meet in coffee shops, hotel conference rooms, restaurants, homes, community centers, and other locations. Some are nationally accredited associations designated as real estate investor associations, or REIAs. Some are open to all real estate investors, and others are geared toward specific groups such as beginners, house flippers in a particular location, or private money lenders. A quick search on meetup. com or any search engine should provide information for groups near you.

Investment clubs often bring in speakers, encourage members to attend conferences, and offer other educational resources. Attending such events not only provides knowledge you can use but also introduces you to people with similar interests and goals.

Some investor groups encourage members to pool financial resources and buy properties as a group. This might work for some people, but I'd urge you to be very cautious and consider carefully before getting into it, because I've heard some scary stories about fraudulent investments and people losing money this way.

There are also Facebook groups for real estate investors, some with more than 100,000 members. Most of them are private, meaning you'll need to apply for membership by providing your name and contact information and agreeing to abide by the group rules. One of the largest of these Facebook groups, Real Estate Investors Group, was created in 2009 and recently surpassed the 160,000-member mark. These groups vary in their content but are generally a great place to get in touch with other investors, both in your area and from around the country. Some are open to anyone, and others focus on specific groups of investors.

When I was starting out, I joined as many local real estate clubs as I could find, and I diligently went to at least three meetings every month. For two and half years I volunteered to help with admission at one of the biggest local real estate clubs, which meant I was present at every event from start to finish. I found tremendous value in those meetings. I often felt pumped when hearing other people's success stories, and I couldn't wait to implement tips and tricks I learned into my own venture. My dedication paid off, as I was later invited back to the same club as a guest speaker, and over a hundred attendees showed up to hear how I went from being a meeting volunteer to a successful flipper.

Find a Mentor

I've repeatedly remarked on the value of mentors. That's because I really can't stress enough how important it is to have someone who can advise you and guide you through your early deals. Let's discuss a little more about what to look for in a mentor figure.

First of all, seek out someone who has a good track record and has successfully flipped numerous houses. Ask the person you're considering about their experience, and talk to other investors—the real estate investing circle is small and everyone who flips within a certain area knows everyone else. You should be able to not only get a sense of your prospective mentor's track record for flipping houses, but also glean some insights into their personality and character. Be sure the person you're considering has experience with the same types of flips in the same geographic area that you're planning on pursuing. Within house flipping, there are different preferences: some flippers mainly do wholesale deals, some work exclusively with houses that need only cosmetic work, and others look for properties they can improve with an addition or ground up construction. Someone whose specialty area differs from where you want to end up ultimately won't be helpful to you.

It's advantageous to have more than one mentor, because you can learn a lot from people with different areas of expertise. Having a mentor who employs a different flipping strategy or invests in a different area than you do can help you learn about that other strategy or location and perhaps use it to find more deals. Also, having multiple mentors enables you to get second or third opinions about decisions you need to make.

Look for a mentor who is honest and reliable, avoiding anyone who is in the house flipping business with the sole goal of making money. As with any profession, there are some flippers who are less than scrupulous. A mentor must have patience and be willing to teach you; someone who is singularly focused on profit isn't likely to offer a nurturing relationship. Finally, the relationship between mentor and mentee is a two-way street. Just as you'll expect your mentor to be reliable, trustworthy, and show up when they say they will, they'll expect the same from you.

Be careful that you don't overstep boundaries with a mentor by demanding too much of their time. I didn't realize when I first started working with my mentor that I was taking up too much of his time by sending him my analyses of all the deals I was considering and asking him to review them. He finally addressed the issue of his time with me, and I apologized for my mistake. Having more than one mentor can lighten the load for everyone.

Although a mentor will provide advice and direction along the way, you should not depend on that person to teach you about house flipping from the ground up. Don't approach someone about being your mentor until you've educated yourself by reading and taking some courses. Having taken these steps demonstrates to prospective mentors that you are motivated and serious about learning the business.

The relationship between you and your mentor should not be one-sided. Make it a mutually beneficial relationship when possible by offering to invest in a deal your mentor is considering or providing services in an area in which you have expertise, such as photography, marketing, or social media. What you're able to offer will depend on your circumstances, obviously, but the important thing is to make the effort. A great way to create mutual benefit is to do as I did: find a deal and bring your mentor in as a partner in exchange for guidance throughout the flip.

Finally, after you've gained some experience and have some successful flips behind you, consider serving as a mentor to someone else. Many people ask me to mentor them, and I do so whenever I'm able to. I'll always remember and be grateful for the invaluable help my mentor provided during my first flip, and I consider it my responsibility now to help someone else who is just getting started.

Start Looking at the Market

The more you can learn about real estate and familiarize yourself with the market, the better prepared you'll be when you're ready to start flipping houses. Sites such as Zillow and Redfin can provide a lot of information about real estate for sale in your area, and they also contain valuable information about the overall housing market, interest rates, inventory, list and sales prices, home value forecasts, and other timely topics. You can learn about price points for different areas and neighborhoods, get familiar with various layouts and home styles, and view how people have finished their homes. You can see which properties are selling quickly and which ones remain on the market for a long time. Ask yourself what might be appealing or not appealing about the homes you look at, and try to predict the sales prices of pending listings. Notice trends. Are buyers snapping up homes in a certain area while other homes remain on the market? Are homes selling for well over asking prices or are price reductions common? Do open-concept homes fetch higher prices than those with other types of floor plans? Save your search criteria to get notifications when new homes are listed or sold, or if there's a price reduction. All these things can help you develop a sense of where the market is headed and what buyers are looking for.

You can also benefit from attending open houses in your area. Talk to the agent who is hosting the open house to learn about the activity level and the seller's expectations. In addition to learning about the market, this gives you an opportunity to network with agents you could possibly end up working with in the future. I met one of my best agents at an open house she hosted five years ago, and she still vividly remembers our conversation. Observe potential buyers at the open house, watching their reactions to different features of the home. Do they all remark about how they like the open design or complain that the kitchen is too small? You can gather clues about what home buyers find appealing—or not.

Learn How to Analyze a Deal

Once you've gotten a feel for the real estate market in your area, you can start learning about analyzing a deal. It takes a lot of effort to become proficient at analyzing deals, so practicing with homes you can keep track of online can be helpful and give you an advantage when you're ready to begin flipping houses. Remember from chapter 3 that the first step in analyzing a deal is determining what the property will be worth when all the rehab work is done.

You can practice analyzing deals by using Redfin or Zillow to locate houses for sale in your neighborhood or other areas you'd like to work in. Once you've identified a house for sale, learn as much as you can about it from online photos and information, or, if possible, go to an open house to see it in person. Once you've gathered as much information as you can, use it to compare the house to others that are for sale and analyze the deal based on the comps. You won't come up with an ARV at this point because you're not considering repairs that must be done; you're just estimating the sales price based on the existing features and condition of the home.

Keep notes about your analysis and the numbers you've come up with, and sign up to get notifications when the house is sold. Compare the sales price to the price you estimated to see how close you got. If there's a big difference between the two, review your analysis to try to figure out what went wrong. Practicing the process of analyzing a deal will help you get comfortable with it and increase your confidence.

You can also try your hand at estimating the cost of repairs, another topic that's covered in chapter 3. You can use your primary residence (whether you own it or not) as a test. Come up with a list of renovations you'd like done to the home, and invite a few contractors over to provide bids. Ask a lot of questions to learn about different possibilities for creating a beautiful house. Compare the bids to learn how much things cost in general. Coming up with repair costs can be daunting when you're just starting out, but you'll soon be able to judge what you'll need to spend to get a house ready to put on the market. There are also some tools you can use, or a contractor will be able to guide you. Getting an idea of what things cost before you start flipping houses will make your work easier when you're ready to begin.

Learn from the Stars

I told you earlier in the book about how I got inspired to flip houses by watching the flipping shows on HGTV. Sure, it's television meant primarily for entertainment purposes, so there are plenty of details that get fudged to make the show more enjoyable and sometimes less messy. But you can still learn a little (or a lot) from shows like *Flip or Flop* or *Fixer Upper*. Watching how flippers/home renovators on these and other shows work gives you an idea of the home remodel process from start to finish and helps you understand the basics of home construction. I always enjoy the design aspects of the shows and have gotten some good ideas from what I've seen on them. One time I got inspired by a show and realized I could simply replace the glass light on a front door instead of replacing the entire door, which enabled me to save almost a thousand dollars on a flip.

You certainly won't learn everything you need to know from TV shows, but they're fun to watch and can help you stay inspired until you're ready to get started on your first flip. Plus, you might get some ideas to use in your own home!

Chapter Recap

» Even if you don't feel ready to start flipping houses, there are things you can do to prepare for when the time is right.

» The more education you can get, the better prepared you'll be for a house flipping career.

» Meeting the right people is crucial to the success of house flippers.

» Learning as much as you can about the real estate market and getting a feel for how to analyze deals will give you a good head start when you start your business.

Conclusion

When I started flipping houses nearly five years ago, I had no idea that I was embarking on a venture that would change my life. I liked the idea of flipping houses and was anxious to try it, but I never expected it would turn into a full-time career that yields a great income and enables me to be my own boss, take control of my life, and do what I love.

My hope for you is that flipping houses will present a range of possibilities, whatever you'd like those to be. Whether you want to be a full-time house flipper or flip as a side hustle, I hope that what you've learned from this book will give you the confidence to give it a try or, if you've already started flipping, to go into the next deal with additional tools you can use.

When I do a presentation for people who are just getting into house flipping, I always offer some advice. I'd like to share it with you.

Dream Big, Start Small

I encourage you to dream big, but it takes a lot to make a big dream a reality. I remember watching the flipping shows on HGTV and dreaming I would one day be as proficient at house flipping and home remodeling as the TV stars. I have made a lot of progress in that direction, but it wouldn't have happened if I hadn't formulated a plan and acted on it by making thousands of phone calls to recruit agents, attending hundreds of real estate meetings, interviewing dozens of contractors, and doing all the other things that were necessary to get me started. Start out by going to a real estate meeting, listening to a podcast episode, or reading a book like this one, working to make some progress every day and to build a good foundation before you attempt to complete your first flip. Remember that a lot of work is essential to achieving any big dream, so don't attempt to take shortcuts. Dreaming big, working hard, and always acting to move forward until you've gained knowledge and have a plan in place are all necessary to get started in house flipping.

Fake It 'Til You Make It

Someone gave me this advice when I was just starting out, and it flipped a switch in my mind. Being a newbie can be frustrating. Until you have experience with house flipping, it can be difficult to get agents and lenders to work with you. I found that it helped to let people know about any real estate-related experience I had, even though I hadn't yet done any flips. For instance, I had remodeled a property, so I had some experience in that area. I had bought and sold properties and managed a rental and was able to cite those actions as real estate experience even though they didn't involve flipping. I believe that presenting myself as someone with experience in real estate activities, even though they weren't house flipping, made agents and lenders more willing to work with me. Present yourself with confidence but never arrogance. Rely on knowledge you've acquired, but don't be afraid to ask for advice when you need it. There are a lot of experienced investors who are more than happy to help those who are just getting started.

Take Massive Action to See Results Quickly

I've met lots of people who want to flip houses but don't quite know how to start. So they test the waters a bit, making a cold call now and then or attending a real estate meeting once every few months, without ever seeing any real results. With no results realized, they get discouraged and give up. If you're serious about flipping houses, my advice is to take massive action by doing as much as you can every day to achieve results in a relatively short time. As mentioned, I took decisive action when I was starting out by cold-calling agents whenever I had free time from work. I was able to recruit over a hundred agents in just one month, which made my first deal possible in a short amount of time. Because I saw results so quickly, I was able to keep up my momentum and continue the hard work toward my goal without ever wanting to give up. I'd encourage you to do the same. Use every free minute to build your network and look for deals. Attend a lot of investor meetings so you can make contacts and get to know people. Putting in the work up front pays off and puts you on the road to success.

Take Calculated Risks

You've read about risks associated with flipping houses. But without risk there is no reward, and you can minimize your risk exposure by being diligent about your numbers, managing contractors, and making renovations that set your houses apart and get you top dollar for them. I consider calculated risk when making any important decision. To cite an example I mentioned in the introduction, when I bought my first property—a condo that was a short sale and came with pending litigation—I knew I was taking a risk. Short sales require a lot of paperwork and a lengthy closing process, and many lenders are reluctant to loan money for them. Also, the homeowners association was suing the developer for water damage at the time of the sale. The worst-case scenario for me was that if the HOA didn't win its lawsuit or didn't get enough money to cover the repairs, each homeowner would have to come up with money to help repair the damage. Many buyers were scared off by the litigation because they thought the downside risk was uncertain and could be significant. I was not as concerned, however, because I knew there were one hundred units in the complex, and if every unit put up $10,000, there would be $1,000,000 available to cover the damage. I figured I could handle that worst-case scenario of having to come up with a $10,000 payment.

The upside to buying the property was that the condo was offered at a great price, $100,000 below what it would have cost if it had been in a different complex and was not a short sale with pending litigation. I compared the downside risk with the upside potential and realized that even if I ended up having to pay $10,000 toward repairs, I was still way ahead of the game because of the deal I'd get on the sale. I decided to take this calculated risk, and it ended up paying off nicely. The litigation was soon resolved, and my worst-case scenario became reality: I had to pay $10,000 to the HOA. Because I had budgeted for that, I was prepared and perfectly willing to make the payment. As I expected, the value of the condo went up immediately without the pending litigation, and my equity in the house went up by $100,000. My calculated risk had clearly paid off.

I also knew I was taking a risk when I decided to start flipping houses full time. I had done a few deals, learned a whole lot, built up a network, and believed in my ability to be successful, but not pursuing another full-time job with benefits after I was laid off still seemed like a leap of faith. When I weighed all the possible outcomes, however, I determined that my chances of being successful were greater than my chances of failing. Acting on that conviction, I took the calculated risk of starting my own business.

As a house flipper, there will be plenty of times when you'll have to decide whether you want to take a risk. Each flip is a risk, and you are going to have to weigh the upside potential against the downside risk before deciding what to do.

Partner with an Experienced Investor on Your First Deal

Finding an experienced house flipper to walk you through your first flip or two is an important piece of advice that I hope you'll carefully consider. The value of a mentor cannot be overstated, and I highly recommend that you find one. I believe that real estate investment groups are great, and I belong to several of them. Often, you'll meet someone in a group who will be willing to mentor a house flipper who is just starting out. The person who agreed to be my mentor was a guest speaker at a meeting I attended. I got his contact information and got in touch with him the next day to introduce myself. When I got my first deal, I asked him to provide mentoring in exchange for part of whatever profit we made, and he agreed. His input, advice, and direction during that first flip, which was problematic from start to finish, was invaluable.

Build Your Brand and Protect It Like Your Life

There are a few ways to build a brand in the house flipping business, but the most important is to establish a reputation of trustworthiness, dependability, and fairness. As I've mentioned, the circle of house flippers in any given location is small and everyone knows each other. Those who try to cut corners or take advantage of people quickly get a reputation for being dishonest, and that reputation sticks. Establishing yourself as an honest person who says what you mean and means what you say earns you a brand that is respected and allows you to stay in business for a long time.

Another aspect of building a brand is spreading the word about your business to set yourself apart and get others to recognize your work. I've spent a lot of time building my brand with YouTube videos, Instagram and Facebook posts, speaking engagements, and other methods. My YouTube channel has over 50,000 subscribers and is growing, and some of my videos have been viewed more than 100,000 times.

With help from others, some good luck, and a whole lot of hard work, I've been able to grow a successful house flipping business in just a few years. I'm confident that if you're willing to use the information in this book, take time to plan, start out slowly, take calculated risks, and give your all to your business, you can do the same.

REMEMBER TO DOWNLOAD YOUR FREE DIGITAL ASSETS!

 Case Study Library

 Prepare for Closing Checklist

 House Flip Deal Analyzer

 Staging Examples

TWO WAYS TO ACCESS YOUR FREE DIGITAL ASSETS

Use the camera app on your mobile phone to scan the QR code or visit the link below and instantly access your digital assets.

SCAN ME or **VISIT URL**

go.quickstartguides.com/flipping

Appendix I
Scope of Work Document

<table>
<tr><td colspan="2" align="center">CONTRACTING COMPANY</td></tr>
</table>

_____   _____
Client   *Client's Contact Information*

_____   _____
Company   *Company's Contact Information*

CONTRACT PROPOSAL

Prepared by: _____   Date: _____

Total Construction: _____

SCOPE OF WORK

fig. 84

Landscaping:
· Pull weeds in backyard
· Prune trees in backyard

Subfloor - According to Plans:
· Build subfloor to level existing bathroom next to stairway
· Build subfloor to even in master bathroom

Underground plumbing:
· 2" Main water line
· 2", 3", 4" ABS sewer
· (2) Toilet
· (3) Sink in bathroom
· (1) Tub (if possible)
· (1) Kitchen sink

1

<u>Rough framing:</u>
· 2x4 Walls in master bathroom
· 2x4 Walls for new bathroom downstairs
· All posts will be 4x4 and 4x6 for exterior balcony
· Replace existing beam for balcony
· Replace balcony with redwood and redwood handrail in back of home
· Repair damaged siding
· New headers for master bedroom for two (2) new openings

<u>Rough plumbing - (as per plan)</u>
· All plumbing shall be done for sewer 3" and 2" ABS
· ½", ¾" and 1" water service
· All hot water shall be insulated
· All vents shall be ABS 2"
· Main water for four (4) units will be 1"
· 3" ABS for toilet
· (3) Sink only
· (1) Tub (if possible) in master
· Prep for range and dryer in kitchen

<u>Rough electrical - (as per plan)</u>
· Compact	Qty: 30
· Ceiling mount	Qty: 3
· 1x4 LED	Qty: 2
· Chandelier	Qty: 1

· Prep for dryer and range
· Rewire in old area that needs Romex downstairs
· Rerun wiring in master bedroom conduit, put inside wall
· All wire shall be #12

FINISH WORK & ALLOWANCES

<u>Finish framing - (as per plan)</u>
· ½" and ⅝" Sheetrock
· Taped Sheetrock and medium texture knock-down
· Roof asphalt, sheet metal, and gutter repair
  only where needed
· Cabinets/millwork (prefab cabinets
  and marble top)   **Allowance: $7,000.00**
· Carpet (in all bedrooms, hallway, and stairs)   **Allowance: $20.00 per yd installed**
· Paint Shermin-Williams (3 colors)
  inside and exterior
· Tile in bathrooms and kitchen   **Allowance: $2.00 per sq ft**
· Resurface existing hardwood to
  match floors (living and dining)

2

- Siding   **Total: $4,000.00**
- Casing doors and baseboard   **Allowance: $1.00 LF**

Finish plumbing - (as per plan)
- Toilet and seat (Toto)   **Allowance: $200.00**
  Qty: 2   **Total: $400.00**
- Mirror and glass   **Total: $500.00**
- Sink and faucet   **Allowance: $800.00**
- Bathtub and valve   **Allowance: $1,600.00**
- Custom shower tile   **Allowance: $3.00 per sq ft**
- Water heater   **Allowance: Owner supply**

Finish electrical - (as per plan)
- Exhaust fan   **Total: $200.00**
- 1x4 LED lights   **Allowance: $150.00**
- Compact or LED   **Allowance: $1,800.00**
- Ceiling mount   **Allowance: $150.00**
- Chandelier   **Allowance: $150.00**
- Outlets   **Allowance: $0.50 per**
- Standard switch

Includes:
- General liability $1,000,000.00 per occurance $2,000,000.00 total
- Worker's comp policy 9164880-2016
- Maintain auto insurance

Exclusions:
- City permit fees
- Structural engineering fees
- Surveying fees
- Any additional work city requires
- Modifying of appliance
- Site improvements
- PG&E fees
- Landscaping

_____ _____ _____
Please Print Name   _Customer Signature_   _Date_

_____ _____ _____
Please Print Name   _Contractor Signature_   _Date_

3

Appendix II
Sample Contractor's Contract

CONTRACTING COMPANY

_____   _____
Owner's Name   *Owner's Address*

_____   _____
Project Name   *Address*

A. Description of the Work: Contractor will furnish all labor and materials to construct and complete in a good, workman-like and substantial manner.

_____

(Describe the work to be done. Look on Scope of Work page for more details and scope of work.)

Upon the following described property (hereafter called "the project"):

_____

(Insert Legal Description And Street Address If Known)

GRAPHIC

fig. 85

A substantial commencement of the above-described work shall be deemed to be physical performance at job site. (Per Sec. 7159(c) of the California Business and Professions Code, a plan and scale drawing showing the shape, size, dimensions and description of materials and equipment must be attached to this contract.)

B. Property Lines: Owner shall locate and point out property lines to contractor. Contractor may, at his option, require owner to provide a licensed land surveyor's map of property.

C. Arbitration of Disputes: Any dispute arising out of or related to this contract or the interpretation or performance thereof shall be decided by arbitration under the Construction Industry Rules of the American Arbitration Association and judgment shall be entered on the award. The arbitrator shall award reasonable attorneys' fees and expenses to the prevailing party. If any party after due notice fails to appear at or participate in arbitration proceedings, the arbitrator shall make an award based upon evidence presented by the party or parties who do appear and participate. In the event that there are court proceedings arising out of or related to the performance or interpretation of this contract, the court shall award reasonable attorneys' fees to the prevailing party.

D. Payment – Total Contract Price To Be: _____

Down Payment* (if any) _____

(*By California law, cannot exceed two hundred dollars (\$200) or 2 percent of the contract price of swimming pools, or one thousand dollars (\$1,000) or 10 percent of the contract price for other home improvements, excluding finance charges, whichever is the lesser.)

1

Schedule of Payments shall be per Sec. 7159(e) and (f) of the California Business and Professions Code

WHEN	AMOUNT
1. _____	$ _____
2. _____	$ _____
3. _____	$ _____
4. _____	$ _____
5. _____	$ _____
6. _____	$ _____

(Shall be specifically referenced to the amount of work or services to be performed and to any materials and equipment to be supplied)

E. Commencement/Completion of Work: Owner shall have job site ready for commencement of the work of improvement no later than 30 days from the date of this contract – and so notify the contractor in writing.

F. Commencement/Completion of Work: The terms and conditions on the reverse side are expressly incorporated into this contract.

G. Upon satisfactory payment being made for any portion of the work performed, the contractor shall, prior to any further payment being made, furnish a full unconditional release** from any claim or mechanic's lien pursuant to Section 3114 of the Civil Code, for that portion of the work for which payment has been made. **BNI Form 110-UP, "Unconditional Waiver and Release Upon Progress Payment," meets this requirement.

NOTICE: By initialing in the space below, you are agreeing to have any dispute arising out of the matter included in the "arbitration of disputes" provision decided by neutral arbitration as provided by California law, and you are giving up any rights you might possess to have the dispute litigated in a court or jury trial. By initialing in the space below, you are giving up your judicial rights to discovery and appeal, unless those rights are specifically included in the "arbitration of disputes" provision. If you refuse to submit to arbitration after agreeing to this provision, you may be compelled to arbitrate under the authority of the Business and Professions Code or other applicable laws. Your agreement to this arbitration provision is voluntary. We have read and understand the foregoing and agree to submit disputes arising out of the matters included in the "arbitration of disputes" provision to neutral arbitration.

I agree to arbitration _____   I agree to arbitration _____
(Initial Owner/ Owners)   *(Initial Contractor)*

You, the owner (buyer), have the right to require that your contractor have a performance and payment bond, and the expense of the bond may be borne by the owner. You, the buyer, may cancel this transaction at any time prior to midnight of the third business day (in the case of disaster repairs, seventh business day) after the date of this transaction. See the attached Notice of Cancellation form for an explanation of this right.

2

Date _____

(Contractor shall make a substantial commencement of the
work no more than 50 days from the foregoing date)

X _____   X _____

(Owner sign here – see and read Notice to   *(If more than one owner,*
Owner on next page before signing)   *second owner sign here)*

Contractor License No.   _____   X _____ **V.P.**

(Contracting company
representative signature)

Time. The approximate dates of commencement and completion are filled in on the first page of this proposal. Delivery of building materials to the site or the issuance of a building permit constitutes substantial commencement of work under this contract. Failure to substantially commence work within 20 days from the approximate date of commencement will violate Contractors' State License Law.

Failure to complete by the approximate completion date shall not entitle Owner to any damages for delay or consequential damages of any kind. Owner's sole remedy shall be to withhold progress payments and retention amounts until completion. The time for completion shall be extended or reduced by such time as Owner and Contractor agree in a written change order or extra work order. The time for completion shall be extended by the number of working days equal to the number of days between the oral issuance of a change order or extra work order and the delivery to Contractor of an approved and signed written change order or extra work order. The time for commencement and completion shall be extended by the number of working days equal to the number of days between the date Owner executes this contract and the date all required governmental permits and approvals are obtained.

Should the Owner, Owner's architect/design professionals, or any public agency direct or request that additional work not shown on the present plans and specifications for the project be done by Contractor, the cost of the additional work shall be added to the contract price and paid by the Owner on completion of such additional work. Contractor is entitled to be paid for all such additional work requested or directed, whether requested or directed in writing or orally, and any expenses incurred by Contractor because of unusual conditions shall be paid for by Owner as additional work done by Contractor.

The term "unusual conditions" includes, but is not limited to, the presence or suspected presence of asbestos, asbestos products, hazardous materials, hazardous wastes, pest infestation, dry rot, subsurface rocks which cannot be removed by a one-half-cubic-yard power shovel without continuous drilling or explosives, hardpan (any material which cannot be removed with hand pick or hand shovel), subsurface water (whether standing, seeping, or flowing), buried or hidden pipes, wires, cables, conduit or the like not visible without excavation or destructive inspection, utility lines, and easements.

The term "cost" means the amount agreed to between Contractor and Owner or Owner's architect/design professional, if the extra work is performed pursuant to a written change order signed by Owner or Owner's architect/design professional. The term "cost" as used in this paragraph means the actual cost to the Contractor of the labor, materials, or subcontracts required for such additional work increased by 30 percent, if the extra work is performed and no written change order was signed by Owner or Owner's architect/design professional.

Unless otherwise specifically provided herein, Contractor shall not be responsible for any patch or repair work to Contractor's work or the work of others on the premises to the extent such is

3

caused by the presence of Owner, other contractors, subcontractors, their employees, agents, invitees and the like during Contractor's performance. Any such patch or repair work shall be extra work. Payment for extra work is due immediately upon completion of the extra work. No retention shall be withheld from said amount.

Permits and Approvals. Unless otherwise provided herein, it shall be the obligation of Owner to obtain any and all necessary permits and government approvals of the work contemplated herein. This obligation includes any fees charged by the governmental entity. Should Contractor pay any fees, Owner shall reimburse same with no markup. Should Contractor's time be required to seek any permits and approvals, Contractor shall be paid at the rate of $100.00/hour.

Correlation Between Plans, Specifications, and Contract. The plans and specifications for the project, if any, and this Contract are intended to supplement each other. Should a conflict arise between the instruments, the specifications shall control over the plans, and this Contract shall control over both the plans and the specifications.

Fire Insurance. Owner, at Owner's own cost and expense, shall procure promptly after execution of this Contract and maintain during the continuance of this Contract a policy of fire insurance with course of construction, vandalism, and malicious mischief clauses attached, insuring the project and all materials delivered to the site of the project for their full insurable value with loss thereunder payable to Owner, any beneficiary of a deed of trust encumbering the property on which the project is located, and Contractor as their interest may appear.

Destruction of Project. Should the project or any part thereof be destroyed by fire, theft, vandalism, accident, act of God, or other cause not the fault of Contractor, any work done or materials furnished by Contractor in restoring or rebuilding the project shall be paid for by Owner as extra work performed by Contractor pursuant to the provisions regarding "Extra Work and Change Orders."

Owner's Power to Terminate Contract. Should Contractor commit any of the acts specified in this paragraph, the Owner may, by giving ten days' notice in writing thereof to Contractor, without prejudice to any other rights or remedies given Owner by law or by this Contract, terminate the services of Contractor under this Contract; take possession of the project and the premises on which it is located; and complete the project by whatever method Owner may deem expedient. Contractor shall be deemed to have committed an act specified in this paragraph if Contractor shall:
(a) File a voluntary bankruptcy under Chapter 7 of Title 11 U.S.C. or have an involuntary bankruptcy imposed upon Contractor;
(b) Make a general assignment for the benefit of Contractor's creditors;
(c) Persistently disregard any law or ordinance relating to the project or the completion thereof; or
(d) Otherwise commit a substantial violation of any provision of this Contract.

Rights on Termination by Owner. (a) Should Owner terminate the services of Contractor under this Contract for any reason other than delay, and complete the project, Owner may only withhold amounts reasonably necessary to complete the project. Owner must pay Contractor the balance of the contract price, less such reasonably withheld amounts, within fourteen days of the termination. On completion of the project by Owner, if the unpaid balance of the contract price is less than Owner's cost of completion, such excess shall be promptly paid by Owner to Contractor. On completion of the project by Owner, if Owner's cost of completion exceeds the unpaid balance of the contract price, such excess shall be promptly paid by Contractor to Owner.

(b) Should Owner terminate the services of Contractor under this Contract for delay and complete the project, Owner must pay Contractor the balance of the contract price within fourteen days of the termination. After completion by the Owner, Contractor shall pay to Owner the reasonable cost of completion within thirty days of the recording of a Notice of Completion.

4

Appendix III
Renovation Tasks

This appendix provides a list of renovations you might encounter when getting a house ready to flip. It is extremely unlikely that you will face all these tasks during any one flip, but I want you to be aware of the many renovation possibilities you may at some point have to consider. This is by no means an exhaustive list, but it should give you an idea of what your scope of work document may include. The renovations listed are organized by exterior, interior, and general tasks.

Exterior

- ❏ **Roof** – Depending on the age and condition, a roof could require repair or replacement.

- ❏ **Rain gutters** – Gutters should be cleaned and, if necessary, painted, repaired, or replaced. Check downspouts to make sure they aren't clogged and are operating properly.

- ❏ **Soffit and fascia** – The soffit is the material underneath the eaves of a roof, and fascia is the board along the edge of the soffit that supports the rain gutters. Depending on age and material, there may be damage that will require repair or replacement.

- ❏ **Chimney** – Have the chimney inspected and cleaned or repaired if necessary.

- ❏ **Windows** – Windows that are old, don't close or latch properly, have fogged glass, or have other issues should be replaced.

- ❏ **Paint** – I almost always paint the exteriors of homes I buy; it instantly improves curb appeal.

❑ **Siding** – Siding may need to be repaired or replaced. At the very least, make sure it is clean and have it pressure washed if it is not.

❑ **Garage** – Garage doors that are damaged or don't open properly should be replaced. Check to make sure electric garage door openers are working. Detached garages should be assessed for damage and repaired if necessary.

❑ **Doors** – Exterior doors that are beat-up, unattractive, or not working properly should be replaced.

❑ **Fencing** – Fencing should be freshly painted or cleaned and any broken or otherwise damaged sections replaced. I sometimes add fencing to create a shield if the property next door is not well maintained.

❑ **Pools** – Pools can be an asset or a liability, depending on their condition and what buyers are looking for. If you have a property with a pool, you'll need to make sure it's in good condition and operable and that it meets safety standards of the municipality in which the property is located.

❑ **Porches or decks** – Porches or decks that are not structurally sound or code-compliant will need to be repaired, or in some cases replaced. If most other houses in the neighborhood have a deck and mine does not, I'll often have a deck added to match the comps.

❑ **Lighting** – Exterior lighting is important for both appearance and safety. Make sure it is adequate and in working condition, replacing fixtures if necessary to update the house's appearance.

❑ **Foundation** – Check for and address moisture or mold problems, cracks, and other issues affecting the foundation.

❑ **Concrete** – Concrete that is stained with oil or other substances can be cleaned and minor cracks patched. Concrete can also be resealed if necessary, a process that greatly improves its appearance.

❑ **Sheds and outbuildings** – Like detached garages, any buildings separate from the main house should be inspected for damage and repaired if necessary. On occasion I've had unsightly sheds and other structures removed from the property.

❏ **Landscaping** – Landscaping can go a long way in improving curb appeal. Some possible tasks include reseeding the lawn or installing sod; planting bushes, small trees, and flowers; trimming existing shrubbery; spreading mulch; and cleaning up dropped leaves, sticks, etc.

Interior

❏ **Demolition** – Nearly all flips require some demolition work, such as removing old and cracked tubs from a bathroom or ripping out kitchen cabinets. You'll need a large roll-off dumpster to dispose of everything you remove from the home.

❏ **Floor plan** – I often open up a house by changing the floor plan, but this requires planning, and you might need permits to do so. As I mentioned in chapter 6, I depend on Home Designer software to experiment with different floor plans.

❏ **Electrical** – It's important to make sure the electrical system in any home meets all standards and to properly upgrade it as needed. New circuits might need to be added if you're finishing an area of the house that was previously unfinished, and outlets may need to be added or upgraded. Make sure smoke and carbon monoxide detectors are installed and in working order. Check to make sure all exhaust and ceiling fans are operational.

❏ **Plumbing** – Addressing the plumbing might require fixing leaks, replacing old appliances such as water softeners or dishwashers, and replacing showers, bathtubs, toilets, and sinks. If you're fortunate enough not to have to replace everything, consider getting new hardware to give appliances an updated look.

❏ **HVAC** – It's not unusual to have to upgrade the HVAC system. Have someone assess the condition of the furnace and air conditioning systems to make sure everything is in working order. You'll also want to be sure the ductwork is in good shape.

❏ **Insulation** – There are codes and standards that pertain to insulation, and they vary depending on climate zones and other factors. Be sure your contractor is aware of the codes for your area and that all insulation meets applicable requirements.

- ❑ **Framing** – If you're finishing an area of the house, you'll need to address framing.

- ❑ **Drywall** – Any heavily damaged drywall should be replaced, and you'll need to install new drywall in newly finished areas.

- ❑ **Fireplaces** – Have fireplaces inspected to make sure they are in good working order.

- ❑ **Flooring** – Different types of flooring are popular in different geographical regions, but in the Bay Area I usually install hardwood, as that seems to be what buyers prefer, and I feel that it helps to set my properties apart.

- ❑ **Doors** – Any interior doors that are damaged, old, or cheap-looking should be replaced. If the doors are okay, you still might want to consider updating the hardware to refresh them.

- ❑ **Trim** – New trim can make a big difference, so replace any baseboards or molding that is dated or damaged. New trim will be necessary for newly finished areas.

- ❑ **Patching and painting** – I normally repaint the entire interior of my flips in colors that I know are popular based on comps. I have favorite brands and colors that I like to use, but they're always in the same palettes of what the comps tell me are popular.

- ❑ **Light fixtures** – Modern light fixtures, especially in kitchens and bathrooms, can set your flip apart. I often replace all light fixtures.

- ❑ **Cabinets** – Don't be tempted to skimp on cabinets. I once thought I could get by with repainting kitchen cabinets rather than replacing them but found that even after being painted, they still looked like old cabinets and needed to be replaced. But if the cabinets are fairly new and in good shape, they may only need to be painted. Be sure to pay attention to the hardware.

- ❑ **Countertops** – I like marble countertops, but they're not always necessary. Know what the comps have and plan accordingly, but remember that you want your kitchens and bathrooms to impress potential buyers.

❑ **Vanities** – Bathrooms are important when it comes to selling houses, so replace any vanities that are dated, damaged, or too small. Double vanities are popular among many home buyers.

❑ **Backsplash** – Installing modern-looking backsplashes can create a wow factor, and you can find some good values at specialty shops or online venues.

General

❑ **Permits** – Make sure you know what permits you'll need for your rehab. Discuss the need for permits with your contractor, who is responsible for obtaining them.

❑ **Pest control and termite inspection** – Have a pest control technician check the property for any pest problems. I normally have a termite inspection done when renovations are completed but before the house is sold in order to provide peace of mind for potential buyers.

❑ **Mold** – Check for evidence of mold or water issues and arrange to have a professional address any problems.

About the Author

ELISA ZHENG COVINGTON, MBA

Elisa Zheng Covington is an author, real estate investor, developer, and real estate influencer. She is also the founder and CEO of Transform Real Estate Investments LLC, a Bay Area local real estate solutions company that purchases and improves all types of homes in various conditions and locations.

In 2017, Elisa transitioned from a comfortable nine-to-five job to become a full-time investor. With over forty successfully completed projects under her belt, Elisa became her own boss and used her real estate investment activities to improve her lifestyle and earn more than she ever could have by staying in her former role—she's been making a seven-figure profit consistently since 2019.

Elisa enjoys helping people and sharing her knowledge with others. She mentors aspiring investors and hopes to empower more women to get started in real estate. Her YouTube channel, Transform Real Estate, teaches people how to invest in real estate and achieve financial freedom and has received 3.6 million views and counting.

Elisa was born and raised in Beijing, China. After working briefly for Google China, she came to the US to pursue her MBA at Kellogg School of Management at Northwestern University. Elisa loves designing her own flips and using unique design features to appeal to buyers. When she isn't prospecting for new properties or supervising projects, she loves hiking, swimming, and traveling. She has been to more than twenty countries across six continents.

Instagram @transformrealestate | YouTube.com/transformrealestate | www.transformrealestate.com

About QuickStart Guides

QuickStart Guides are books for beginners, written by experts.

QuickStart Guides® are comprehensive learning companions tailored for the beginner experience. Our books are written by experts, subject matter authorities, and thought leaders within their respective areas of study.

For nearly a decade more than 850,000 readers have trusted QuickStart Guides® to help them get a handle on their finances, start their own business, invest in the stock market, find a new hobby, get a new job—the list is virtually endless.

The QuickStart Guides® series of books is published by ClydeBank Media, an independent publisher based in Albany, NY.

Connect with QuickStart Guides online at www.quickstartguides.com or follow us on Facebook, Instagram, and LinkedIn.

Follow us @quickstartguides

Glossary

1031 exchange
An exchange of one investment property for another of a similar nature that enables capital gains taxes to be deferred. The term gets its name from the section of the Internal Revenue Code in which it is contained.

After-repair value (ARV)
A property's estimated market value after the rehab work is done.

American Society of Home Inspectors (ASHI)
An association that provides education, information, and other services for its home inspector members. It also has a lobbying presence in Washington, D.C.

Assign the contract
The act of transferring a sales contract from a wholesaler to a dealer, typically with the dealer agreeing to pay the wholesaler more for the contract than what the wholesaler agreed to pay the seller for the house.

Broker tour
A showing of a property that's intended for other real estate agents, not potential buyers. It enables agents to gain firsthand knowledge of a property and determine which of their clients might be interested in purchasing it.

Business entity
An organization formed to conduct business.

C corporation
A legal structure for a corporation in which owners are taxed separately from the corporation.

Change order
Work that is added or removed from the original scope of work of a construction contract.

Close of escrow
The point in a real estate transaction at which the sale is final and the transaction has been completed.

Comparable sale (comp)
A home in the same neighborhood as one's flip that has similar features and is in approximately the same condition. Data about comps is used to obtain helpful information such as what home features are popular in a particular location and what is a fair price to ask for a flip once the renovation is done.

Comparative market analysis (CMA)
An analysis agents use to determine the value of a target property by comparing it to similar ones that were recently sold.

Contingency
A clause in a real estate contract that states certain conditions must be met for the contract to be binding, and if they are not, enables one to back out of the purchase agreement without any consequences.

Contract Assignment
A method of wholesaling in which a wholesaler signs a contract with a property owner or another wholesaler outlining terms for the sale of a property, and then assigns or passes along the contract to another investor who agrees to pay a fee to get it.

Days on market (DOM)
The number of days between the time a house is listed for sale and when it goes under contract.

Double close
The process of a wholesaler purchasing a property and immediately selling the same property to an end buyer for a higher price. So named because the transaction involves two closings.

Due diligence period
The time during which a buyer can inspect a property to make sure there are no problems that would prevent them from moving forward with the purchase. This period usually takes place during the property inspection contingency period after a purchase contract is signed, but it can also occur before an offer is made.

Earnest money deposit (EMD)
A specified amount of money placed in an escrow account to indicate seriousness about buying a home and moving forward with the transaction. Also known as a *good-faith deposit*.

Escrow account
An account in which a third party temporarily holds money or property until a purchase agreement has been completed. Earnest money deposits are ordinarily placed in escrow accounts.

Foreclosure
A legal process in which a lender forces the sale of a home that serves as collateral for a loan. Foreclosure is an attempt by the lender to recoup the balance of a loan on which a borrower has stopped making payments.

Hard money loan
A short-term, asset-based loan commonly used when flipping houses. Issued by individuals or private companies, the loan is secured by the value of the property rather than the borrower's creditworthiness.

Hold time
The time between the close of escrow on the purchase of a flip and the close of escrow on the sale of that flip.

Home equity line of credit (HELOC)
A line of credit that's secured by one's home and allows them to draw funds as needed and repay the money at a variable interest rate. Interest is paid only on the money that's borrowed.

House hack
A real estate investing strategy that involves renting out portions of one's primary residence and using the income to offset the cost of their mortgage and other expenses associated with owning a home.

Installment sale
A type of sale that enables deferral of taxes by selling an investment property and collecting the proceeds in installments instead of all at once.

Lien waiver
A document a contractor signs stating they have received full payment for work completed and they waive their right to file a lien against one's property.

Limited liability company (LLC)
A legal structure that separates a business from its owner, thereby protecting the owner's personal assets from liability and debt.

Listing agent
A licensed real estate agent who represents the seller in a transaction.

Loan origination fee
An up-front charge by a lender that covers the cost of services such as processing, funding, and underwriting. Also known as *points*.

Local market norm
Trends within a particular real estate market that influence buying and selling habits.

Long-term capital gains tax
A tax levied on assets that have been held for more than one year.

Multiple listing service (MLS)
A database established by real estate brokers to provide information about properties for sale.

Notice to perform
A document that spells out purchase expectations for a home buyer and requires the buyer to act within a certain time period. Time allotted varies by state, but many states, including California, typically allow 48 hours for the buyer to address a particular issue.

Offer deadline
A stated day and time by which all offers on a house must be received. A seller typically reviews all offers after the deadline rather than each one as it's submitted.

Personal line of credit
A designated amount of money that a financial institution loans over a designated period of time.

Points
See *loan origination fee*.

Pre-foreclosure
The beginning stages of a foreclosure action, normally initiated because a borrower is 60 to 90 days or more past due on their mortgage payments and has gotten a default notice from their lender.

Preapproval letter
A letter from a lender stating that the lender is willing to loan a specific amount of money.

Preemptive offer
An offer made by a prospective buyer in advance of a designated offer deadline.

Proof of funds (POF) document
A document stating that a prospective buyer has funds available to pay 100 percent of the purchase price of a house.

Real estate owned
A property that is real estate owned (REO) has reverted to the mortgage lender because a foreclosure sale was unsuccessful. Also known as *bank-owned property*, these homes are normally placed for sale on the open market.

Rehabbing
A type of house flipping that involves buying houses, fixing them up, and selling them for a profit.

Residential purchase agreement (RPA)
A legal contract stating one's interest in buying a house and what is required to happen for the sale to proceed.

Retail contractor
A contractor who works primarily for individual homeowners.

S corporation
A corporation that meets certain criteria set by the Internal Revenue Service and is able to pass corporate income, losses, deductions, and credits through to its shareholders for tax purposes.

Scope of work (SOW) document
A detailed outline of all work that needs to be completed in a construction project—for example, during the rehab period when flipping a house.

Seller's market
A real estate market that favors sellers because there is more demand for houses than supply.

Search engine optimization (SEO)

The process of optimizing online content so it appears at or near the top of search results on a search engine such as Google.

Short sale

A sale that occurs when a financially distressed homeowner sells their property for less than the amount due on the mortgage, usually to avoid foreclosure.

Short-term capital gains tax

A tax levied on assets that have been held for less than one year.

Single-source funding plan

A process used during a double close in which the end buyer pays a wholesaler for the property, after which the wholesaler uses that money to purchase the property from the original seller.

Sole proprietor

A person who owns and runs a business on their own.

Supra box

An electronic lockbox containing the keys to a home that's listed for sale. Can usually be accessed by a smartphone.

Title binder policy

A commitment on the part of a title company to provide a title insurance policy at a much lower cost to a home buyer who resells the same property within a certain time period. The same company that first issues title insurance, which protects buyers from problems regarding ownership of the property, must issue the title binder policy. Also known as an *interim binder*.

Wholesale contractor

A contractor who works primarily for investors.

Wholesaling

The process of locating a discounted property, signing a purchase agreement with the owner, and selling the deal, usually as-is, to another investor.

References

CHAPTER 2

Hansen, Louis. 2021 "Bay Area Home Prices, Sales Continue to Surge." *The Mercury News*. August 5. Accessed September 13, 2021. https://www.mercurynews.com/2021/08/05/bay-area-home-prices-sales-continue-to-surge.

Redfin. 2021. "Contra Costa County Housing Market." Accessed November 1, 2021. https://www.redfin.com/county/309/CA/Contra-Costa-County/housing-market

CHAPTER 4

DiLallo, M. 2021. "Best Cities to Flip Houses." *Millionacres*. March 3. Accessed September 21, 2021. https://www.millionacres.com/real-estate-investing/house-flipping/best-cities-flip-houses/

CHAPTER 9

California Department of Real Estate. 2021. "Requirements to Apply for a Real Estate Salesperson License." *CA.GOV*. Accessed November 19, 2021. https://www.dre.ca.gov/examinees/requirementssales.html

National Association of Realtors. 2020. "Quick Real Estate Statistics." November 11. Accessed November 6, 2021. https://www.nar.realtor/research-and-statistics/quick-real-estate-statistics

Statista Research Department, S. R. 2021. "Number of National Association of Realtors members in the United States from 2009 to 2021." April 20. *Statista*. Accesssed November 3, 2021. https://www.statista.com/statistics/196269/us-national-association-of-realtors-number-of-members-since-1910/

CHAPTER 10

Campisi, Natalie. 2021. "Housing Market Predictions 2022: Will Prices Drop?" *Forbes Advisor*. August 10. Accessed September 6, 2021. https://www.forbes.com/advisor/mortgages/when-will-the-housing-market-cool-off/

Zillow. (n.d.) "Property Descriptions 101: How to Write Listing Descriptions That Sell." Accessed November 8, 2021. https://www.zillow.com/sellers-guide/listing-descriptions-that-sell/

CHAPTER 11

He, Bin. 2020. "What is the Impact of a Recession on the Housing Market?" *CoreLogic*. April 1. Accessed March 1, 2000. https://www.corelogic.com/intelligence/what-is-the-impact-of-a-recession-on-the-housing-market

Mack, Emily. 2021. "Millennials are Fueling the Housing Boom – Will it Continue?" *Chicago Agent Magazine*. November 2. Accessed December 7, 2021. https://chicagoagentmagazine.com/2021/11/02/millennials-are-fueling-the-housing-boom-will-it-continue/

CHAPTER 12

Alcalay, Megan. 2017. "S Corp vs LLC: Should You Incorporate?" *Stride*. May 22. Accessed March 2, 2022. https://blog.stridehealth.com/post/s-corp-vs-llc

CHAPTER 14

Evangelou, Nadia. 2020. "How Long do Homeowners Stay in Their Homes?" *National Association of Realtors*. January 8. Accessed January 7, 2022. https://www.nar.realtor/blogs/economists-outlook/how-long-do-homeowners-stay-in-their-homes

Friedman, Nicole. 2021. "Millennials Are Supercharging the Housing Market." *The Wall Street Journal*. December 14. Accessed January 7, 2022. https://www.wsj.com/articles/millennials-are-supercharging-the-housing-market-11639496815

Niemeyer, Brooke. 2016. "There Have Been 6.3 Million Foreclosures in the U.S. in the Last Decade." *MarketWatch*. May 31. Accessed December 27, 2021. https://www.marketwatch.com/story/there-were-63-million-foreclosures-in-the-last-decade-2016-05-31

Rexrode, Christina. 2019. "Financial Crisis Yields a Generation of Renters." *The Wall Street Journal*. July 27. Accessed January 7, 2022. https://www.wsj.com/articles/financial-crisis-yields-a-generation-of-renters-11564228800

Schneider, Howard. 2021. "U.S. Recession Ended in April 2020, Making it Shortest on Record." *Reuters*. July 19. Accessed January 7, 2022. https://www.reuters.com/business/recession-ended-april-2020-making-it-shortest-record-2021-07-19/

Index